BEING

THE EFFECTIVE LEADER

LIFESUCCESS PUBLISHING, LLC
8900 E Pinnacle Peak Road, Suite D240
Scottsdale, AZ 85255

Telephone: 800.473.7134
Fax: 480.661.1014
E-mail: admin@lifesuccesspublishing.com

ISBN (hardcover): 978-1-59930-093-1
ISBN (ebook): 978-1-59930-247-8

Cover :   LifeSuccess Publishing, LLC
Layout: LifeSuccess Publishing, LLC
Edit: AllIvy Editing Services

COMPANIES, ORGANIZATIONS, INSTITUTIONS, AND INDUSTRY PUBLICATIONS: Quantity discounts are available on bulk purchases of this book for reselling, educational purposes, subscription incentives, gifts, sponsorship, or fundraising. Special books or book excerpts can also be created to fit specific needs such as private labeling with your logo on the cover and a message from a VIP printed inside. For more information, please contact our Special Sales Department at LifeSuccess Publishing, LLC.

BEING

THE EFFECTIVE LEADER

"*Before you can do something
you first must be something*"
~*Goethe*

MICHAEL NICHOLAS

TESTIMONIALS

A great book, an important book for it convincingly states the crucial fact that true leadership comes from inside ourselves, if we have the courage to look; not from business schools – or books, except for this one.

~ Sir John Whitmore, author of *Coaching for Performance*

This detailed and rigorous exploration of the impact of thinking processes and beliefs on leadership is very much overdue. Michael Nicholas uncovers the habits of thinking and behaviors that will enable you to become a world class leader.

~ Steve Siebold, author of
177 Mental Toughness Secrets of the World Class

In this book Michael Nicholas clearly explains how to get things done more quickly and effectively. It is built around the solid principles adopted by the most successful leaders. Don't just read this book -- use it everyday to put you on the fast track to superior results.

~ Vic Johnson, Founder, www.asamanthinketh.net

Do you want to really understand the essential principles necessary to transform your capability as an individual and as leader and equip yourself with the skills in how to put them into practice? If so, then I can't recommend *Being The Effective Leader* highly enough.

~ Richard Millman, Group Strategy Director, Danoptra Gaming Group

Few people are aware of the enormous potential that we are all born with, and even fewer take advantage of it. Everything that we achieve stems from the use of the mind – *Being The Effective Leader* will show you how.

~ Paul Martinelli, President, LifeSuccess Consulting

Do you want to be able to dramatically improve your influencing skills, and with them your leadership? Then *Being The Effective Leader* is a must read.

~ Kate Burton, author of *NLP for Dummies*

If you want to make a change in your life, *Being The Effective Leader* will make a difference in your approach and give you information that will not only show you how to change, but will also inspire you to do so.

~ Jim Sloane, Vice Chairman, Deloitte & Touche UK

Simple and profound. The advice in *Being The Effective Leader* offers everybody, whether they consider themselves to be a leader or not, the opportunity to improve the way that they work with and influence others.

~ **Ben Bengougam, HR Director, DSGi**

If you want your business to compete, then its people must collaborate. Michael Nicholas clearly describes why this behavior is so rare and how to motivate people to be the best that they can be. A must-read for leaders at all levels.

~ **Keith Jones, Managing Director, PC World Stores Group**

I found *Being The Effective Leader* to be a must read for anyone who leads others. Not only does it explain why we are getting our current results, it offers sound business advice about how to improve them.

~ **Peter Thomson, One of the UK's Leading Strategists on Business and Personal Growth**

Michael Nicholas blends a wealth of both established and new leadership ideas, together with his own extensive experience, to present a straightforward formula that anybody can use.

~ **Julie Harding, European HR Director, HSBC Bank plc**

DEDICATION

This book is dedicated to my two children,
Amy and Hannah, who seem intuitively to be
aware of so much of its content already.

I love you both very much.

ACKNOWLEDGEMENTS

I have increasing gratitude to the many people who have contributed to my professional and personal journey. They are the coaches, mentors, friends, and colleagues from whom I have had the opportunity to learn for more than 20 years. Many of them have made an indelible imprint on my thinking and capabilities. Then there are my clients, very few of whom, I suspect, realise how much they are helping me as we work together. Their enthusiasm for this project has been an enormous encouragement in getting it finished. It is with deep appreciation that I would like to specifically mention the following people:

Thank you to my partner, Bridie. Without your love, tolerance of the long hours involved, and help, the whole project would have been so much more difficult.

Thank you, Dad, for your endless support and, in relation to this book, the way that you challenged my ideas and held me to the highest standard.

Thank you, Mum, for always being there for me.

Thank you to my sisters, Sarah and Debbie. You are such an important part of my life.

Thank you, Kandi Miller, Dee Burks and Sophia Heller from my publisher, for your reviews of my work, your ideas, and your ongoing support and coaching. Thank you also Daniela Savone and Lloyd Arbour, for your fantastic design work and for your patience with me in incorporating my ideas.

Thank you, Sir John Whitmore. Your teaching profoundly impacted me and may well have altered the course of my life.

And finally, thank you to the many authors and teachers from whom I have had the privilege to learn, particularly Tony Robbins, Dr. David Hawkins, Wayne Dyer, Deepak Chopra, John C. Maxwell, and Daniel Goleman. Your contributions have been immeasurable.

BEING THE EFFECTIVE LEADER

INTRODUCTION

There is genius in all of us. We were born with it and it is still available to us by reconnecting to the unimaginable potential of our unlimited minds.

~ **Michael Nicholas**

Almost 25 years ago, while undergoing leadership training in the military, the team that I was part of had just completed a gruelling, three-hour exercise. In competition against several other teams we had run to exhaustion, eluding "the enemy" and attempting to pass through various checkpoints at specific times. For me personally, the challenge had been intensified because I had been assigned the role of leader and the tasks set pushed me far beyond anything that had been required of me before.

We did not win – and on this occasion that did not matter. As we sat down to debrief with our instructor, my overwhelming feeling was one of spine-tingling elation. Overriding the physical exhaustion and the knowledge that this was just the first of three exercises that day, there was a deep sense of joy, excitement, and peace that infused everything that was happening. To this day it still feels fantastic to think about it.

I have reflected on that experience and others like it many times, wondering just what it was about it that felt so good. What are the specific factors in our peak experiences that stimulate such emotional highs? I believe that the answer to this question, when integrated into our lives, can give real meaning to what we do and greatly enhance our sense of fulfilment.

On that day in training, when tested beyond my mental and physical limits as I perceived them at that time, I discovered a reservoir of internal resource of which I had no previous awareness. Simultaneously, I experienced an effortless feeling of being "in flow" as the team worked cohesively and harmoniously toward our collective goal. This was definitely a team accomplishment, yet the sense of individual achievement and fulfilment was intense. It easily overcame any discomfort that my physical exhaustion might otherwise have generated, and my self-belief took a huge leap forward. The emotional response that went with it was due to the awareness of having achieved something of significance, the sense of personal growth and having got a glimpse of my own innate potential.

This is closely related to the reason why sport has the ability to generate such passion and loyalty. Superficially, this may appear to be due to the enjoyment of the competition or the pleasure of watching your team win. However, such factors would be unlikely to generate the respect and awe with which athletes who have mastered their sport are regarded. A more complete explanation, as I have come to understand it, is that we have an intuitive awareness of the dedication, sacrifice, and commitment to goals that such people must be able to draw upon as they strive to overcome human limitation and establish new standards. As we watch them succeed in surpassing their own previous limits, it can inspire us by reminding us of what we, too, are capable.

Whenever any of us moves beyond the comfort zone of our past achievements to a new level of performance, we become increasingly aware of our potential. This is transformation at its most fundamental: the creation of a dramatic change in who we perceive ourselves to be. When this happens, the awareness that we gain brings with it the possibility of a rapid advancement in performance because, as you will see later in this book, changes in our beliefs are always reflected in our external results. Consequently, my primary intention in writing this book has been to seek to offer you a set of techniques so that **you can transform your level of awareness about yourself, the way you manage yourself, and your interactions with other people. These are the core elements of leadership**. As your belief in your potential in any one of them increases, your capability as a leader will automatically improve, as will your results.

The starting point is to become more effective at leading yourself – it is simply impossible to lead others well in any other way – yet this is not the area targeted by most of the books and courses on leadership that I've been exposed to. Indeed, I have seen highly respected experts in the field quoted as saying that in seeking to improve performance we should focus on behaviours rather than trying to change ourselves at a deeper level, because we would be unlikely to succeed in personal change. This line of thinking breeds limitation and is one of the reasons why many people are not able to effect significant and rapid change. Its impact is highly visible each time people return from a training course and find themselves unable to sustain the new behaviours that they have learned. When this happens their results, too, remain fixed.

I hope to demonstrate to you that by working first on yourself it is possible to make the shifts necessary to be successful at the personal level and, if appropriate, in your business. I aim to assist you in creating a nonlinear leap in performance, not by working harder or making minor adjustments to the way that things have been done before, but primarily by transforming yourself so that all of your interactions become more effective and profound.

One of the challenges that you are certainly going to face is to overcome the set of self-imposed limitations that you have, almost certainly unknowingly, accepted for yourself. These can create huge resistance as you seek to change and grow. Yet it is self-evident that unless you can adapt and learn new skills, improved results will be forever elusive. Worse still, in an ever-moving environment, remaining stationary is impossible; therefore, failure to move forward results in inevitable decline.

To grow we must be prepared to venture beyond the edge of our proven area of expertise and explore the unknown. I've observed over and over again in my business experience, especially since I've been coaching professionally, the way that people are held back by imaginary stories that they tell themselves, stories that evaporate once the first few steps have been taken in a new direction. In other words, **the biggest block to our progress is our own beliefs about what we are capable of**. Christopher Logue, the contemporary poet, captures this beautifully in this brief dialogue:

> Come to the edge.
>
> We might fall.
>
> Come to the edge.
>
> It's too high!
>
> COME TO THE EDGE!
>
> And they came,
>
> and he pushed,
>
> and they flew.

It is the very nature of change to create uncertainty, doubt, and fear at first and for this reason it is generally resisted. In other words, most of what holds people back is internal. I have found that usually people have no awareness what they are capable of until they are confronted with a problem. At this point, where they experience huge motivation to find a better way, they may discover their resourcefulness. When we are forced to make changes in this way and leave some of our old methods behind, then we may uncover capabilities that were always there but were hidden behind our habits and established patterns of doing things. This strategy is not the most effective because it relies on a problem occurring before change takes place, but it is often the one used. As Christopher Logue so eloquently describes, almost everyone discovers their wings on the way down.

As you progress through the book I shall explain to you why this happens and give you some techniques to allow you to break the cycle. This is important because true masters in every field are able to make changes without having to be **pushed** past the edge of their **perceived** capabilities. They step out willingly to take on new challenges even when the things in their life appear to be going well. In doing so, their rate of progress is dramatically increased.

One of the simplest and quickest ways to effect behavioural change is to adjust the way that you look at things. As your interpretation of the situations and challenges that you find yourself facing shifts, so you will automatically take different actions. This is clearly evident, for example, in the diversity of responses in a crowd exposed to a major incident. Some may attempt to run while others remain to the end to help; some may experience terror that immobilises them, while others overcome this with courage and take charge. Although everyone is faced with the same external conditions, their perception drives very different responses. Therefore, by seeking to shift your perception of things as they happen to you, the process of achieving behavioural change can be much simplified. To do so is primarily a question of training yourself to use your mind differently.

This is not to say that change will necessarily ever be easy – it takes courage to do things differently, to seek to take command of your life and break away from established patterns of thinking that have been ingrained for many years. Even realising what needs to be done can be hard; our natural tendency is to refuse to believe, or at least to think odd, anything that is not familiar or that we don't understand. It is the trait that English poet W. H. Auden was referring to when he wrote, "We would rather be ruined than changed; we would rather die in our dread than climb the cross of the moment and let our illusions die." The impact of our inability to recognise our own development needs can be highly detrimental to our progress, not least because it will tend to cause us to believe in our own misguided assessment of our capabilities.

I encourage you to frequently remind yourself of this point as you read. Although is it important to question everything that we hear or read rather than to accept things at face value, it is also vital to learn not to reject ideas simply because they are different from our own. I'm sure you can think of times when something that you were absolutely certain about was proven to be wrong. The question is, how willing are you to deliberately seek to identify areas where your thinking is flawed? This will have a major influence on your rate of progress. If you prefer to hold rigidly to your current ideas and beliefs you will block your future growth. Conversely, the faster you are able to shift your thinking the more rapidly you will progress.

I am well aware that this may sound obvious; however, simple observation demonstrates that there is a huge difference between what we know and what we do. The challenge is to understand why it is so common that people fail to put into practice what they know, even when they are aware of the benefits to be gained from doing so. This requires a better understanding of how the mind works.

In medicine it has been known for years, and is now widely accepted, that the mind controls the body. Research in immunology has clearly demonstrated that there is a direct correlation between our state of mind and the immune function, with immunity being improved significantly by positive states of consciousness. The same thing is also true in relation to our results in the world. I will demonstrate the mechanism by which the mind creates all of our results and in the process, enables you to maximise your ability to take advantage of your opportunities.

A major element in improving effectiveness is the ability to overcome blocks to progress. Most people don't realise that moving past their doubts and fears to expand self-awareness and self-confidence can be exhilarating. The challenge is to prevent our doubts from gripping us in a way that inhibits action and makes us powerless. Many aspects of this book are aimed at helping you to recognise your power and step into it.

I want to clarify what I mean by the word "power" in this context. In the sense that I shall use it there is no relationship to the way that many people think of it; that is, as having control over others. This is the goal of egomaniacs and is force, not power. Force has limited ability to affect anything for the good because it always produces opposition and automatically creates an opposing counterforce. By polarising rather than unifying it escalates conflict and creates a system of winners and losers. Winners then have to perpetually be on the attack or defence to maintain their position; thus, the egomaniacs don't realise that their actions actually block them from experiencing the feeling of power that they are seeking. They will always struggle and never be satisfied. At the same time, the "losers" that they create are dissatisfied and underperform. This is exhausting for everyone and in business is extremely costly as it can never produce the best results.

Power refers to an internal capability that, like gravity, does not move against anything and cannot be resisted. The type of power that I am talking about is total and complete in itself, requiring nothing from the outside. This is what Nelson Mandela accessed to remain strong, even to become stronger, during 27 years of incarceration. Accessing your true power will have the impact of making you less controlling and manipulative of others. You will care more and gain the ability to empathise with many more people – a skill that is critical if you are seeking to influence them. Essentially, you gain the ability to create the win-win solutions that most inspire others to be their best. It is the power within yourself that enables you to change your perceptions, get yourself to do the things that you want to do, take charge of your growth, create joy and satisfaction in your life, open up to other people, and allow yourself to operate from a place of authenticity. Instead of resisting, as force does, power works synergistically with all other things so that the whole becomes much greater than the sum of its parts.

If you do not own your power you will always experience fear because you will have set up a dependency on the outside world being a certain way in order for you to experience happiness. This automatically creates the fear of loss, together with a sense of helplessness, because it is impossible for anyone to control what happens outside them – and attempting to do so can be massively stressful. Although this may happen at a subconscious level, this does not diminish its impact. There is a real fear of losing the good feeling that has subconsciously been associated with something in the outside world.

The solution to feeling good more of the time, therefore, is to realise that the source of the feeling is actually inside you and that it is created by your interpretation of what is going on outside. It is within your capabilities to change your experience at any moment by using your mind differently.

Your internal power is the foundation of the kind of leadership that I encourage you to develop. This is the reason why the most effective starting point is to take responsibility for leading yourself. Furthermore, once you learn to liberate your own inherent power you will gain the capability to release it in other people. This process never works the other way around – you have to start with yourself.

For many people this is a massive paradigm shift. I hope that as you read you will learn to push through your own self-doubts and in the process, let go of the underlying fear of helplessness that automatically arises if we believe that we cannot change our circumstances. This deeper level of fear can be absolutely paralysing, as I describe in Chapter 3. However, if we can learn to accept our fears and observe them from a position of power, their influence on the choices that we make is removed, and they lose their control over us. We then gain the ability to lead much more effectively.

I hope that this book will offer some new ideas to anyone who has an interest in leadership. It is also my intention that it may provide a wake-up call for many people who haven't yet realised that they are leaders, whether or not they are in a leadership position, and that by developing more of their potential they will be able to transform their capabilities. I will be delighted if I can help you to generate a deep motivation to learn, especially if that desire then becomes an ongoing part of your life; this is the only sure path to greatness.

Three of my relatives were top-class orchestral musicians up until their retirement. To first develop and then retain this standard that enabled them to play at the highest level took persistence and dedication to their instruments on a daily basis for over 40 years. I believe that we can all learn from this approach: to be the best that we can be in any field of endeavour requires constant practice and application.

There are many things we do daily that we accept as requirements for a healthy life, such as eating, keeping ourselves clean, and maintaining our living environment. We know that none of these activities has a lasting effect, and we unquestioningly accept the need to repeat them on a frequent basis. Unfortunately, I know from working with my clients that there is often huge resistance to practicing the personal development skills that I suggest in this book in the same way. This is normal and to be expected; however, personal development and leadership are inextricably linked. Very few people make significant progress without first being prepared to put in some additional effort toward personal growth. Just as getting fit requires discipline and repetition, so it is with creating the changes in the mind that lead to higher performance.

There is an old saying that champions don't become champions in the ring – they are merely recognised there. The thing that enables world-class performers to develop the skills necessary for success is the discipline of their daily routine; their success is, in fact, just a collection of habits. What many people do not realise is that, unfortunately, so is failure.

If you wish to become world-class in leadership you will need new habits, so I hope that you will practice the disciplines suggested in the eight techniques associated with Chapters 2 through 9. Any one of them is powerful enough to transform your results by installing the habits of success into your daily activities. There may be all sorts of imagined obstacles in your way, but if you will practice even a subset of these ideas until they become automatic, you will see improvements in your life.

The evidence that we all have a startling ability to effect such change, once we allow ourselves to believe in our potential, is overwhelming. The foremost brain research in the world today has demonstrated that it is impossible to even identify a definable limit to this potential. Therefore, above all, I hope that as you progress through the book you will experience an increasing awareness of your capabilities and belief in yourself. I am not aware of any other single factor that will create a bigger transformation in your life and the fulfilment that you are able to get from it.

We cannot solve a problem from the level of consciousness that created it.

~ Albert Einstein

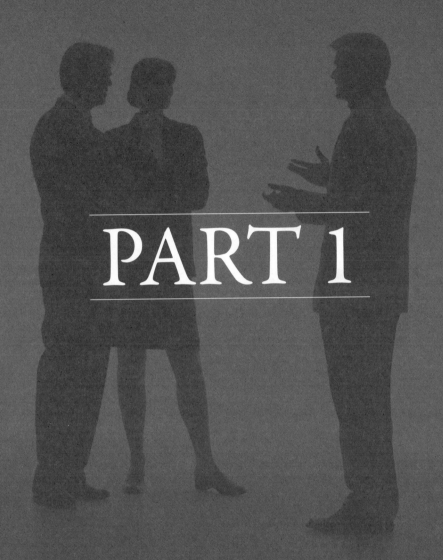

PART 1

AWARENESS - WHERE IT ALL STARTS

LEADERSHIP FOR THE MODERN AGE

When you're finished changing, you're finished.

~ Benjamin Franklin

There is a seismic change taking place in the economy that is having a dramatic impact on what it takes to be successful. In a little over a century, three great waves of technological change have broken over first world economies. These bursts of innovation fuelled the rise of manufacturing in the 1890s, mass production and national corporatism in the 1940s and 1950s, and high-tech entrepreneurialism in the global economy of the 1990s.

Each of these pivotal events saw the demise of one type of economy and the emergence of another. Each changed the nature of work, the organisation of enterprises, educational methods, the places where people live, the role of government in promoting economic growth and social justice, and even traditional conceptions of family and morality. Each spread confusion and conflict as it took hold – but also ultimately led to vast improvements in people's quality of life.

That cycle is repeating itself today, only this time at warp speed. Computers and the Internet are ubiquitous at work and at home. Bureaucratic organisations are yielding to decentralised networks, not only in the private sector but in the public one as well. National economies are being absorbed into a global marketplace open for business 24/7. Employment is continuing its shift from heavy manufacturing to new, knowledge-intensive ventures that scarcely existed a decade ago.

Those companies and individuals that can't respond, or won't, will get left far behind. A recent McKinsey Global Survey highlighted the fact that the vast majority of executives believe their companies are facing a much tougher environment now than they were five years ago, with 85% saying that it is "more" or "much more" competitive.

To compound this problem, a study by Harvard University discovered that for as far back in history as they could go, the pace of change has been accelerating every year. The world is changing at an unprecedented rate, and it is reasonable to assume that this trend will continue.

These changes have unleashed tremendous creative energies and rapid economic growth, but they are also profoundly disruptive for many business leaders and their employees. The need to respond is intense, and many companies have a huge challenge because they have built up such a formidable set of rules, regulations, and chains of command that people can no longer communicate effectively. This rigid structure is not suited to keeping pace or encouraging employees to think outside their current activities. It smothers creativity and severely restricts the ability of the organisation to compete.

The Emerging Environment

In his book, *What Leaders Really Do*, John Kotter presents the idea that the activities of management, which tend to keep things the same, will reduce the ability of companies to respond and keep pace. Many of these activities have remained unchanged since the Industrial Revolution, such as controlling people as things, where employees are told what to do, how to do it, and are punished for any deviation

> TO GET THE BEST OUT OF THEIR EMPLOYEES COMPANY LEADERS CAN NO LONGER MANAGE ACTIONS; THEY MUST STIMULATE THOUGHT.

from those instructions. As the external pace of change accelerates, so the need for internal change becomes ever more pressing, requiring that strong leaders are embedded in all levels of the organisation.

The new economy is being shaped around people and ideas – around leaders. There is increasingly wide acceptance that, overwhelmingly, the work involved will be mind work. Machines built around expert systems will replace people in many knowledge-based roles and as this happens, softer, interpersonal skills that cannot be replaced by a system will become the most valued attributes. There are many signs that this process is already firmly underway.

This people-driven economy has been called The Age of The Mind or The Age of Thinking. Just a few years ago, when I was a director in one of the leading strategy consultancies, a linear extrapolation of historic data trends provided a reasonably reliable forecast for the future. The major nonlinearities in corporate and economic evolution that are being enabled by the rapid advance of technology mean that in many industries this use of historic data is no longer valid. More than ever before, we must be able to cognitively evaluate data and apply a healthy dose of intuition in setting direction. **The awareness, understanding, and insight of individuals will determine the level of success achieved.**

This is a radical shift and means that company leaders will need to encourage different competencies in their staff. **To get the best out of their employees they can no longer manage actions; they must stimulate *thought*.**

Consequently, knowledge can never qualify anyone to be a leader. No one is inspired by a person's education, position, or title. They are inspired by the leadership qualities that shine through in the course of the daily activities. Individuals stepping into a senior position cannot assume that people will follow them merely because of their title, yet many do seem to hope for just that.

Most people accept that, in any field, if we identify the factors that contribute to success, around 80% can be attributed to **attitude**. In leadership, these are often described as "soft skills," or more recently, Emotional Intelligence. This emotional intelligence is much more important than IQ or technical knowledge but is rarely taught. In general, the leaders who succeed will have either natural skills or will have learned them through trial and error, while spending the majority of their time learning and developing technical skills and knowledge.

> THE ONLY ROUTE TO IMPROVED RESULTS OVER THE LONGER TERM IS TO HAVE A TEAM THAT IS BETTER ABLE TO CREATE VALUE.

As the new economy gains pace, personal and interpersonal skills are increasingly becoming critical for success. To have a great impact you must have great influence with other people. Extensive studies have shown that these skills account for 80 to 90% of the leadership competencies that differentiate the best from the others.

The higher you want to climb, the greater will be your need to develop outstanding interpersonal skills. Ultimately, your impact will be determined by your ability to influence and inspire others. However, unless you know how to lead yourself it is almost impossible to lead others effectively. Furthermore, if you choose not to lead yourself, or don't know how, then you will need someone else to follow. This is why it is possible to find so many people drifting through life taking guidance and direction from others. In my experience, few people realise the vital importance of developing a higher level of self-identity that enables them to move beyond the reactivity of the ego, if they wish to change the whole nature of their interactions with others.

Bringing Out the Best

It is common to hear people refer to the employees of a business as its greatest asset. However, the test is not what is said but how the company actually behaves towards its staff. Unfortunately it is less common to find a company where leaders actually treat them as though they mean it. Often the focus on results is so direct as to be counterproductive. One of the easiest ways to observe this is in the often savage cutting of Human Resource department budgets for staff development when corporate profits are under threat. Actions do indeed speak louder than words, and **this action seems to miss the rather obvious fact that the only route to improved results over the longer term is to have a team that is better able to create value.** That means that it must learn and grow.

People who do not have the opportunity to grow will never give their best – and they are beginning to become aware of this. Whereas in the past people may have been satisfied with showing up for work to earn money to allow them to provide for their family, enjoy their time off, and save for retirement, this is no longer the case. They are now looking for professional fulfilment as well. They want to be able to pursue their own dreams, to be challenged and asked to think, and to have the latitude to show creativity in solving problems. They are seeking the ability to express more of themselves, and they have an intuitive awareness of their desire to grow. This is one of our deepest needs. If it is not met, we will always struggle to feel a sense of fulfilment and will have a tendency to withdraw our commitment.

Part of the problem is that employees do not identify with their organisation, its mission and goals. In fact, one quarter of workers admit they show up only to collect a paycheque. This matters with the shift of power that is taking place from corporations to individuals. Employees are realising that they have the power to choose where they will devote their time and energy. If the company they are with doesn't offer the environment and lifestyle they are seeking, they will move – and take their intellectual skills with them. We can see this from the high mobility that now exists in the workforce showing up as high employee turnover, particularly among poor employers. In The Age of the Mind this is critically important. So what can a company leader do?

At the heart of the issue are the relationships that bosses have with their people. It is a well-known axiom that people don't quit their jobs, they quit their bosses. In fact, dissatisfaction with the boss is the number one reason why people leave a company. Such relationships will always create limitation. To move beyond this situation and bring out the best in people, it is necessary to meet employees' needs at a much deeper level. This can be termed "holistic management"; it engages the hearts and minds of the people.

CHAPTER 1: LEADERSHIP FOR THE MODERN AGE

Essentially, greater fulfilment simply comes down to finding ways to feel good. This is the essence of why anyone does anything. There is a shift going on in people's awareness of what will enable them to feel good, to which companies must respond. More employees than ever are looking for fulfilment at work, and some are becoming less willing to trade the quality of their work experience to earn more. By taking an active interest in the needs of employees beyond their pay and benefits, a relationship can be created that extends beyond a superficial exchange of value. Everyone has much more to give if their motivation can be increased.

To deepen people's commitment and increase their motivation it is necessary to change the way that people think.

The Value of the Right Thoughts

We all know that there is a huge difference in the quality of the results that people achieve, but very few people understand why. It cannot simply be factors such as education, location, IQ, or upbringing because we all know of people who have overcome apparently

THE BIGGEST DIFFERENCE BETWEEN WINNERS AND LOSERS IS THE FACT THAT THEY USE THEIR MINDS DIFFERENTLY – THE WINNERS DOING SO IN SUCH A WAY THAT THEY CAN LEARN EFFECTIVELY FROM THEIR MISTAKES.

adverse circumstances to achieve great success. Neither is it luck – too many people who acquire huge fortunes lose it all again. The single factor that fully accounts for all of these differences in results is the way that people use their talents: the way they think.

The impact of differences in thinking is extreme. If we consider financial wealth, only because it is easier to quantify than other factors such as quality of relationships, we find huge disparities. According to the annual government Family Resources Survey, in 2006 the richest 10% of the U.K. population earned 30% of total income, while the poorest 10% and the bottom 50% earned only 2% and 25%, respectively. Even more strikingly, if we look at individual net worth, in 2001 in the U.K., the richest 1% owned 23% of the total wealth whilst the bottom half of the population owned only 5% of the total. The wealthiest individuals did not all inherit their fortunes: 75% of those on *The Times'* rich list have made their money on their own. In the U.S. this is even more apparent, with almost all of the richest people having created their own fortunes. Immigrant populations also demonstrate how a positive attitude allows their apparently severely adverse circumstances and huge disadvantages to be overcome, often to the point that they overtake the established population.

So if thinking offers the answer to the critical question of how to improve results, why is it so hard for people to raise their level of performance? Why are training programs, which work at the level of the conscious, thinking mind, so ineffective? Following such courses, performance may indeed improve for a short time but the gains are rarely sustained. If people simply need to think differently, why don't people do a better job once they have been taught how?

As will become clear later in this book, the reason comes down to the fact that it is not our conscious mind that creates our results. It is not possible for a conscious change in awareness alone to create a change in behaviour. There are several stages of learning through which we must all pass as we go from incompetence to peak performance. These dictate that at the first stage of conscious knowledge people will still be incompetent. Then, as they practice, they move to a state of conscious competence and finally to where their new behaviours become habitual.

Prior to the point that it becomes habitual and therefore automatic, any new behaviour may require a lot of effort to sustain and master. I have frequently seen this with my clients. Once they have started to make progress, the inevitable setbacks that they experience while working on a new skill can be very discouraging. To persevere in the face of these difficulties requires tenacity, resilience, focus, and determination.

Such qualities, and the high performance that follows, comes from just one place – the proper use of the mind. Unfortunately, most people spend more time learning how to use their latest electronic gadget than they spend learning how their mind works and how to use its enormous potential to their advantage.

The fact that we have this huge, innate potential presents an incredible opportunity. It is our greatest untapped resource, and we have the ability to decide to capitalise on it at any time. We simply need to learn to use it differently. Take a look at the people who have been exceptionally successful: it is almost never the result of them working harder, having a better education, or a fortuitous upbringing. It is also clear from studies that they have made similar numbers of mistakes as everyone else. **The biggest difference between winners and losers is the fact that they use their minds differently – the winners doing so in such a way that they can learn effectively from their mistakes.** This requires honesty and a willingness to make changes.

Very few people begin their careers, or anything else that they do, as stars. They must learn along the way, and that takes effort and determination. To keep the body fit and strong requires dedication to regular and challenging exercise. The mind is no different. If you do not properly exercise it, you are very likely to suffer from the common affliction of the mind becoming weaker with age. This becomes particularly evident in people once they retire from work. Conversely, with regular stretching, we now know that the capacity of the mind will continue to become stronger. Simply by making a practice of something as simple as reading educational material on a regular basis, we can make a huge difference – as we can see from studies that have found that readers earn on average two and a half times as much as nonreaders.

Unfortunately, few people have learned how to learn well. Throughout our formative years we are taught to conform to a series of tasks but we are not explicitly taught learning as a skill. We are encouraged in our tasks until we reach a level that is considered acceptable and then, for many people in many areas, we never seek further improvement for the rest of our lives. Take the example of command of the English language. Once we have finished taking exams, most of us never again revisit the subject. As long as we can do it well enough, we tend not to recognise the rewards that are available for becoming excellent – yet there is a direct correlation between command of language and success.

The result is that people have learned to accept mediocre standards for themselves, or have an attitude of just getting by with minimal effort. To break away from mediocrity it is necessary to think differently – to lay waste to the paradigm of generations of conditioning. Generally, ingrained thought patterns are passed from parent to child where, if the patterns are negative, they then limit the mindset of the next generation. For example, overweight parents often have overweight children, and poor academic achievement also tends to run in families. At some point someone has to gain the higher level of awareness necessary to realise that they can break the pattern and make a change and then **decide to do it**.

In the mid-90s in the U.K. a large survey found that, while 80% of the population believed that learning was important, less than one-third had any plans to do anything about it. This provides yet more evidence of how human beings do not do the things that they know they should if they are to be successful. As a result of this study, in 1996 a massive

"Campaign for Learning," supported by the government and business, was launched. In the words of its chairman, Sir Christopher Ball, its aim was, "to care about their learning … and to help create a learning society in the U.K. in which every individual participates in learning, both formal and informal, throughout their lives."

Unfortunately there is little evidence that anything has changed as a result of this campaign. Nonetheless, the initiative highlighted a key point. If we are to move ahead in any field we must ensure that our education does not end when we leave school. We must seek it out, maintaining an attitude of constant and never-ending improvement throughout our lives. As we move into The Age of the Mind the new "poor" in society will be those who cannot learn or who are unwilling to do so.

The Future Belongs to the Learners

In times of change the learners will inherit the earth,
while the learned will find themselves beautifully
equipped to deal with a world that no longer exists.

~ Eric Hoffer

There is no doubt that the ability to learn well is essential in the modern world and that those who do it most effectively are likely to be the most successful. What seems strange is that although most people recognise its importance, very few pursue it with energy and commitment.

Clearly there are many factors that impact the choices we make in this area. One of the most important is that we may not **feel** that the effort is justified by the rewards for winning. In other words, **the long-term gain may not seem to be worth it compared to the cost in terms of our ability to meet our short-term pleasures and pressures**.

This is a common dilemma that lies behind many of the poorer decisions that people make. Any time we are insufficiently connected emotionally to potential long-term gain, we are most likely to choose the immediate payoff, even if, as is usually the case, the benefit is only transitory. This explains why people who would say that they are attempting to lose weight still reach for a chocolate bar. It might well also be the reason why some people appear lazy. I don't believe that anyone is truly lazy – it is just that some of us have not found anything that we feel sufficiently passionately about to motivate a change in current behaviour in order to achieve something meaningful to us in the future.

> IT IS CRITICALLY IMPORTANT THAT A LEADER OPENS UP TO THE POSSIBILITY THAT HE OR SHE HAS IMPORTANT BLIND SPOTS.

Both of these examples demonstrate that **the motivation to learn a new behaviour requires a desire to achieve something greater**. If we are to move into the ranks of the learners, therefore, we must have some clear purpose in doing so. The lack of desire to learn that we can observe in most people is a strong indicator of a general lack of direction and life goals. This is a critical area to address if the energy and commitment that I mentioned earlier are to be achieved.

Another reason why so few people commit themselves to learning lies in their confidence level. Contrary to what many people may think, **supreme confidence is not a good foundation for growth**. Learning effectively requires **a certain degree** of confidence but an individual with too much confidence may think they don't need to learn; too little and they think they can't.

This becomes an increasingly critical issue as people progress through their careers. Studies have found that the further up the corporate ladder a leader climbs, the less accurate his or her self-assessment is likely to be. This is primarily because the quality of feedback that executives receive decreases as they ascend the ranks. Furthermore, because of the way the mind works, it is very difficult for executives to become aware of their weaknesses on their own. As a result, senior leaders as a group will have the highest tendency to lack the "certain degree of confidence" that growth and learning require.

To resolve this issue **it is critically important that a leader opens up to the possibility that he or she has important blind spots** and develops the willingness to receive feedback, learn, and change. Even if major blind spots do not exist, we all have a multitude of opportunities for growth outside our current conscious awareness. As we become more receptive to feedback and seek growth, we place ourselves among the ranks of the learners. This maximises our ability to capitalise on the accelerating economic change that is sweeping through the marketplace and looks set to continue to do so. As Peter Drucker, who was considered by many to have been one of the world's most influential business gurus, said, "We now accept the fact that learning is a lifelong process of keeping abreast of change. And the most pressing task is to teach people how to learn."

The Leading Decision

Often people think that their potential as a leader is limited, that they lack the special qualities necessary. This is usually founded on a false belief that there are essential skills of leadership that must be inherited at birth – charisma, for example. This is simply not true. Although some people may have a higher level of natural aptitude than others, **every skill necessary to become an extraordinary leader can be learned.**

Take the example of Sir Winston Churchill. He became the British Prime Minister during the Second World War while in his 60s, and is regarded as the greatest British leader of the 20th century; yet he did not obviously show these traits from the start. Despite a highly privileged birth he spent his early years at school rebelling. He generally performed badly, for which he was punished, was very headstrong and stubborn, and did not get along well with the other students. He did not have an imposing stature, being only 5 feet 6½ inches tall, and he suffered from a speech impediment. When he left school and applied to join the army he required three attempts before he passed the entrance exam. Nevertheless, by the time he reached the end of his 20s and entered politics, he was a national hero due to his exploits in the wars in the Sudan and South Africa. He went on to make a major impact as a leader, not only in politics but also in literature, winning the Nobel Prize for Literature in 1953.

> TO BE REALLY STRONG
> IN THE EMERGING ECONOMY,
> ORGANISATIONS REQUIRE LEADERS
> FROM TOP TO BOTTOM.

Part of the reason that Churchill was able to be so successful can be attributed to the fact that there is no single way to be effective as a leader: we all have the opportunity to develop the style most suited to our individual strengths. Churchill's approach was highly distinctive and at the same time incredibly effective. The same could be said of Gandhi, Bill Gates, Richard Branson, or a host of other notable leaders. Each may have had a very different background, environment, and set of goals. Yet each was able to learn the skills necessary to have a long-term impact on the world through their own style of leadership.

Leadership, therefore, is about acting in such a way so as to be able to significantly influence the thoughts, feelings, and behaviors of others. It is a collection of behaviors, not a role, title, or birthright. Extensive evidence demonstrates that if we can tap into the motivation necessary, every one of us also has the potential to be a leader. By developing our own personal talents it is possible for us to reach a high level of leadership skill no matter what level we are at or what we are doing right now. Most important is the **decision** to be the best that we can be – to be prepared to lead rather than follow.

For anyone who is prepared to make this decision, the opportunity to make a difference is huge. Every one of us is thought to influence at least 10,000 other people during our lifetime. For those in senior positions it will generally be many more.

Unfortunately, many people believe that leadership is only for the few people who are already at the top of the corporate ladder or in senior public positions. They often fail to recognise that leadership came first and the position was the result. Therefore, they completely miss the importance of developing the ability to inspire and influence. They are oblivious to the opportunities they may be passing by in failing to lead themselves effectively, and they end up passively following other people. For an organisation this matters enormously. **To be really strong in the emerging economy requires leaders from top to bottom.**

You can make a massive difference once you decide to develop your potential as a leader. The first prerequisite for success is to set inspirational goals in order to provide direction and meaning for all of your activities. As we will cover in detail later in the book, it is essential to know what you want, and why.

The second prerequisite is to know where you are now. This is the part that many people seek to avoid and which training courses rarely explore except superficially. As the next chapter covers in detail, it is essential that you raise your level of self-awareness about what drives you; in particular, why you do the things that you do. The speed at which you will be able to create better results will be determined by your preparedness to be honest in this area, as well as by your willingness to make the necessary changes.

2

THE FOUNDATIONS OF OUR RESULTS

What is necessary to change a person is to change his awareness of himself.

~ Abraham Maslow

W hen people begin to think about raising their level of performance, they often turn first to developing their skills or knowledge. This is perhaps to be expected, given the emphasis placed on these areas by our education system. However, as suggested in the quote above by Abraham Maslow, the well-known psychologist most noted for his proposal of a hierarchy of human needs, the only means by which to improve at anything is actually to raise your level of self-awareness. Awareness is the foundation of all of our results and determines how well we will perform in any given set of circumstances.

This understanding is critical because it establishes that it is impossible for you to change your behaviour in relation to any area where you have a blind spot. Anything that you are unaware of will control you. Therefore, **greater awareness is the essential ingredient that empowers** personal transformation.

Awareness is generally understood to mean having a conscious knowledge of something. However, there is a more sophisticated understanding that makes the distinction between our "thinking mind" and our "aware mind." In this context, awareness can be seen to be automatic and fully inclusive of all of life's experiences. Much as all normally functioning people effortlessly comprehend at least one language, awareness provides us with a "knowingness" that does not require logic, analysis, or calculation. It functions completely spontaneously, recognising the whole picture and responding accordingly.

> PEOPLE PERFORM AT THE LEVEL THAT THEY DO BECAUSE THEY ARE NOT AWARE OF WAYS TO PERFORM BETTER.

In relation to personal growth, this capability to generate awareness of any area on which we focus provides the vital foundation for our understanding of self: our personality, strengths and weaknesses, how we are feeling, what we are doing, and how this impacts people and events around us. Developing self-awareness can help us to recognise when we are stressed or under pressure. It is also a prerequisite for developing empathy for others, effective communication, and all interpersonal relations.

A corollary of this understanding of the role awareness plays in determining behaviours is that in any environment, **people perform at the level that they do because they are not aware of ways to perform better**. No one goes to work to intentionally do a bad job – they simply do not know how to do better. Even those who may appear to have a disruptive intention will change if shown a better way and helped to believe in their ability to follow through.

Many people exposed to this suggestion for the first time rapidly conclude that it must be wrong because most of us can easily identify people who appear to already know how to do better but who aren't doing it. In my experience, with awareness it is possible to look at anyone and identify areas in their professional and personal lives where they **know** how to do better. For example, every student knows how to study more effectively, every salesman knows how to sell more, and everyone who wants to be slimmer knows what they must do to be successful. I frequently ask clients or seminar attendees to think of three things that they already know that would enable them to do their job better, but which they are not doing. So far, everyone that I've asked has been able to do this with ease.

The explanation for this apparent contradiction lies in the fact that it is not conscious knowledge that drives the choices people make. Instead, our actions are the consequences of all of the habits and beliefs that reside at the subconscious level. If improved performance could be achieved simply by gaining knowledge, there would be a higher correlation between education and performance, and people would benefit more from training courses. Unfortunately, from the early days of our formal education we are encouraged to focus on our grades above all else and conditioned to believe that knowledge will determine whether we succeed or fail. As a result, too many people have accepted the premise suggested by Sir Francis Bacon, that knowledge is power.

Although this may have been the case when he lived and information was scarce, it is certainly not true now. Our society has reached information overload, and many very knowledgeable people achieve only limited success.

The sad consequence of this conditioning is that far too many have reduced their awareness by focusing on the left brain activity of accumulating knowledge. What really makes the difference is what we do with what we know. As we shall go on to explore, this is controlled by an entirely different part of the brain from that which we use for learning.

Because many organisations do not understand this, development efforts are often targeted ineffectively. For example, trainers are often engaged in response to poor sales with a remit to improve sales skills or processes. Unfortunately, most of their audience probably already know how to sell – the real issue is that they are not doing what they know. Rather than more sales training, what they need is greater awareness of why they are not doing what they already know and an understanding of how to use that awareness to do things differently. Once that has been achieved, regular skills-training becomes much more valuable because people have the ability to put their new learning into practice. If you are spending money on teaching your staff new skills but have not first given them the awareness necessary to be able to put the teaching into practice, then you may be wasting both time and money.

The most dramatic change in individual performance occurs when a person gains a raised awareness of their own potential. This is normally accompanied by a dramatic shift in approach and is a huge enabler to leadership.

Emotional Intelligence is Vital

*Even in such technical lines as engineering, about
15% of one's financial success is due to one's technical
knowledge and about 85% is due to skill in
human engineering, to personality and the
ability to lead people.*

~ Dale Carnegie

Daniel Goleman, one of the best known writers on the body of knowledge that has become known as "emotional intelligence," defines it as the ability to be intelligent about emotions in ourselves and others. It requires that we have the capacity to recognise our feelings and those of others, and to use this awareness to manage both our emotions and our relationships with others.

The starting point, a heightened sensitivity to emotions in ourselves and others, comes from the development of something called Sensory Acuity. Everyone is constantly monitoring and reacting to their environment but there are huge variations in our ability to use our sensory input effectively. With sensory acuity our ability to become aware of the inputs from our sensory organs can become extremely refined.

If you look at the top people in any field, they always have very highly developed sensory acuity. For example, wine tasters have an incredible ability to notice subtle differences in wine to pinpoint the grape, vineyard, and year of production; bird watchers recognise the tiniest differences in appearance of a bird or its movements; and golfers putting are highly tuned to subtle slopes of the green, the strength and direction of wind, the moisture on the ground, and even the grain of the grass.

Similarly, highly developed sensory acuity is also essential in business, where it underpins the ability to develop emotional intelligence. As you become more senior, so the human element of your job will become increasingly important, and you will need to become highly aware of how others are reacting to you, thus allowing you to modify your behaviours to achieve optimal results.

The first people to coin the term "emotional intelligence" were Peter Salovey, a Yale psychologist, and John Mayer of the University of New Hampshire. They defined its main tenets as follows:

- Self-awareness: observing yourself and recognising a feeling as it happens. This is fundamental to emotional intelligence. People who are aware of their feelings have greater mastery of their lives.

- Managing emotions: handling feelings so that behaviours remain respectful and appropriate, and finding ways to deal with fears, anger, sadness, etc. People who lack self-restraint tend to do whatever their impulses suggest. Effective management of emotions enables people to better cope with life's adversities and to bounce back faster than those who lack this ability.

- Motivating oneself: channelling emotions towards a goal, having emotional self-control, delaying gratification, and stifling impulses. This underlies accomplishment on every level.

- Recognising emotions in others: sensitivity to others' feelings and concerns and appreciating the differences in how people feel about things. This is only possible from an established foundation of emotional self-awareness. In other words, if we are in touch with our own feelings, we can then empathise with others and sense their needs.

- Handling relationships: managing emotions in others, social competence, and social skills. For example, the ability to calm distressing emotions in others can help resolve many conflicts.

Most of us are aware that the need to develop the right psychology is critical to success in sports, yet few consider the significance of their emotional state in the work environment. In fact, there is extensive research to indicate that it is every bit as important in business as anywhere else. Overall, it has been found that for all jobs, in every field, emotional intelligence is at least twice as important as pure cognitive ability.

Of course, it would be absurd to suggest that cognitive ability is irrelevant for success in, for example, science-based vocations. One needs a relatively high IQ just to be admitted in these fields. However once admitted, how you perform in relation to your peers will depend less on IQ differences and more on social and emotional factors. It is more important, for example, to persist in the face of difficulties and to get on well with colleagues than it is to have an extra few points of IQ.

Note also that emotional and cognitive skills are related, even at the biological level. One important aspect of this is that when people are experiencing negative emotions, the hormones that are created literally block access to the reasoning parts of the brain. In the "marshmallow studies" at Stanford University, 4-year-olds were asked to stay in a room alone with a marshmallow and wait for a researcher to return. They were told that if they could wait until the researcher came back before eating the marshmallow, they could have two. Ten years later the researchers tracked down the participants in the study. They found that those who were able to resist temptation had a total SAT score (a U.S. test that students take before they can go to college) that was 210 points higher than those kids who were unable to wait.

Although intellect and clear thinking are generally the most important competencies early in people's careers and may be responsible for getting them up the first rungs of the ladder, this situation does not last. Progressively, the ability to make a contribution through other people becomes increasingly important.

Despite this obvious and well-recognised importance of interpersonal skills, few businesses provide the training needed to become proficient in this area. Consequently, even though it is critical to success, few people are even aware of the skills necessary to be strong in emotional intelligence; they don't know how to positively express themselves with integrity while listening to, understanding, and communicating effectively with others. This is hardly surprising since the educational system rewards learning, and emotional intelligence skills are rarely taught.

> ALL OF THE NECESSARY EMOTIONAL COMPETENCIES FOR EFFECTIVE LEADERSHIP CAN BE LEARNED.

I believe that the most important aspect of emotional intelligence is the ability to harness emotions for our benefit and the benefit of others. For instance, in a study at Yale University by Sigdal Barsade, a group of volunteers played the role of managers who came together in a group to allocate bonuses to their subordinates. A trained actor was planted among them. The actor always spoke first, in some groups projecting cheerful enthusiasm, in others relaxed warmth, in others depressed sluggishness, and in still others hostile irritability. The results indicated that the actor was able to infect the group with his emotion. Furthermore, good feelings led to improved cooperation, fairness, and overall group performance. In fact, objective measures indicated that the cheerful groups were better able to distribute the money fairly and in a way that helped the organisation. Similar findings come from the field. As far back as 1988, Bachman found that the most effective leaders in the U.S. Navy were warmer, more outgoing, emotionally expressive, dramatic, and sociable.

The good news is that **all of the necessary emotional competencies for effective leadership can be learned** and in many cases, they are complementary and mutually supporting. In their book on leadership competencies, *The Extraordinary Leader*, Jack Zenger and Joseph Folkman describe how "competency companions" rise and fall together. As one competency is improved others automatically rise with it. They build upon each other and are highly interrelated.

Figure 2.1 illustrates the relationship between the major emotional competency areas. In the following pages each is explored in turn to provide insight about how to approach improving skills in each competency area, focusing particularly on leadership.

Figure 2.1 – An Emotionally-based
Leadership Model

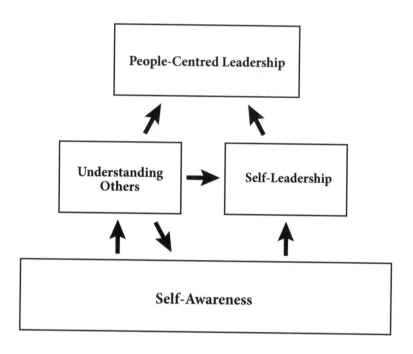

The foundation is the need to understand why people do what they do. This can come from two main sources: self-awareness to understand our own emotions and an understanding of others and what motivates their behaviours. These two are closely related and are, in fact, inseparable. As you gain greater personal understanding through feedback, contemplation, and reflection, an improvement of your understanding of others will be automatic. Similarly, by seeking greater understanding of the behaviours of others, self-understanding will also be enhanced.

> THE VERY FIRST ELEMENT TO FOCUS ON IN BUILDING A PLATFORM FOR SUCCESS IS SELF-AWARENESS.

As we understand more fully why people behave as they do, we can become more compassionate about the challenges they experience as they move outside their comfort zone by taking on new things and seeking to grow. We can also recognise how their behaviours impact our emotional state. As a consequence of this higher level of awareness of self and others, our own self-leadership improves.

Finally, an understanding of others combined with the ability to manage our own emotions effectively allows for people leadership based on strong relationships. Therefore, **awareness of self provides the foundation for, and is fundamental to, becoming a better leader.** Let's look at each of these competency areas in more detail.

Self-Awareness

If you desire to have great people skills you will need to develop the competency of self-awareness. This is generally overlooked, both by people seeking to develop their leadership skills and by the organisations that train them. It is essential to know why you do the things that you do before it becomes possible to make rapid and effective changes. To take an alternative approach is to fail to address the underlying cause and would be rather like attempting to learn calculus without mastering basic algebra first. Tall buildings require robust foundations.

The ancient scholars understood the importance of this particular area to one's success – almost 2,500 years ago Socrates advised, "Know thyself." More recently, the importance of self-awareness was demonstrated in a study by Ashridge Business School that asked leaders what they knew now that they most wished that they'd known 10 years ago. The most common response was that they wished they'd known more about themselves. **The very first element to focus on in building a platform for success is self-awareness.**

Many of the struggles that leaders encounter early on in their careers are not issues of the marketplace or corporate environment but are issues of emotional self-control and evaluation of circumstances. With greater awareness leaders later come to realise that much of what appeared to be a crisis at the time was only a lack of people skills and self-knowledge on their part.

In raising self-awareness for leadership, there is little that is more important than becoming more sensitive to your emotions and those of others. In their investigation of emotional intelligence, Salovey and Mayer developed research programs intended to develop valid measures of emotional intelligence and to explore its significance. In one such program they studied a group of people who were shown an upsetting film. They found that those who scored highly on emotional clarity (the ability to identify and give a name to a mood that is being experienced) recovered more quickly. In another study, individuals who scored higher in the ability to perceive accurately, understand, and appraise others' emotions were better able to respond flexibly to changes in their social environments and build supportive social networks.

These examples provide evidence of the degree to which emotions can provide enormously useful feedback to help you enhance your interactions with others, yet this is an area where many people are surprisingly weak. The simple exercise of keeping an emotional diary, a record of feelings together with what triggered them, can stimulate significant changes. Emotions are not something for leaders to avoid. Instead there are huge benefits to be gained from embracing them: they will help you to gain the most from the situations that arise for you.

Take the example of one of my clients who regularly found himself in conflict with his Board colleagues during meetings. He was convinced that everyone else lacked his ability to see the answers to problems as quickly and intuitively as he could. Consequently, when new ideas were proposed he would quickly take a position, adopting a persuasive approach initially but becoming rapidly quarrelsome and belligerent if he did not get his way. Finally he would become very quiet and cease contributing.

The biggest issue in resolving this behaviour had nothing to do with the other members of the team or the degree to which his problem-solving capability was real or imaginary. It came from understanding that the breakdown in communication with his colleagues stemmed from his own inability to recognise and manage his own emotions and to have empathy for how the rest of the team were feeling. Before any change was possible, he had to realise that even if he was right, and he often was, this approach reduced his ability to achieve his desired outcomes. He had to learn to become aware of the negative emotions that he experienced whenever his initial attempt at persuasion failed so that he could adopt a different approach and avoid the hostility that had historically obstructed his progress.

Most people have trouble managing emotionally charged situations, especially those involving intense emotions such as anger and anxiety. These are a major cause of stress both at work and at home. As a result, difficult communication issues can arise and escalate, producing deep problems for those individuals who are unable to function effectively in this area.

If you overlook or shy away from managing your emotions there is a danger that your leadership capability will be severely inhibited. It is simply not possible to lead others unless you are first prepared to lead yourself. In the absence of self-leadership there will be times when you will need to follow someone else. This is why throughout history dictators have been able to gain power, and why many people in business become content with letting someone else think for them and continuing to follow very poor leaders. On the other hand, if you can learn to handle your emotions, from the perspective of both their expression and their regulation, as well as develop the ability to generate the kinds of emotions in others that are productive and effective, you will have a major advantage.

Self-awareness is not about allowing someone else to tell you that you are wrong. It is about recognising your strengths and weaknesses, being prepared to look proactively for your own flaws and opportunities for growth, and then having the ability to handle them accordingly.

Understanding Others

With improved self-awareness also comes a deeper connection to the motivations of others. Our most important capability in understanding others is empathy: the ability to understand how someone else is likely to be feeling in any particular situation. Researchers have known for years that it contributes to occupational success. Robert Rosenthal and his colleagues at Harvard discovered over two decades ago that **people who are best at identifying others' emotions are more successful in their work as well as in their social lives**.

> PEOPLE WHO ARE BEST AT IDENTIFYING OTHERS' EMOTIONS ARE MORE SUCCESSFUL IN THEIR WORK AS WELL AS IN THEIR SOCIAL LIVES.

It is empathy that enables us to put ourselves into another person's place and feel the same emotions. This is why we cry at movies, laugh at funny stories, and are horrified by tragedies we see. The psychotherapist Carl Rogers described empathy as, "entering the private perceptual world of the other and becoming thoroughly at home in it … to be with another in a way that means for the time being you lay aside the views and values you hold for yourself in order to enter another's world without prejudice." **Understanding people from an empathetic perspective will dramatically improve your ability to deal with them effectively.**

Often the resentments or misunderstandings that occur between people are issues of communication. When something hurts or annoys us, we make up entire stories about what the other person's potential motives were. These are usually not only wrong but very often they will not serve us in any way either. However, they do create a build-up of negative emotions in us that diminish our ability to function effectively.

A very simple example of this in daily life is when someone cuts in front of us in traffic. How do you react to such situations? For many people, they immediately become angry, and this feeling may stay with them for some time.

> IF WE REACT WITH INTOLERANCE AND NEGATIVITY TO ANYTHING THAT IS HAPPENING AROUND US WE INSTANTLY LOSE OUR ABILITY TO EMPATHISE WITH OTHERS.

Meanwhile, the person responsible is likely to be unaware of the incident, or could even be taking pleasure from it. In such circumstances, we continue to suffer for as long as we continue to brood over what happened. We can rise above the situation by seeking a different interpretation of what we have experienced. Perhaps the other person was having a bad day or was rushing to hospital to be with a loved one.

Stephen Covey presented a story in *The Seven Habits of Highly Effective People* that illustrates this point powerfully. He was on a subway train when a man and his children got on. The children were extremely loud and disruptive, yelling, throwing things, and disturbing the other passengers. As Stephen found himself getting increasingly irritated by the unruly behaviour, and the lack of action to deal with it by the father, he decided to have a polite word with the man to raise his concerns. "Oh, you're right," replied the man. "We just came from the hospital where their mother died about an hour ago. I don't know what to think, and I guess they don't know how to handle it either."

I'm sure you can imagine the magnitude of the shift in Stephen's emotional state upon hearing these words. Immediately, his perception of the situation changed, and all judgment that he was feeling gave way to enormous compassion for how the man and his children would have been feeling.

This may be an extreme example but the principle is very sound. **If we react with intolerance and negativity to anything that is happening around us we instantly lose our ability to empathise with others** and as a result, become much less effective in our interactions with them. This severely limits the ability of a leader in this most critical area of leadership.

We can never fully understand what may be going on in the mind of another person; however, developing a higher level of understanding of what drives their behaviours builds on your foundation of self-awareness in an extremely powerful way. The combination of these two areas has a synergetic impact on your self-leadership capability.

Self-Leadership

Nothing so conclusively proves a man's ability
to lead others as what he does from
day to day to lead himself.

~ Thomas J. Watson

The value and importance of self-leadership is that it enables us to break away from allowing our external environment to determine how we feel. To behave otherwise is to be controlled by our emotions. If we look again at the previous example of someone being cut off whilst driving: without self-leadership the anger that begins on the drive to work can translate into a short temper for the entire day. This could inhibit their ability to make progress, or potentially even cause lasting damage to their relationships because of the behaviours that it tends to promote.

Once you are able to recognise your emotions and let the negative ones go, it frees you from being controlled by them. By becoming more self-aware, you give yourself the opportunity to shift your state from a negative emotion such as resentment to a powerful alternative, such as forgiveness. We are all human and mistakes will always be made. The inability to forgive errors, whether they are made by you or someone else, hurts no one but you in the long run.

It is impossible for a leader to be authentic to others in relation to their feelings without mastering this area. Make no mistake: **those who you deal with and who surround you on a daily basis are very aware how you handle your feelings and emotions**. This is not something that can be hidden or swept under the rug, and it always has a damaging impact on others' performance under your leadership if not managed well.

It is a privilege when we have the opportunity to lead a team of people but with it comes many responsibilities, at the forefront of which is **managing moods**.

In a *Harvard Business Review* article called "Leadership That Gets Results," Daniel Goleman cites research that shows that up to 30% of a company's financial results (as measured by key business performance indicators such as revenue growth, return on sales, efficiency, and profitability) are determined by the "climate" of the organisation. Broadly described, climate refers to the perception of employees about how it feels to be part of the organisation.

So what is the major factor that drives the climate of an organisation? In *Primal Leadership: Realizing the Power of Emotional Intelligence,* Goleman states that roughly 50 to 70% of the way in which employees perceive their organisation's climate is attributable to the actions and behaviours of their leader. A leader creates the environment that determines people's moods at the office and their mood, in turn, affects their productivity and level of engagement.

Witness the number of times you may have driven home with an internal glow, reliving a positive encounter with an upbeat and supportive boss, perhaps savouring recognition or a good word about your performance that he or she left with you. Think how great you felt and how eager you were to get out of bed on the following morning to get back to the office and give that man or woman the very best that you had to offer. That's the "afterglow" that lingers and gives you renewed energy to be more productive, bringing your finest talents to your work.

> A LEADER IN A BAD MOOD IS LIKE A SOURCE OF INFECTION WITHIN THE ORGANISATION.

Now think about that same scenario in reverse – the bad experience of an encounter with your boss that has undermined your self-confidence or security. This creates what Susan Scott, in *Fierce Conversations: Achieving Success at Work and in Life, One Conversation at a Time,* calls

"The Emotional Wake." The aftermath or bitter aftertaste of being the recipient of acrid remarks from a leader in a negative mood may have lingered with you for a substantial period of time. How did that affect your determination to overcome difficulties in a project, to keep your heart fully engaged in the process and to want to continue to give that person your very best?

Leadership literature is full of studies attesting to the consequences of a leader's mood. One such study involving 62 CEOs and their top management teams showed that the more upbeat, energetic, and enthusiastic the executive team was, the more cooperatively they worked together and the better the company's business results. The study also showed that the longer a company was managed by an executive team that didn't get along well, the poorer the company's market returns.

Perhaps nowhere is a leader's mood more crucial than in the service industry where, without fail, employees in a bad mood adversely affect business. One of a multitude of studies in this area looked at 53 sales managers in retail outlets. They led groups ranging in size from four to nine members, and it was found that when managers themselves were in an upbeat, positive mood, their moods spilled over to their staff, positively affecting the staff's performance and increasing sales. It is clear that **a leader in a bad mood is like a source of infection within the organisation** that eventually spreads across people to entire units and wrecks performance. Ultimately, people take their cues from the behaviour of the leader, whether it is positive or negative, causing the formation of equivalent habits in an organisation.

Some people seek to avoid addressing their poor self-leadership by arguing that their occasional bad mood or display of anger on "a bad day" is to be expected, or they overlook it in staff they consider to be stars in other areas. We may hear this type of behaviour excused or minimised with statements such as, "She can't always control her temper, but she is so brilliant," or, "He has an amazing mind and he only really shouts at people when it's stressful," as though brilliance somehow makes bad behaviour more acceptable. Unfortunately, the impact bad behaviour has on other parties doesn't stop with the end of the mood. Even if leaders are balanced and reasonable most of the time, deviations will have a toxic effect on their ability to engender trust.

I saw this powerfully demonstrated by one of my clients. He was very unhappy with a comment given to him during a 360-degree feedback survey. Despite the fact that all of the comments were intended to help him and were unattributed, he believed that he knew where the one in question came from and went and confronted this person. During the exchange that ensued he lost his self-control, became angry, and made a number of statements in an open-plan office environment that caused much unnecessary hurt. Despite the fact that this was an infrequent behaviour pattern, the person who was on the receiving end of his bad mood never trusted him again. Furthermore, because he did not even demonstrate the control necessary to find somewhere private for the meeting, he also severely damaged the way that he was regarded by a number of other people.

An unpredictable leader elicits anxiety, even fear, which negatively affects performance and productivity. **It is literally impossible for anyone to maximise effectiveness whilst continuing to leaving a trail of damaged relationships behind them caused by their inability to manage their emotions.**

Of course, no leader steps out of the elevator in the morning with an intention of spreading a bad mood but this is life – events inevitably occur that can derail even the most calm and self-assured among us. The only solution is to develop the capacity to manage emotions more effectively as they happen so that when the negative ones do arise we don't need to live with them for as long. This is a definite skill that can be learned.

We can draw some further advice on the management of moods from another *Harvard Business Review* article by Daniel Goleman titled "Primal Leadership: The Hidden Driver of Great Performance." First of all, it's important to note that a leader's mood has the greatest impact on performance when it is upbeat but it must also be in tune with those around him. Goleman calls this dynamic *resonance*. He suggests that "Good moods galvanise good performance, but it doesn't make sense for a leader to be as chipper as a blue jay at dawn if sales are tanking or the business is going under. The most effective executives display moods and behaviours that match the situation at hand, with a healthy dose of optimism mixed in. They respect how other people are feeling – even if it is glum or defeated – but they also model what it looks like to move forward with hope and humour."

Accordingly, I am not advocating that leaders lack authenticity with false smiles and fake cheerfulness. Constituents recognise a non-genuine smile and are very adept at noticing when a leader wears one. I also fully acknowledge that there are no easy solutions to managing emotions on an ongoing basis in the often difficult circumstances in which leaders must operate and make decisions. It may require considerable personal growth – but there is really no alternative. You must start by working on yourself.

The operative words in the statement from Goleman above are "optimism," "hope," and "humour." Leaders that behave this way have learned to control their mood such that they can determine how they respond. They are no longer simply reacting to their surroundings based on conditioning; rather they have developed the emotional resilience and behavioural flexibility to optimise their performance.

This capacity to maintain a responsive rather than reactive state is one of the ultimate goals of self-leadership. When people are reacting to their environment their conditioning is determining what they do. The problem here is that every situation is different, so any reaction based purely on the past will limit their ability to create better results in the future. This tendency to react occurs most strongly when people are in a poor emotional state and it rarely results in appropriate action.

In contrast, responsiveness will allow you to bring your full intellect to identifying the most appropriate action in the circumstances that you are facing. Thus, it means not being controlled by conditioned behaviours but being able to assess each situation on its merits.

A great example of the effectiveness of moving beyond reactivity comes from research that tested the effectiveness of a compassionate response to difficult people and circumstances. In such situations most people's conditioned reaction is to match what is happening to them and become emotionally negative themselves. It was found that these negative states, such as anger or resentment, produced a negative reaction 100% of the time. In contrast, the study demonstrated that where a compassionate response was used to meet the difficulty, a positive reaction was achieved 70% of the time.

With self-awareness you can become a much more successful leader by raising the standards of behaviour that you expect of yourself and responding in a way that is consistent with them. **The effect of this change on your ability to influence and inspire others has the potential to be transformational.**

People-Centred Leadership

It sounds obvious doesn't it – leadership is about people. The problem is that what many people pass for leadership is really management. They are constantly seeking efficiencies, but **leadership**

must be effective, not efficient. Efficiency never brings out the best in people. Often one of the most effective changes that people seeking to improve their leadership can make is to shift this focus.

At the heart of this change must be an alteration to the way that you interact with others. For example, if you want to increase your impact, shift from seeking praise from others to focusing on the things of value that you can achieve instead, such as giving praise. This alone could create dramatic results because it would lift you from the competitive to the creative plane of action. So many people limit their success through competitive behaviour, potentially even preventing others from being successful, to enable them to feel better through comparison. This is easy to do, for example, by undermining their actions through criticism or withholding help that could have been provided. However, advancement comes from focusing on how you can add more value, never from comparison with what others are doing.

> LEADERSHIP MUST BE EFFECTIVE, NOT EFFICIENT.

The metaphor of how crabs behave when placed into a basket illustrates the impact of this way of competitive thinking. If a single crab is in the basket a lid is needed to stop it from climbing out; however, if there are two or more crabs this is no longer necessary. Instead, the other crabs will drag any down that try to climb up the sides, thereby stopping them from getting away.

You may not realise that you do the same thing each time you express views that limit possibility for others. This is a widespread tendency and explains why virtually everyone who has made great advances in their lives or in society at large did so by ignoring the opinions of the masses. To move from competitiveness to creativity it is essential to avoid unquestioningly accepting the belief systems of others, particularly as they relate to yourself. You should seek instead to become more interested in the voice of your own intuition rather than the opinions of others. Leadership always involves diverging from popular opinion and being prepared to be the first to tread new ground.

So how good do you want to be? All of the skills of leadership and self-awareness can be learned if you are prepared to dedicate yourself to personal growth. One of the basic laws of the universe is that everything is in a perpetual state of either creation or disintegration. Just as every seed disintegrates until it is placed in an environment in which it can grow, when you choose to stop learning, either actively or through neglect, you are allowing the disintegration process to set in. It is simply impossible to stand still in a world that is changing constantly and at such a rapid pace. The half-life of knowledge in the current business environment is typically somewhere between three and five years, depending on the industry, and complete paradigm shifts that utterly change the competitive environment have become more frequent. Whether at the level of a huge corporation, such as IBM in the 1980s, which seemed to have an unassailable lead in the computer industry then rapidly came close to bankruptcy, or an individual – try getting a job in a typing pool today – the message is the same: **you must change, or risk becoming irrelevant**.

Consequently, ongoing learning is essential if you are to be able to get ahead and stay ahead. How much you will need to learn and how hard these changes will be to implement depends on how good you want to be. Generally, those who get average results have put in little or no extra effort, whilst those in the top 10% will have at some time devoted considerable energy to deliberately learning and growing. Unfortunately, however, few of them maintain this success formula throughout their careers and therefore many never make it to the top. To be a peak performer requires focused effort – you simply must be prepared to put the work in. The key to unlocking the creative process that underpins performance at this level is the understanding and awareness that comes from study.

Some of this may seem a bit obvious – but is it really? If it were so obvious why is it that so few people, including many intelligent and very well-educated people are doing it? Jim Rohn provided useful insight and advice when he said, "Success is the study of the obvious. Everyone should take Obvious 1 and Obvious 2 in school." Unfortunately, when it comes to seeking success, it is often the obvious that is most overlooked.

Jim Collins undertook a study at Stanford University of what separates good companies from great ones; his findings were published in the book *Good to Great*. Many executives have read this book, and I'm sure some have thought, "There's nothing new here – we know this." They may have been right. One of the most important points Collins makes is precisely the fact that the great companies he studied **didn't** have revolutionary ideas or management techniques. They did many little things very well and very consistently created outstanding – and sustainable – results. It seems surprising that despite the fact that very few companies met Collins' criteria for what it means to be great, those that did excel did not do so by virtue of a huge breakthrough of some description. And one of the biggest surprises to Collins was that **the quality of leadership was critical in every case**. Clearly, the real challenge of building a world-class business is not the knowing what to do but being able to put it into practice.

To really understand what it takes to develop the quality of leadership necessary to reach the top we first need to understand why we do the things that we do in more detail and why we find it difficult to change. This is the starting point for growing self-awareness, the foundation of leadership.

Transformational Technique:
Build Self-Awareness

The key principle in this chapter is to recognise that all aspects of personal performance are built on self-awareness. If this is missing, any growth becomes more difficult. The greater your understanding of yourself, the stronger your foundation will be for all other areas of your life, particularly leadership. Quite simply, you must learn to lead yourself first.

To this end I recommend that you develop the study of yourself into an ongoing practice. Proactively seek feedback to identify your blind spots and deliberately reflect on what you find out and, together with what your results are showing you, identify the most beneficial areas in which to concentrate your growth efforts. Also, focus specifically on developing your sensory acuity around emotional intelligence issues to improve overall leadership awareness.

3

THE FORCE THAT CONTROLS US

Great spirits have always found violent opposition from mediocrities. The latter cannot understand when a man does not thoughtlessly submit to hereditary prejudices but honestly and courageously uses his intelligence.

~ Albert Einstein

No one likes to believe that they are controlled by anyone or anything. We are more likely to want to picture ourselves with our backs firmly to the wall ready for whatever life throws at us, our attention fixed on the external world. However, what if the force that shapes our destiny is internal? What if the multitude of experiences that we have had in our lives, many of which were not of our choosing, has shaped our mind such that it controls our behaviour?

Have you ever caught yourself saying something to an employee without thinking and then remembered that same phrase coming from one of your parents, or perhaps from an earlier boss? What we do and how we do it is determined by the numerous events that have shaped our mind and, over time, accumulated into patterns of behaviour. These patterns are ingrained so that they produce our reactions to situations, usually without conscious thought on our part. The only way to manage these behaviours is to first become aware that they exist.

There is a powerful case to argue that everyone in the developed world started pretty much even on the day they were born. We can see from numerous examples that whether people mature into happy, healthy, and wealthy adults is not the result of luck, or even circumstance. How many people have you ever heard of that have overcome incredible adversity to succeed? How many have pulled themselves from the depths of despair and failure to rise to the pinnacle of success? Conversely, how often do you see individuals with every material advantage destroy their lives?

At age 21 Art Berg lay in hospital bed with a broken neck, listening to the doctors list for him all of the things that he would no longer be able to participate in due to his injury. He was told he would never walk again or work or live independently. He was encouraged to believe that his life was as good as over. As Art listened, he decided that while there may be 1000 things that he could no longer do, before his accident he could do 5000 things. That meant there must be 4000 activities that he could still do – and he made the conscious choice to focus on them. As a result, Art went on to be a world-renowned speaker and successful businessman, running two multimillion dollar companies, set a world record for being the first quadriplegic of his level to race in a 325-mile ultra-marathon, and was the father of two children. He persevered against the odds and he succeeded.

Then there is the case of Kathy Buckley. As a child Kathy was misdiagnosed and labelled as retarded because she had undetected hearing loss. She was sexually abused and seriously contemplated suicide throughout her teens. Then she was run over by a Jeep while sunbathing on a beach (she could not hear it coming), which resulted in broken bones and intermitted paralysis in her legs (not to mention being pronounced dead by the attending paramedics). After five years of recovery, once she could walk again, she discovered she had ovarian cancer. All of this before the age of 30! Kathy has been through many trials but now, as an award-winning comedienne, she shares her wonderful zest for life. People laugh and cry at the same time as she demonstrates her extraordinary ability to face her challenges with dignity, courage, and laughter. Kathy could have given up and let the bad events of her life overtake her but she didn't. What made the difference?

Oprah Winfrey provides another great example. She began life in relative poverty, reared by her grandmother on a farm. From age 6 to 13, she lived in Milwaukee with her mother. After suffering abuse and molestation, she ran away and was sent to a juvenile detention home at the age of 13, only to be denied admission because all the beds were filled. As a last resort, she was sent to Nashville to live under her father's strict discipline. But none of this barred her from extraordinary success. By the age of 50 she had been named one of the 100 Most Influential People of the 20th Century by *Time* magazine, received a Lifetime Achievement Award from the National Academy of Television Arts and Sciences, had been presented with the National Book Foundation's 50th anniversary gold medal for her service to books and authors, and was the first African-American woman to become a billionaire.

So many of us get really good at focusing on the things that we think we cannot do, and in the process we provide evidence for ourselves about why we should not even try. As I cover later in the chapter, we learn to be helpless and as a result we lose before we even get started. Yet none of us is really any different from Art, Kathy, or Oprah. Although they are exceptional examples of people who have overcome more adversity than most will ever experience, surely they are also evidence that we all have the ability to create extraordinary lives for ourselves. **The difference in the results they achieved has nothing to do with circumstance; the major factor they possess over others is their mindset.**

The Man Who Thinks He Can

If you think you are beaten, you are,

If you think you dare not, you don't,

If you like to win, but you think you can't

It is almost certain you won't.

If you think you'll lose, you've lost,

For out in the world we find,

Success begins with a fellow's Will ~

It's all in the state of mind.

If you think you are outclassed, you are,

You've got to think high to rise,

You've got to be sure of yourself before

You can ever win the prize.

Life's battles don't always go

To the stronger or faster man,

But soon or late the man who wins

Is the man WHO THINKS HE CAN.

~ Walter D. Wintle

Ultimately, when we examine human motivators they all boil down to a desire to feel good. For most people, this means seeking fulfilment externally in activities, possessions, and the other people in our lives. This sets up a whole set of negative consequences.

People strive toward a particular external want because of their internal feeling of being unfulfilled. If a person or event then gets in the way of them attaining the object or relationship of their desire they are likely to get angry and frustrated. Once they finally obtain the thing that they want, they then become paranoid and worry that they will lose it. Because they believe their happiness is dependent on having that item, the risk of losing it represents a threat to their happiness. And this whole chain of actions and reactions is based on the delusion that their source of happiness is outside themselves.

Notice how all of the negative feelings are linked. You may think, "When I get that title, car, job, income, relationship, recognition, etc., then I'll be someone." However, if anything then stands in the way of getting what you want, you will then react negatively. This attitude results in a lifetime of false emotional highs followed by sadness as life becomes a constant chase for the next thing that will bring that "feeling" of happiness once again. The central problem is that living in this manner always puts the fulfilment of your desires in the future, meaning that you will always be moving from one reason to feel incomplete to the next. Even when you do get what you are chasing, there is always something better to strive for and the fulfilment that you experience will be transient at best.

Man is not disturbed by events, but by the view he takes of them.

~ Epictitus

Perception Creates Our World

How we feel is dependent purely upon an interpretation of reality. No event, no circumstance, no object is anything until we make it such by the label that we put on it. Our perception of the situation within the exact context of its surrounding events, and how we think that will affect us, determines the label we give it and the emotions that result. You can clearly see this in many areas. Do you find a roller coaster exhilarating or terrifying? Is a desire for wealth greedy, a great way to stimulate personal growth, or an enabler to a life of philanthropy? Do relationships bring love and happiness or misery and loss of independence? Are children the greatest blessing or a source of problems? Whatever situation you consider, you will be able to find people whose opinions of it are polar opposites.

> HOW WE FEEL IS DEPENDENT PURELY UPON AN INTERPRETATION OF REALITY.

René Descartes, the highly regarded 17th-century French philosopher, mathematician, scientist, and writer stated that there is the world as we perceive it (res interna) and the world as it is (res extensa). What this really means is that there are no rights and wrongs – just interpretations. But not all interpretations are equal, because the feelings that they generate and the consequent actions may differ widely.

The real issue is not one of right versus wrong, but whether the interpretation and the consequent behaviours serve us. As Wayne Dyer says, when we change the way we choose to look at things, the things that we look at will change. Then we can move ourselves from a reactive to a responsive state.

So our perception literally creates the world as we experience it. Once this is understood it is simple to realise that nothing outside ourselves has any power over us except that which we allow it to have. It is not life's events that create our experience but the rules that we use to determine whether they have positive or negative implications for our lives. This is when we choose to view them as opportunity or threat.

Unfortunately **most people's thinking is controlled by what goes on outside themselves** and how it subsequently makes them feel. When they find a situation that they perceive makes them happy, because they don't understand that it is their interpretation that's determining this happiness, they seek to put themselves into that situation as often as possible. The almost inevitable result is that people

> MOST PEOPLE'S THINKING IS CONTROLLED BY WHAT GOES ON OUTSIDE THEMSELVES.

attempt to control their circumstances, conditions, and environment to reproduce the desired feeling. In my coaching and training practice, this is one of the most common misconceptions that it is necessary to address: people generally believe that they can control their world!

Figure 3.1 – Control and Influence Circles

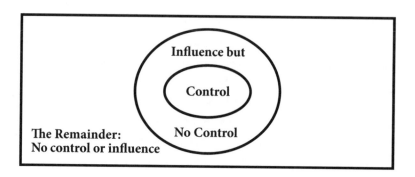

Consider the simple diagram in Figure 3.1. The rectangle represents everything that is in your life, and within it there are three areas: things that you can control, things that you can influence but over which you have no control, and everything else that you can neither control nor influence. I regularly discuss with clients the implications of the fact that the only thing in the central area is one's self. Many people challenge this suggestion at first but under examination, they always recognise that this must be true. We have control only in respect of our thoughts, feelings, and actions.

We have literally no control over the external world, and attempts to control it are a prime cause of stress. We will return to this idea later in the book. For now, the essential point is to remember that you have authority only over yourself. You cannot control your circumstances to make you happy – life has to be approached the other way around. First change your perception, how you evaluate and interpret things, and then you will change the feelings associated with them.

How We Have Been Conditioned

All people are born with an innate capacity and desire to learn, and almost everything that you believe to be true about yourself, your world, and your potential, you almost certainly learned from someone else. As children we get this message from close family. As adults it can be more subtle but the key people in your life, along with the media and society, are subtly but consistently sending you messages about what to believe. With repetition we can accept almost anything as truth, and having done so our world changes; we have been programmed.

To look at this in more detail, a child is immediately introduced to the "rules" of how we live by adults that capture its attention and put information into its mind through repetition. This is how we learned a huge proportion of what we currently know. Through this process we are introduced to ideas about appropriate ways to spend our lives. It is suggested to us what would be suitable lines of study in further education, which careers we should consider, and perhaps even what type of partner would be most suitable for us.

I remember a career advisor at school concluding that I should be a teacher – based on a set of responses that I gave to some simple questions. Back at home this idea was quickly rejected. I don't think I gave it a moment's serious thought – I was going to follow a scientific path, just like my father, and that view was fully backed up by the family. It amuses me now to see just how many of the things that my father did I also went on to follow. After working my way up the corporate ladder, I finally decided to leave that life and start my own business. As was recommended so many years ago, I am now a teacher (and a student). Before I left salaried employment there were not many people who were supportive of my plan but fortunately, by then, I had learned to follow my inner guide; I had worked out what I loved to do and had decided to do it regardless of the opinions of others.

So we were taught what to think through repetition from others and as we grew, we learned our picture of "reality" – how to behave in society (usually in the same way that our parents did), what to believe, and the whole concept of duality: what is good and what is bad, what is beautiful and what is ugly, right versus wrong, what we should and shouldn't do, and so forth.

For generations we have been taught to hate someone – the French, the Germans, the Russians. Think about it – before the end of the Cold War we were all supposed to hate the Russians, yet how many people would have even known a Russian, never mind actually hated one? As a result we learned to judge people because they live on the other side of an imaginary line, speak a different language, have different colour skin, look different to us, have different beliefs, even for the car that they drive or the clothes that they choose to wear. Many of these beliefs started hundreds of years ago and often no one can even remember what the original issue even was.

I recently heard a story that illustrates just how easily we can unknowingly become programmed. It involved a couple of newlyweds. As the husband was watching his wife preparing to bake a ham he noticed that she cut the ends off prior to putting it in the oven. When he enquired why she did this her reply was, "Because that's the way my mother did it." His interest sparked, he went to her mother and on asking the same question also received the reply, "Because that's the way my mother did it." Fascinated now, he sought out his wife's grandmother, who was by then quite old and fragile, and asked the same question, why did she cut off the ends of the ham? The reply was astonishing and at the same time illuminating about human nature. This old lady's explanation was, "Because we didn't have a baking pan large enough, so I cut the ends off to make it fit."

Through such interactions, behaviours ingrained within us by our surroundings and passed down from generation to generation may bear no relation to logic or truth. They may no longer make sense in the current environment, yet they can become so habitual and unquestioned that they continue to be passed on to children who believe what adults tell them. You may well be living the beliefs of your great, great, great, grandparents.

We train children through a series of rewards and punishments, just as we would train a dog – "you're a good boy." When we, as children, go against the rules we are punished but if we follow them we get a reward. Studies show that most children are punished many times a day, often many times more than they are rewarded. We become afraid of being punished and missing out on our reward, often the attention of

PEOPLE BECOME A PERFECT MATCH WITH THEIR ENVIRONMENT AND THE PEOPLE IN IT.

our parents. As a result we come to depend on attention. It feels good, so we start to focus on what others want us to do in order to get the reward we desire.

Let's look at how this generally progresses as children grow up. By the time a baby is able to think cognitively it will already produce thoughts in harmony with its conditioning. Given the impact of the automatic system that develops within the mind for filtering its environment, unless the individual finds a way to break out of the pattern, it will retain these thoughts for the rest of its life. Therefore, although our parents gave us the best that they had, they will automatically have limited us by what they taught us because of what they were taught themselves.

With greater maturity, soon the desire to get attention and fit in extends beyond our parents to other people. We want to be accepted, to have a sense of belonging, which can be especially strong through school. In much the same way that caterpillars will crawl around the rim of a plant pot following the one in front of them until they die of starvation or exhaustion, even if food is available right next to them, so people become experts at following the follower to avoid being seen as different. A very strong tendency to conform is developed.

Before long, we pretend to be what we are not so that we can please others – so that we can be good enough for them. We want to please everyone, and if we are unsuccessful it will often lead to feelings of inadequacy. We commonly attempt to be what we are not to avoid rejection – and this continues to be one of the most powerful drivers of behaviour for many people through the entirety of their lives. It prevents them from ever seeking to express who they really are.

Many times, people caught by this need to fit in will even do things to harm themselves, such as take drugs or drink excessively, in order to be perceived as one of the crowd. It takes a great deal of willpower, especially as a teenager, not to do something that all of your friends are doing, even when you know that what they are doing is harmful. Hence, **people become a perfect match with their environment and the people in it**. They are not aware that the true root of this behaviour – the poor choices made out of a desire to conform – is that they don't accept themselves. Therefore it is very difficult for them to make changes.

It is also probably true that you have abused yourself through negative internal dialogue. As Princess Diana once said, "If I talked to my friends the way that I talk to myself I would have no friends." This trait will impact you in many areas because if you don't have respect for yourself, you will likely be more accepting and tolerant of someone else who behaves badly toward you, such as a boss, because it fits with your internal picture of your self-worth.

Often Our Programs are Wrong

"Great minds think alike, and that's the problem" is the tagline to an intriguing advert used by the Harvard Business School. The reality is that the problem is broader than they suggest: **minds think alike; all minds, not just great ones.** We are subject to the same repetitive programming whether good or bad. Carl Jung, the esteemed Swiss psychologist, coined the term "collective unconscious," also known as "a reservoir of the experiences of our species," referring to the shared thought patterns and experiences of the human race.

> MINDS THINK ALIKE; ALL MINDS, NOT JUST GREAT ONES.

These shared experiences result in people tending to agree on things in huge numbers. This is sometimes referred to as "groupthink." Unfortunately the masses are wrong about many things of importance, for example:

- Most people are wrong about money. The minority captures the vast majority of the wealth, and the remainder always feel that they don't have quite enough and face retirement dependent on support from others or the state.

- Most people are wrong about health. Obesity is on the increase, as is malnutrition, and huge swathes of the population are slowly killing themselves every day through harmful habits such as smoking.

- Most small business owners are wrong about business. They struggle financially and work too hard, yet still almost all of them go out of business in the first few years.

- Most people are wrong about how to have a fulfilling relationship – divorce rates are climbing ever higher.

First they will ignore you, then they will laugh at you,
then they will fight you, then you will win.

~ **Mahatma Gandhi**

Throughout history we can also see that, once societal paradigms have been accepted, anyone who challenges the accepted wisdom is resisted, ridiculed, rejected, and at times, even tortured and killed. For example, when in the early 1400s Marco Polo returned from his 24th year of travel in Asia, many doubted the authenticity of his accounts, and this continued for centuries afterward. Today topographers have called his work the precursor of scientific geography. In the 16th century, Galileo, who, according to Stephen Hawking, probably bears more of the responsibility for the birth of modern science than anyone else, spent the last years of his life under house arrest on orders of the Inquisition for

OUR PERCEPTION FEELS
LIKE REALITY TO US.

supporting the theory that the planets revolved around the Sun rather than the Earth. In the 20th century the Wright brothers were ridiculed for attempting to develop a machine capable of powered flight, and Marconi's friends had him taken to a psychological hospital for tests when he suggested that it would be possible to transmit the sound of the voice over large distances.

Ultimately, anything that gets repeated enough times is likely to gain wide acceptance. For example, for over 60 years it was reported that our genes are the controlling mechanism for life. Despite the fact that no proof had ever been found for its core theories, an entire science was built up around this belief. However, in the year 2000, when the first map of the human genome was completed, the entire hypothesis was shattered. In summary, what the project discovered was that we do not have nearly enough genes for the old explanation of how the body is constructed and regulated to have validity. The new information demonstrated that there must be some fundamental aspects of what controls life that science has yet to begin to recognise. The search is now on.

Once a paradigm is installed and accepted it can control everyone in society, including the most enquiring minds, without them ever becoming aware of it. Until Roger Bannister's four-minute mile, it was universally accepted that this feat was impossible. Bannister did not write himself into history because he broke the world record – people do that all the time – but because he delivered an expanded awareness of human possibility by breaking through the paradigm that had controlled everyone else's thinking until that point.

There are many, many examples of the fact that even the opinion of the "experts" should be treated with caution when we start to consider what is possible for us. They will often be proven wrong over time, as the following list shows:

- "It would appear that we have reached the limits of what is possible to achieve with computer technology, although one should be careful with such statements, as they tend to sound pretty silly in five years." John von Neumann, 1949

- "Everything that can be invented has been invented." Charles H. Duell, an official at the U.S. Patent Office, 1899.

- "Stocks have reached what looks like a permanently high plateau." Irving Fisher, economics professor at Yale University, 1929.

- "It will be gone by June." *Variety*, passing judgment on rock 'n roll in 1955.

- "Democracy will be dead by 1950." John Langdon-Davies, *A Short History of The Future*, 1936.

- "... good enough for our transatlantic friends ... but unworthy of the attention of practical or scientific men." British Parliamentary Committee, referring to Edison's lightbulb, 1878.

- "The Americans have need of the telephone, but we do not. We have plenty of messenger boys." Sir William Preece, Chief Engineer, British Post Office, 1878.

We can see that history makes it abundantly clear that we struggle with ideas that fall outside our paradigm and that we are unable to rely on the agreement of experts or the masses to help us to establish what represents truth. The problem is that **our perception feels like reality to us**, so it is difficult to move beyond it and be sufficiently open-minded to allow real creativity.

Our Biggest Handicap is Invisible

Your vision will become clear only when you can look into your own heart. Who looks outside, dreams; who looks inside awakens.

~ Carl Jung

The conditioning we receive throughout life is so pervasive and powerful that we cannot possibly be aware of the psychological influence that it has on our decision making – even for relatively minor decisions. For example, in his book, *Influence: The Psychology of Persuasion*, Robert Cialdini quotes one study where "men who saw a new-car ad that included a seductive young woman model rated the car as faster, more appealing, more expensive-looking and better designed than did men who saw the same ad without the model. Yet, when asked later, the men refused to believe that the presence of the young woman had influenced their judgments."

Gary Craig, the founder of Emotional Freedom Techniques, an alternative therapy with an amazing power to deal with a range of emotional and physical traumas, describes this conditioning as "the writing on our walls." When we are born the "house" that we are born into, which represents our belief systems, is bare. Before long, people come into our house and write things on our walls that we subsequently accept to be true. Whenever things happen to us we go and consult the writing on our walls and use that to determine what action we should take. Unfortunately though, much of the writing will not get us the results that we want in life because the person who wrote it did not know how to be successful. We would never seek to learn to fly an aeroplane from someone who did not have the skills themselves. Yet in many areas of our life we unwittingly accept the advice and beliefs of people who are not experts and as a result, we limit ourselves. Very few people ever go back and examine what people "wrote on their walls" to identify the elements that serve them and throw out the aspects that don't.

> OUR CONDITIONING HANDICAPS EVERY ONE OF US BUT WE DON'T RECOGNISE IT BECAUSE IT IS INVISIBLE.

Thus, **our conditioning handicaps every one of us but we don't recognise it because it is invisible**. Think about the implications of this. For example, people who display what we might term "bad behaviours" are really just following their conditioning. Their inability to recognise that they are doing wrong is an inherent element of the nature of human beings – at our core we are like the hardware of a computer. We all start out with similar capabilities and possibilities but we do not have the option to choose which software gets loaded, and unfortunately, we can easily be programmed with a psychological "virus." This can happen even if the people doing the programming have good intentions because, as you are now aware, they don't know any better. They are just passing on what they were taught.

This inability to recognise things as "wrong" affects whole societies. We can see this because as society evolves, the nature of the past events becomes recontextualised and reinterpreted from the new, higher level of awareness, often reclassifying them as atrocities, even though they weren't considered so at the time. Wherever mass behaviour is involved it follows that the people involved in it were behaving in a way that was generally acceptable at the time. It is thought-provoking to realise, therefore, that there is no way that we can say that this is any less true today than it has been throughout history. The realisation, then, that **the classification of anything in terms of opposites, such as "right" or "wrong," or "good" or "bad," relies upon a comparison relative to an arbitrary point of observation** is transformational. As the point of observation moves, so does the interpretation and therefore we can see that what we consider to be "true" depends entirely on context.

Accordingly, we must face the humbling proposition that human beings, individually or on mass, literally cannot identify the truth. The mind has no quality control mechanism to allow us to identify and root out beliefs that are false or do not serve us. Therefore, to maximise our growth, when we come to evaluate ourselves we must accept the premise that a great deal, possibly most, of what we have come to believe about life, and particularly our own potential, is likely to be based on ineffective thinking. This will allow us to examine every area of our beliefs and to choose those that serve us while working to replace those that don't.

THE ONLY THING
STOPPING YOU IS YOU.

Learned Helplessness

One of my friends and business colleagues, Paul Hutsey, tells the story of when, as a youngster, he would see the circus come to town. He liked to watch an elephant being used to help set up the circus tent. The elephant would pick up the 40-foot long central pole and hold it in place while they erected the tent around it. Once it was up, they would take a 4-foot rope, tie it to the elephant's leg and attach the other end to a 12-inch stake that was used to restrain the animal. Only minutes earlier the elephant was lifting a 40-foot pole but now he couldn't pull up a 12-inch stake. **Why is this?**

The process by which elephants are trained involves attaching the baby elephant firmly to a big tree with a strong chain. At that age it isn't strong enough to break free so it learns that it can't. As the elephant grows, the size of the chain can be reduced until ultimately the full-grown elephant is held only by a rope attached to a stake in the ground. The elephant could easily walk away but for its belief that it is helpless, and so is kept in a prison by the power of its own mind, tied to a stake for the rest of its life.

The first person to fully recognise and explain this phenomenon was Martin Seligman of the University of Pennsylvania. As he describes in his book, *Learned Optimism*, he observed an experiment with laboratory dogs where, in Pavlovian fashion, the dogs were exposed to two types of stimulation – high-pitched tones and brief, harmless shocks. The idea was that the dogs would feel fear on hearing a tone and would react to it as though it were a shock.

Next the dogs were placed into a box with two compartments divided by a low wall. The investigators wanted to see if a dog would jump the barrier on presentation of the tone. The first stage was to teach the dogs to jump the partition to escape a shock, then they were planning to see if the same reaction could be provoked using the tone. However, when the dogs were shocked they made no attempt to get away. During the early stages of the experiment they had learned to be helpless. As they experienced the shocks going on and off irrespective of their own reaction, they learned that nothing that they did made any difference. Therefore, they made no attempt to try.

Seligman coined the term "learned helplessness" to describe this destructive mindset, and over the next few years demonstrated its applicability to people. He discovered, for example, that depressed people became that way because they learned to be helpless – that whatever they did was futile so they developed a sense of terminal discouragement.

Although depression is a fairly extreme example of how disempowering beliefs can affect us, **we have all learned to be helpless to some degree**. This is why Henry Ford was undoubtedly right when he said, "Whether you believe you can or you can't, either way you are right." The main obstacle we face in achieving our desires isn't whether the possibility of success exists. We can achieve virtually anything. What stops us are the reasons that we give ourselves why we can't do or have what we want, backed up by a set of beliefs that we are convinced are true but that, as with the elephants and dogs in the earlier examples, only constrain us because we have accepted them. The power of your mind will prevent you from doing anything unless you first believe you can. In other words, **the only thing stopping you is you**.

Almost all of our beliefs about ourselves and others that limit us have been learned from someone else. Our challenge is to unlearn them so that we can gain access to our true potential. To do so we need to realise that most of the time we are not actively choosing how to behave. Our actions are unconscious, effectively dictating that we live our lives habitually, on autopilot.

Many people would be 100% in favour of improving their circumstances, yet very few are willing to be sufficiently honest with themselves and others to look inside themselves for the things that have created their current circumstances. If we are not prepared to examine the beliefs that drive our daily actions we cannot create meaningful change in our lives. The starting point for all achievement is the mind.

How the Mind Works

To change your ingrained beliefs you must first understand how the mind works. This will require a picture that we will refer to as the Stickperson:

Figure 3.2 – The Stickperson

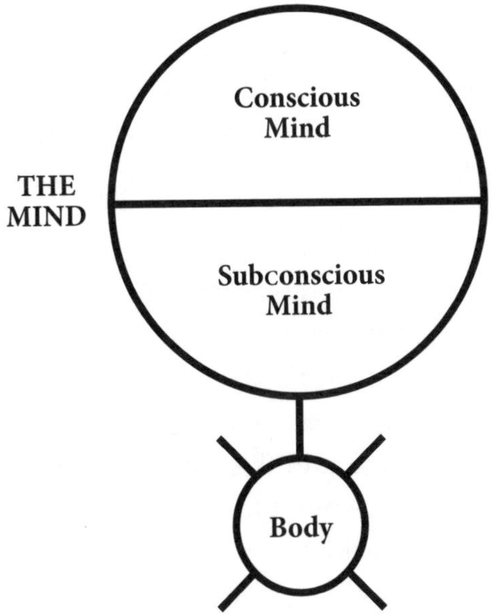

The Stickperson was developed by Dr. Thurman Fleet of San Antonio, Texas in the 1930s. Dr. Fleet was the founder of the Concept Therapy movement and realised that the treatment of illnesses and infirmities could be made much more effective by treating the whole person, rather than just the symptoms themselves. This meant treating the mind as well as the body. This is also what the ancient Greeks and Romans believed; hence their promotion of the idea "a healthy mind in a healthy body."

The influence of the mind on our state of health is now almost universally accepted, with extensive research confirming repeatedly the interactive relationship of the mind and the body. For example, if you test your mental skills when you are physically unfit, then test them again after you have trained to become fit, there will have been a significant improvement. Likewise, I'm sure that we have all experienced times when we were feeling particularly tired, then something happened to change our thinking and the feeling of tiredness was instantly forgotten.

The Stickperson provides a deceptively simple model by which to understand how the mind works and the impact that it has on the body. The understanding that it offers has allowed many thousands of people, including me, to rapidly transform their lives.

The Stickperson represents us in two parts: the mind and the body. The mind is drawn to be much larger than the body to reflect the fact that this is the most magnificent and significant part of us. This description by Dr. David Hawkins, a renowned psychiatrist, physician, researcher, and pioneer in the field of consciousness research, taken from the book *Power vs. Force*, beautifully captures this concept: "The identification and experience of self could be limited to a description of one's physical body. Then, of course, we might well ask, how does one know that one has a physical body? Through observation, we note that the presence of the physical body is registered by the senses. The question then follows, what is it that's aware of the senses? How do we experience what the senses are reporting? Something greater, something more encompassing than the physical body, has to exist in order to experience that which is lesser – and that something is the mind."

In the image of the Stickperson, the mind is also divided into two parts, the first of which is the conscious mind. The conscious mind is the thinking mind. It is the area that gathers information and gives us the reasoning capability that allows us to decide on and initiate action. By definition, it holds the information that we are aware we know (i.e., our conscious memories), and it is in this part of us that our free will resides. The conscious mind is also the part that gives us the ability to originate new thoughts or to accept or reject thoughts that we receive from an outside source.

However, the conscious mind is not our power source, and if we were to restrict ourselves to what we are able to do consciously, no one would be able to walk, drive, ride a bike, or hit a golf ball. In fact, we could not engage in any learned skill at all. You will be able to observe this clearly by remembering what it was like when you tried to perform a complex skill for the first time, like hitting a tennis ball or learning a dance step.

The conscious mind knows what to do – it may have seen other people do it thousands of times – but this is not nearly enough. Someone learning to touch-type could learn in just a few minutes which finger should press each letter but much practice is required before they can type at speed. This is because it is not the conscious mind that is engaged in touch-typing. This is taken care of by the part of the mind we call the subconscious, unconscious, other-than-conscious, and other similar terms. In this book I am going to use one term, subconscious, to refer to this part of the mind.

As we accept any thought in our conscious mind, or perhaps just neglect an idea from outside and accept it uncritically, it becomes impressed upon the subconscious. This part of our mind is the power centre that controls every function of the body and every action we take.

Just consider for a moment some of the tasks that it is capable of conducting, all simultaneously: maintaining the chemical balance of the 100 trillion cells in our body; constantly evaluating the input from 130 million light receptors in each eye and constructing a picture from what they receive; coordinating the actions of the 500 muscles in our body so that they propel us effortlessly from A to B; repairing the body whenever it gets injured; monitoring the hundreds of thousands of sensors in or on our body all the time; and keeping the heart beating even when we are asleep.

> THE STRONGEST FORCE IN THE HUMAN PERSONALITY IS THE NEED TO REMAIN CONSISTENT WITH THE WAY THAT WE DEFINE OURSELVES.

I once saw a metaphor for the power of the subconscious that compared it to having the capability to open up an e-mail account to find 30,000 new mails waiting and being able to deal with them all instantly and simultaneously. It has been estimated that, from the perspective of memory alone, the subconscious is 10 billion times as powerful as the conscious mind!

There are few people that recognise this power and seek to capitalise on it to create the results that they want. As Guy Claxton suggests in his book, *Hare Brain Tortoise Mind*, "The modern mind has a distorted image of itself that leads it to neglect some of its own most valuable learning capacities. We need now a new conception of the unconscious – one which gives it back its intelligence, and which reinstalls it within the sense of self." He then goes on to say, "Highlighting the ways of knowing that are associated with consciousness, control and articulation enabled the extraordinary explosion of scientific thinking and technological advances of the last two centuries; but the cost was a disabling of other faculties of mind that we cannot afford to be without." In other words, making the conscious mind predominant in determining our actions has enabled huge advances through science, but to continue to restrict ourselves to only using this part of our mind will greatly limit our progress in the future.

The subconscious programs that we receive all our lives mould the critically important beliefs that make up our self-image. As Tony Robbins has frequently stated, **"The strongest force in the human personality is the need to remain consistent with the way that we define ourselves."** This definition is a result of our beliefs. Any statement that you make starting with the words "I am..." is a function of these beliefs: I am smart, I am funny, I am successful, etc. The opposite statements are even more common and we hear them, or say them, almost daily: I am stupid, I am poor, I am ugly, I am unlovable... Such statements become unquestioned and control every action that we make.

The impact of "I am" beliefs on behaviour is always significant and for this reason I am always on the alert for them in my coaching interactions with clients. For example, one of my clients once revealed to me that he was highly dependent upon positive feedback because it enabled him to think, "Maybe I'm not such an idiot after all." I'm sure that you can see that the underlying belief that this revealed, which could then be addressed, was, "I am such an idiot." This belief about himself manifested itself in both his work and home life in many ways. At work he would tend to see new challenges as being beyond his capability and therefore worry that someone would notice and find him out or, worse, that he wouldn't be able to meet the demands put upon him. To list just a few of the areas where this impacted him: he would also avoid responsibility wherever possible, procrastinate on important activities, feel inferior, tend to be critical and intolerant of others, and find it very difficult to participate in activities in which he was not the best.

In such situations it is only by getting to the primary cause of limiting beliefs that effective resolution is possible. In the example above, as we began to explore the belief in detail it rapidly became clear that it was rooted in his childhood and mirrored very strongly his parents' beliefs. With that knowledge it was possible to help him to make the changes necessary to overcome his limiting thoughts.

We are so well conditioned that we no longer need the programming and control that we got from our parents and other authority figures when we were young – we maintain it ourselves using the same system of punishment and reward. We punish ourselves when we do not follow the rules according to our own belief systems. We are like a judge, except for the important stipulation that in a case of law we do not allow anyone to be punished more than once for the same crime. In our case we often make ourselves pay over and over again, potentially thousands of times. Furthermore, because the subconscious mind cannot tell the difference between something that is actually happening and something that we vividly imagine, each time we recall the event, we impress our judgment of ourselves deeper onto our subconscious. Each time we remember the event in question, or someone else reminds us, we judge ourselves and repeat the cycle.

The result is that most people are "two weeks ago" people. They are constantly thinking about what happened in the past. "Why didn't I do this?" or "I should have said that." According to Deepak Chopra, a renowned endocrinologist and former Chief at Boston Regional Medical Center, who has become a world leader in mind/body medicine, 95% of our thoughts will match those that we had the previous day, and for most people, two-thirds of their thoughts will on average be negative.

The internal judge is wrong because the belief systems are wrong. We cannot tell the difference between truth and falsehood, yet we behave all the time as though we can, and in the process, determine what we will be capable of in the future.

The starting point of all of our results is our thoughts, because what people do or don't do is based on the meaning that they associate with something. In his magnificent book, *Man's Search for Meaning*, Viktor Frankl, the Jewish psychologist who spent the war years in one of the German concentration camps, described just how powerful this conscious ability that we have is. Unlike most of the books about the Holocaust, he does not seek to capture in graphic detail the atrocities that he and the other prisoners went though. Instead he describes the impact that this level of human suffering had on the mind of the people who experienced it. I believe that it is this that makes the book so powerful. He noticed that as long as people had a compelling future they could survive anything or, conversely, they would die when they gave up hope.

> NO OTHER PERSON CAN CAUSE YOU TO THINK ANYTHING THAT YOU DO NOT CHOOSE TO THINK.

Probably the best-known lines from the book highlight examples of men who were able to overcome their appalling conditions to provide care for others. They state that these men were proof that, "everything can be taken from a man but one thing: the last of human freedoms – to choose one's attitude in any given set of circumstances, to choose one's own way." If this is not powerful enough, consider the next lines, perhaps in the context of challenges that you face in your own work environment: "Every day, every hour, offered the opportunity to make a decision, a decision which determined whether you would or would not submit to those powers which threatened to rob you of your very self, your inner freedom ... It is this spiritual freedom – which cannot be taken away – that makes life meaningful and purposeful."

My belief is that if this principle was true in a concentration camp then it must be true in everyday life today. **No other person can cause you to think anything that you do not choose to think.** Unfortunately, because of our conditioning it is easy to blame others when we feel bad, but with a higher level of awareness it becomes clear that it can never be their fault. No one can make us feel inferior, angry, embarrassed, or anything else, without our permission. All pain, pleasure, and limitation, in fact, originate inside us or are accepted uncritically from outside as a result of what we choose to focus on.

The discovery that the way we think is a choice is one of the most significant findings in psychology of the last 30 years. It makes clear that we have the ability to choose meaning and thereby shape our perception, which is possibly the most important skill of all. Our choice of meaning determines the quality of the life that we will experience as well as our reactions and responses to circumstances. With this ability mastered, external factors such as the quality of a person's relationships, economic status, physical health, or career success no longer need to affect how we feel or control our actions.

Let's take a look at the application of this principle in the context of how people respond to what **they perceive** as pressure in their job. I have been told by clients that they experience pressure from their bosses. Again, with higher awareness it becomes clear this is impossible – the feeling of pressure is as a result of their interpretation of the situation, which in their case is one whose impact is to create stress. Other people in the same situation may well experience it as challenging, or even exhilarating, which substantially improves their ability to continue to operate effectively. It is their choice of thoughts about the expectations of their bosses that creates the feelings as opposed to the expectations themselves.

Taking Action Is Not a Conscious Activity

Returning to the diagram of the Stickperson in Figure 3.2, notice that there is no direct connection between the conscious mind and the body. Before any action can take place an idea must be impressed upon the subconscious. Any thought that resides in the subconscious we experience as a feeling; therefore, it is our feelings that determine what action we take, which in turn creates our results.

It is critical for you to become aware of your ability to consciously choose your thoughts, because, unlike the conscious mind, the subconscious has absolutely no ability to reject any idea presented to it. Whatever we choose to think at the level of the conscious mind will be impressed upon the subconscious mind, creating feelings and ultimately determining our actions.

This explains why we cannot consistently perform in a manner that is inconsistent with our own self-image. Tony Robbins, a recognised expert in the psychology of peak performance, summarises the importance of our conditioning when he says that this self-image, or the identity that we have for ourselves, is the deepest motivator of human behaviour. This identity exists as a set of beliefs that we hold about ourselves that will have the impact of clearly defining the quality of results of which we believe we are capable. A training course, for example, may demonstrate to us ways in which we could do better, allowing us to gain conscious understanding and to raise our level of performance for awhile. However, the subconscious mind will sabotage those new ideas and eventually take us back to our programmed level of achievement if we do not at the same time shift our self-image.

This is the source of a major challenge for anyone seeking to develop and grow. In practice, the task of changing subconscious beliefs is likely to be difficult for anyone who does not have the awareness of the process needed to do so. This is why so many people get stuck.

The reason that changing beliefs can be so difficult stems from the interaction between the conscious mind and the outside world. The beliefs were originally created by the thoughts in the conscious mind, or the ideas of other people that were accepted uncritically. Through our actions these beliefs produce our results, which we then experience via information from our five senses. This experience then controls our thoughts, which automatically reinforce the belief system that generated the results in the first place. This cycle is shown in Figure 3.3. Consequently, without deliberate action to change belief systems, a lasting improvement in results is impossible.

Figure 3.3 – The Self-Reinforcing Belief Cycle

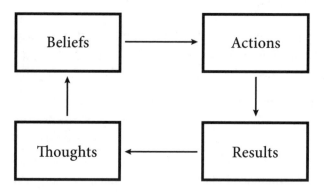

This automatic functioning of the human mind leads to the biggest limitation in people's ability to change and become more successful; it is critical, therefore, to have a much more detailed understanding of it. The next chapter explores in detail how to break out of the cycle described above so that you may create extraordinary results in any area of your life. It will also give you the information necessary to enable you to help others to do the same.

Transformational Technique: Understand Conditioning

To maximise your ability to tap into your potential, it is essential to learn to use the subconscious mind differently, so that you can start to tap into its vast power to serve you instead of limit you. The primary outcome from this chapter is to learn to fully accept that all of your results are the product of the programming that exists in your subconscious mind. This will enable you to focus your development efforts onto the root cause – your conditioning. Until you can achieve this level of understanding you will always be giving away some of your power to your external environment.

Ultimately, your results are determined by your beliefs. One of the most important implications that automatically follows from this is the recognition that because of the insidious way that our mind works, you will generally have little or no awareness of the limited beliefs that are holding you back. It is unavoidable that the mind effectively keeps us in an invisible prison because learned helplessness affects us all to a greater or lesser degree. Evidence that we may choose to accept from external sources, such as experts or "conventional wisdom," certainly cannot be relied upon to provide us with an escape route.

Thus, the invisible force that controls us is totally internal. It determines the way that we perceive the world, in particular, the extent to which we will believe in our potential or our ability to achieve the goals that we set for ourselves. We must constantly examine our beliefs to establish which ones serve us and then seek to change those that do not.

I know of no more encouraging fact than the unquestionable ability of man to elevate his life by conscious endeavor.

~ Henry David Thoreau

PART 2

ACCESSING
YOUR PERSONAL
GREATNESS

THE ART OF CORRECT THINKING

It isn't what you have, or who you are, or where you are, or what you are doing that makes you happy or unhappy. It is what you think about.

~ Dale Carnegie

The True Power of the Mind

The vast majority of all that we know about the mind, and the most advanced techniques for getting the best out of it, have only been uncovered in the last few years. Take the discovery that what we considered to be "speed reading," at up to 3000 words per minute, is positively pedestrian compared to the hundreds of thousands of words per minute (with 75% recall) that has been proven to be possible when we use our mind correctly.

> ONE OF THE MOST IMPORTANT ELEMENTS IN GAINING ACCESS TO MORE OF THE POWER OF THE MIND IS TO DEVELOP OUR INTUITION.

Research has increasingly shown that our potential to generate thought is, in practical terms, infinite. If you are prepared to recognise and accept this, it will create a dramatic shift in the way that you think about yourself and others. We know from the previous chapter that your thinking is the origin of all action and so constitutes the only route to improved results – a shift in thinking can be profound in its impact.

The mind is also synergetic, meaning that as we add more information to our store, the total increases by more than the amount that we have added: where our mind is involved one plus one does indeed add up to greater than two. An excellent example of this can be observed in someone working on increasing their vocabulary. As they consciously learn each new word they are likely to gain the ability to actively use about 10 additional words.

As a result of these discoveries, those who really understand them are forecasting that social and economic advances this century will be dominated by leaps forward in the way we use our mind, in the same way that advancement in the last century was enabled by the Industrial Revolution. To be at the forefront of this trend we need to learn to gain access to more of the power of the mind. **One of the most important elements in doing so is to develop our intuition**, but what does this really mean? Unfortunately, for many this is an area that they are not interested in because they see intuition as unreliable and best left to creative types, with little applicability in business. But they are wrong – let's look at why.

Knowledge is what you know you know. It can be taught and is acquired from external sources. Intuition is more elusive and relates to things you do not know that you know. It cannot be taught. Instead it is accumulated through life, is based on understandings and awareness, and is stored in the subconscious mind. It is only when knowledge is integrated with intuition that we get wisdom. These days, for senior leaders knowledge is pretty much taken for granted, so it is the use of intuition that most enables a leader to differentiate from his or her peers, and moreover, will determine the level of responsibility and compensation that each will command.

Intuition can be transformative because it is not the conscious area of the brain that delivers the best course of action. That part can only access a tiny part of our accumulated experiences and knowledge. When the intuition is engaged, reason is bypassed and a capacity for instantaneous recognition and understanding replaces it, without the need for sequential processing of the particulars of the problem. It requires no logic, reasoning, or rational thought of any kind. Recent scientific evidence has revealed that complex or unfamiliar issues are much more effectively dealt with by approaching them in a patient, less deliberate manner, while the mind is in a peaceful state. I'm sure that you will have experienced that new ideas never come from concentrated thinking – instead they come out of silence, usually while completely relaxed, such as at 4 a.m. in the morning or in the shower as you get ready for the day.

This explains why a behaviour practiced by many of the great geniuses is that of apparently doing nothing. In actuality they are thinking very deeply – allowing their subconscious to provide answers to complex questions. These days most people believe that they are far too busy for this highly productive activity, even though they may recognise that many of our best ideas arrive "out of the blue" or just "pop into our heads." Relaxed concentration gives access to our intuition, whilst being in a state of hurry or stress make this impossible.

Intuition allows for better judgment as it gives access to a lifetime of wisdom and the full power of the subconscious mind. The ability to face complex and rapidly changing situations, to deal with them in their entirety and gain instantaneous understanding is a key skill and is only available by accessing the power of the subconscious mind through intuition. The capacity this offers is not sequential and is therefore unlimited; it opens up the possibility of the full use of previous experience in dealing with new and challenging situations. Perhaps this is the reason why Edgar Mitchell, the Apollo 14 astronaut and moonwalker, said, "Reliance on the intuitive response was the most important part of astronauts' training."

The intuition may tell you that something is a great idea, even when reason says that it is not. Evidence shows that our conscious functions can veto the subconscious, overruling the initial decision even when it is correct – we basically second-guess ourselves even when the first response was correct. Yet studies have found that our snap decisions are often better than those reached by endless pondering because they use the information collected over years in the subconscious. This allows us to make a decision quickly and accurately. We particularly experience the power of this capability in life-threatening situations, when there is no time to think. It will even prompt us that we are in danger if we have no conscious knowledge of why.

Several years ago I saw a powerful example of this in a BBC documentary by Professor Robert Winston, one of the world's most respected medical academics. He presented the account of a fire chief who had arrived at a major factory fire with his team. After many hours in the burning building attempting to control the fire, it seemed that they were beginning to prevail when the chief ordered his team out of the building. Despite their protests – they were reluctant to leave when they were just beginning to make progress – and the chief's lack of ability to justify the decision, he insisted. Seconds after they evacuated the building there was a huge explosion caused by a backdraft, an explosion caused by a fire becoming starved of oxygen, and the building collapsed. Without the chief's sensitivity to his intuition, and his preparedness to follow it, they would all have died.

> INTUITION OFTEN SEPARATES THE GREATEST LEADERS FROM THE ONES THAT ARE MERELY GOOD.

The reason that the chief was able to save his team was that he had experienced three backdrafts earlier in his career. While his conscious mind was not aware of it, his subconscious noticed subtle changes, such as in the colour or behaviour of the smoke, and sounded the alarm.

In any complex situation the subconscious can make a major contribution towards determining the most effective course of action. It communicates this to us through feelings, but without the self-awareness to notice these feelings and the understanding that logic and data can only ever give us part of the story, we will limit our ability to make optimal decisions.

It is possible to improve your awareness of your intuitive guidance, with the result that you will have a heightened awareness of life. The most important factor is to take more notice of how you feel about things. Feelings provide the mechanism by which the subconscious mind communicates with us.

Because of its nature as a mode of intelligence that goes beyond the rational mind, intuition is an area of capability that you must learn to trust. The guidance that you will get from it cannot be verified but if used effectively, it will be one of the most powerful gifts available to you in determining the most appropriate decisions and courses of action. **Intuition often separates the greatest leaders from the ones that are merely good.**

The Mind Can be Improved

Just as the body can be strengthened, toned, and have its endurance increased, so the mind will improve through use and regular activity. It has also been proven, as explained by Tony Buzan in his fascinating book, *Head Strong*, that **the pervading belief that the mind becomes weaker and creativity diminishes with age is incorrect**. We now know that the brain creates new brain cells throughout our whole life to replace those that we lose and that, in the absence of disease, it is lack of mental activity, not aging, that causes the loss of capability.

Even more importantly, every brain cell is capable of developing hundreds of thousands of branches, each with hundreds of thousands of connection points. The more we use the brain, the more of these connections we create, and the more powerful our brain can become. Professor Anokhin, at one time Russia's top brain scientist and the most brilliant pupil of Ivan Pavlov, the Nobel Prize-winning physiologist, psychologist, and physician, calculated that the number of patterns that our brains are capable of, if typed out, would be a one followed by 10½ million *kilometres* of zeros. It is difficult to find anything that we can comprehend to even help us to contemplate a number of this magnitude. I have been told that it is comparable to the number of atoms in the known universe!

Tony Buzan also argues that because of the extraordinary creativity and synergetic nature of the mind, the old expression "garbage in, garbage out" does not apply. In fact, **as we put more garbage into the mind its effect is magnified and grows.** The limiting beliefs of our conditioning, as well as any habitually negative thought patterns, can expand to become the dominant factor in our awareness. Consequently, great care is necessary when we allow things to take up space in our mind. If you focus on flawed ideas, the magnitude of your error will become magnified in your experience.

We should also understand the impact of stress on our incredible minds. The fight-or-flight response developed over millions of years to help keep us alive. At times of extreme need, blood is diverted away from nonvital areas of the body, such as the internal organs, the digestive system, **and the areas of the brain responsible for reasoning**, and sent to areas such as the major muscle groups and **the emotional centres of the brain**. We then experience negative emotions such as anxiety, panic, anger, rage, etc. Our sensitivity to the information from our five senses is heightened, and our ability for complex thought diminishes or is completely blocked. As a result we go into a highly reactive mode – the classic "strike first and ask questions later" situation.

The issue is that this response is highly inappropriate in most circumstances today. The mind works at its best and has effective access to memory, analytical abilities, and intuition only when it is calm. Therefore we must learn to use our mind differently.

Thinking in Reverse

*There is a principle which is a bar
against all information, which is proof against all
arguments and which cannot fail to keep a man in
everlasting ignorance – and that principle is
contempt prior to investigation.*

~ Herbert Spencer

Many people believe that their experience of the world through their five senses gives them a reliable representation of "truth," so it comes as a huge surprise to them when they discover that this is not the case. The amount of information being received via our senses alone is enormous – estimated at around 20 million bits per second. Add to that literally billions of bits of internal data per second that also need monitoring and we can see that staggering amounts of information are processed by the subconscious mind. Meanwhile, the conscious mind can only deal with a few thousand bits per second. Clearly, **at the conscious level we are only capable of dealing with a tiny subset of the total information available to the subconscious.**

To reduce the conscious load to a level that we are capable of handling there must be a huge amount of filtering. The result is that **we delete huge chunks of the information reaching our subconscious mind, distorting and generalising it prior to conscious awareness.**

There is a part of the brain that is responsible for this filtering, known as the Reticular Activating System. What this does is prioritise in order to determine which information to bring to our awareness. The critical thing to realise is the basis of this prioritisation – **all of that subconscious data is filtered based on your existing beliefs about what is important to you**.

Consider this example. You are at a lively cocktail party talking to a friend. The more interesting the conversation becomes the more fully you will block out the noise and activity around you, making it entirely possible to be equally focused on the person you are with as you would be in a quiet environment on a one-to-one basis. Then, while you are listening intently, someone a short distance away mentions your name. Instantly, your attention will go to the source of the event. So how is it that you are able to pick up your name out of all of that background noise? The answer, which can be proven by hypnosis, is that in fact you are hearing every word in your environment all of the time but you filter most of them out because you believe them to be unimportant. Unimportant, that is, until your name is mentioned. Then, your subconscious knows for certain that you are high priority (to you) so it immediately brings the event into your awareness. Once that has happened it will be difficult to fully concentrate any longer on what your friend is saying.

> AT THE CONSCIOUS LEVEL WE ARE ONLY CAPABLE OF DEALING WITH A TINY SUBSET OF THE TOTAL INFORMATION AVAILABLE TO THE SUBCONSCIOUS.

This is the same process that takes place when you buy a new car and suddenly notice the same car everywhere: your subconscious was reprogrammed when you picked up the car. It is also how you become aware of picking up a hot plate. In this case your subconscious, which is monitoring all of the 200,000 temperature sensors in your skin all the time, prevents injury by bringing it to your attention the moment any of them detect heat.

Where we direct our attention will also affect what gets filtered in or out of our awareness. You were almost certainly not aware of the sensation of your feet on the floor until I mentioned it!

Because of the power and extent of this filtering, we are all able to find proof of anything that we strongly believe, irrespective of evidence to the contrary. **Our belief system filter, which began to form with our earliest sensory experiences and which is almost entirely subconscious, will simply block out anything that is inconsistent with it and reinforce that which we already hold to be true.** This explains why it is so difficult to dislodge an existing paradigm, whether individual or mass, once it has been established.

YOU ARE ONLY ABLE TO SEE THAT WHICH YOU ALREADY BELIEVE EXISTS.

Dr. Bruce Lipton, a former medical school and university professor, and best-selling author, summarises this as follows, "The subconscious mind reads around 20 million environmental cues per second and immediately engages previously learned behaviours – all without the help, supervision or even awareness of the conscious mind." It has now been scientifically proven that we literally create the world that we perceive.

What this means is that it is not possible for us to know what "reality" is. All that we can ever become aware of is our thoughts about reality. Please stay with me here – this is important. It follows, therefore, that what we recognise as a tangible experience is actually only the experience of our own thoughts and beliefs. Since our thoughts will always differ from other people's this will inevitably lead to differences of opinion about what is really happening. Unfortunately, our response to this is to attempt to use the evidence of our own experience to establish what is true. What we end up with is completely circuitous: our thoughts determine our experience which we then use to prove that our thoughts about the experience are correct! As demonstrated by the extreme and irrational response of a phobic, all subsequent perceptions then simply reinforce what we already hold to be true.

This makes it very hard for us to move forward in awareness. We have expressions like, "seeing is believing" and "I'll believe it when I see it," reflecting most people's natural resistance when faced with a new idea. I hope that it will now be clear to you that **the process of discovery actually works in reverse**. It is impossible to see anything that is not already in harmony with your existing conditioning; in other words, **you will only see it once you believe it**. Perhaps this explains the apparently baffling ability of a 70-pound anorexic to look in a mirror and proclaim herself to be fat. She believes so firmly in her own distorted body image that she sees exactly what she is expecting. If you don't even have the idea that something may exist, that is, if you have no concept for it, your neurology will not even allow you to become consciously aware of it.

This means that for every one of us, the multitude of things that are in conflict with our beliefs will remain outside of our perception, even if such things would provide the solution to our most pressing challenges. The good news is that if we accept this awareness of how we really experience the world, we will open up our minds such that they are capable of exploring something that may at first seem completely irrational. We now have a new belief in possibility, so we have actually created room in our minds to find evidence as we explore. This is why the quote at the start of this section from Herbert Spencer, the philosopher and social theorist, is so powerful. If we block the possibility of advancement in thinking or awareness prior to investigation we are certain to be able to prove to our own satisfaction that we are right.

Most People See Their Results as Causes

The inherent functioning of the mind that causes us to "think in reverse" prevents most people from even recognising opportunities to change. Let's develop the concept of the thoughts-beliefs-actions-results cycle that was introduced in Figure 3.3 by developing the Stickperson model so that we may explore this in more detail.

Figure 4.1 – The Stickperson's Relationship to the Environment

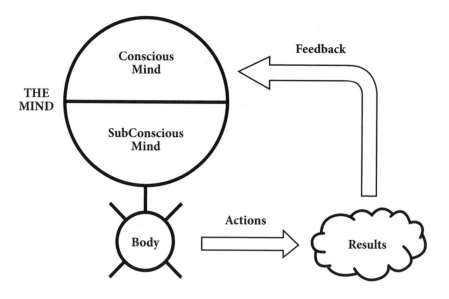

From the explanation thus far you should now be aware that anyone's results are simply a reflection of their thinking to date – and most definitely not of their potential. To recap: thinking creates feelings that determine actions and actions produce results. Therefore, **if we want to change our results we must change our thinking**. In general, however, people allow their thinking to be dictated by the physical results that they see in their world. Since this thinking will then be impressed upon the subconscious mind it will result in actions that will produce more of the same. They then rationalise the reasons why they got those results or look for those reasons outside themselves, and they will rarely fail to find them. It is always possible to find reasonable or logical excuses for failure. The problem is that if you believe the excuses you are destined to get more of the same.

Consider a situation where you think you want something but have a much deeper belief that it is undesirable – perhaps being famous (which could restrict your freedom and privacy), rich (a lot of people are harshly critical of the wealthy), or successful (a guarantee that you would experience rejection). Your subconscious will not allow the creation of something that you do not want, no matter how deeply buried the fear of it might be, so you will remain oblivious to the opportunities to bring that thing into your life. As explained in the previous section, they will be filtered out prior to conscious awareness.

This understanding allows us to fully comprehend the damage done by such simple conditioning as, "He who wants never gets" and "Money is the root of all evil." Though we hear and say some of these common phrases, it is critical in seeking to improve performance to become aware that every time we do so they become ingrained into our filter system. If you believe that money is the root of all evil you will always lack money. Similarly, if you believe that success

IF WE WANT TO CHANGE OUR RESULTS WE MUST CHANGE OUR THINKING.

comes from being "in the right place at the right time" you may never be prepared for the fantastic opening that is certain to come your way at some time, because in waiting for luck to shine your way you will not be looking for the opportunity. Richard Branson was not lucky to find the 350-plus opportunities that he has now turned into businesses. He was actively looking for them and knew that finding them was never a matter of chance. Even if you say such phrases without really believing them, because the subconscious takes things literally (you could think of it as being like a 6-year-old child) they will still become established in your belief system.

To see what type of belief system you have, examine your past results. Are they punctuated with limited financial success, poor health, or a string of unfulfilling relationships? If so, then you must also have corresponding conditioning.

We can only begin to change such results when we change our thinking – there is no value in knowledge. That statement may surprise you since we live in a society that values knowledge so highly; however, examination demonstrates that in and of itself knowledge achieves nothing. It is clearly what we do with our knowledge that matters. Now that you are aware of the power of the subconscious you also know that you cannot improve your results without changing your conditioning. If you are not deliberately working at this level as you seek to create change, then your progress will be slow at best.

As we have seen, most people spend the majority of their time thinking about what they are experiencing through their five senses: their current results. When those results are fantastic that is how they will feel, and when what they sense is unpleasant to them (according to their values), that will similarly determine their feelings. What happens next is insidious and leads to a huge amount of misery. Because people realise that they don't have control over their circumstances, they also believe that they do not have control over how they feel – but that won't stop them trying. They employ the logic that if they can change their circumstances they will feel better and so spend much of their lives trying to force change in things that are outside their control.

No matter how much control we think we are able to gain over events or the actions of others it can never be enough. There will always be another uncontrollable circumstance to cause people with this way of thinking to feel bad.

Happiness Is an Inside Job

There is nothing either right or wrong,
but thinking makes it so.

~ **William Shakespeare**

Instead of thinking, "once this situation changes I'll feel better," realise that what you need is a change of perception. **Feeling better is the result of choosing a different thought, which instantly changes your "reality" and catalyses a completely different set of actions.** This idea is critical, so I make no apology for repeating it more than once. You have the ability to choose how you feel. If you feel bad it is not because of what anyone is doing to you, or the circumstances that you are in; it is because you gave away the feeling of peace through your interpretation of the environment. If you want evidence for this statement, just consider the fact that in any given set of circumstances different people always demonstrate a range of emotional reactions – some positive, some negative. Therefore, the emotion must be caused by the way that people have evaluated what is happening to them, not by the events themselves.

In any situation, you will either recognise that you are fully responsible for your results, or choose to see yourself as passively on the receiving end of the actions of others or of your environment. Remember: the mind works best when it is calm, so the perspective you choose will have an enormous impact on your effectiveness at work. **If you see your external world as the cause of your results, you will be unable to create effective or rapid change in your life or to realise more of your potential.** You will have learned to be helpless.

CREATE A PICTURE OF WHAT YOU DO WANT IN YOUR LIFE.

Once anyone has made a decision, consciously or subconsciously, about the degree to which they will take responsibility for their results, the incredible power of the subconscious mind to delete, distort, and generalise everything that they experience through their five senses will ensure that their perception of the world matches their internal reality. Hence, it is only by taking responsibility that we will be empowered to take different actions.

Figure 4.1 clearly illustrates that if you want to improve your results the only link in the thinking-feeling-action-results cycle that can be broken is the feedback loop between the external world and your thinking. You will have to learn to choose to hold thoughts that serve you irrespective of what your unreliable senses are telling you about what is happening around you.

Let's face it, if we relied upon our senses we would not believe that we are spinning through space at thousands of miles per hour and we would be convinced that railway tracks really do converge as they disappear into the distance. However, our higher awareness allows us to discard such information. You must similarly learn to **create a picture of what you *do* want in your life** irrespective of what the feedback from the senses would indicate to be possible, and to hold that picture until such time as it has been created in the physical world.

If you allow thoughts of what you do not want to dominate your awareness (these may be thoughts about your current results) you will never get the outcome that you desire. Everyone has at some time started a regimen to create change in their lives and failed, whether this was a diet, a new job, a new relationship, etc., even if only their New Year resolutions. Let's take the example of someone starting an exercise plan to lose weight. For most people their effort is focused on their body – the weight that they want to lose. But this focus rarely achieves the results that are being sought after because the excess weight is the effect, not the cause, of the problem. It is the result of harmful patterns of behaviour that become established as a result of the thoughts running around the mind.

The decision to change is a thought and it is thoughts that need to be the focus in driving the desired change. The emphasis should not so much be to try to change the pattern, such as by exercising, but on understanding the mindset that led to excessive eating in the first place. This deals with the primary cause. Thus, the starting point is to uncover the core beliefs underlying the behaviour.

You Must Change Your Beliefs

Because of the power of your beliefs, **change will come only when you begin to expect it, irrespective of how much you want it**. Your expectation determines where the power of the subconscious mind will be focused. Therefore, our only real challenge in the change process is to align our beliefs with what we want. Please note that this is not what we may say we want – our true subconscious desires are what matter. For example, we may believe that we want to run a large business but, as explained earlier, if our mind has accepted the belief system that corporate executives are crooks, which would make this goal undesirable at some level, then we will be unable to achieve it.

A study conducted by Stanford University highlighted this point. A group of people was given a wide range of activities to perform – everything from mathematics to snake charming. Before they began, their beliefs about how successful they would be were assessed and then as they undertook each task their performance was measured. In all cases actual performance was very close to the level of expectation of each test subject prior to starting.

The group was then taught how to perform each task better – experts were brought in to give demonstrations and coach them in the new techniques. When the group's beliefs about how well they would do were assessed again, as expected they were found to have improved. The tests were then repeated. Initially most of the students performed worse, which again was expected because they had to change the way that they were doing things to practice their new skills. One of two things then happened: some people became frustrated with this loss of performance and gave up attempting to use their new skills, whilst other persisted with them. In the first case the test subjects quickly returned to their original level of performance and plateaued there, failing to improve as they repeated the exercise. In the second case, where the subjects persisted with the new skills, after the initial drop in performance they began to improve. Ultimately they surpassed their initial performance to reach a new level of proficiency that matched their new expectations following their period of instruction.

This study provided highly tangible evidence of the extent to which our beliefs dictate the results that we will achieve. I'm theorising now, but I expect that deeper investigation would also have found underlying beliefs to explain why the subjects split into two groups, one of which had much more persistence than the other. For example, those that gave up may have had limiting beliefs about their ability to learn new skills and so, effectively, made the decision not to waste their time trying.

What can be concluded from the Stanford study is that when people are struggling with any activity, the root cause lies in the form of a belief or set of beliefs. So what are these things called beliefs? A belief is simply something that we have a feeling of certainty about, based on our internal evaluation of it. Whether it relates to a person, object, event, or situation, our subconscious mind becomes imprinted with the result of this evaluation, and our assessment of every similar experience will be set against that background.

For example, if you were frequently criticised as a child, you may have decided that this meant you were ugly and unlovable – this would have been your **interpretation** of the situation. When someone now offers a compliment or wants a close relationship, you may react with suspicion and distrust since you decided years ago that you are ugly and unlovable – a great example of an "I am" belief. Consequently you may find yourself being comfortable only with those who view you in the same light: ugly and unlovable. You would repeat the behaviours associated with suspicion and distrust and continue to be attracted to negative situations with people who don't treat you well, even though consciously you would be telling yourself that they were not what you wanted. Without changing the basic belief, in this case your internal judgment of yourself, there is little hope of changing the circumstances.

Once we are aware of what is occurring in our own minds, it gives us the opportunity to re-evaluate the root of our beliefs and diagnose the cause of our behaviour. Since a belief is created by an evaluation in the first place, as we re-evaluate it the belief will change. Different results will then follow.

To begin the process of change, you must choose new beliefs that move you forward. It does not matter whether you can prove those beliefs to be right – we have established that this is close to impossible to do – as long as they serve you by moving you toward what you want and don't violate the rights of, or disadvantage, others. I recommend that you simply test new beliefs with an examination of whether you will like the results that they will create. For example, can we know that we are the cause of everything in our life, as presented in this chapter? This is something that I do feel very certain about but even if I did not, I like the results that taking responsibility for everything in my life generates. It delivers a sense of power and purpose rather than helplessness and despair. We will always benefit from choosing empowering beliefs, such as, "I am smart," "I am talented," "I am worthy," "I am lovable," and "I find opportunity in adversity." These have the potential to transform our self-image and unlock new possibilities in our lives.

> THE PROCESS OF CHANGING BELIEFS FOCUSES YOU DIRECTLY ON THE PRIMARY CAUSE OF YOUR RESULTS.

For many people, negative thoughts are so frequent and familiar that at first it can be tough to recognise and change them. There is an unconscious stream of "I can't…," "I shouldn't…," and "I won't…" type thoughts and they don't recognise how their negative self-beliefs are limiting their own achievements.

Throughout the process of change, open-mindedness is essential. It requires a forced objectivity and knowledge that you must not get attached to your beliefs – many of which will be wrong or unsupportive of your desires. Unfortunately, because beliefs underpin people's identity, there is a powerful tendency to defend them, no matter how limiting or destructive they may be.

The process of changing beliefs focuses you directly on the primary cause of your results. In effect, our results are like the temperature in a room: once a steady state has been reached the thermometer indicates where the thermostat is set. Similarly, the results that you are getting reveal a great deal about your identity. The vital point to recognise is that you have the choice whether your mind operates like a thermometer or a thermostat. If you want to change the temperature of a room it makes no sense to approach the thermometer – everyone knows that they would need to adjust the thermostat. They then wait patiently for the changes to take effect, aware that they have done what is necessary.

Unfortunately, few realise that the mind works in the same way. By focusing on current results we ensure that we will get more of the same. We must treat the mind like a thermostat, working first on the primary cause, the self-image. Each time we visualise a bigger and better picture for the future, the subconscious mind treats this as though it were real and our beliefs about our own capabilities will gradually change.

Bear in mind, as this process is taking place there may be many other people looking at your current results who are likely to want to give you all **their reasons** why you are not capable of achieving your goals. As we have already discussed, when you alter your behaviour to try to please someone else you are not being true to yourself. I can think of no better guidance at this point than to echo the words of Abraham Maslow, who advised that, "The highest quality that a human being can reach is to be independent of the good opinion of others."

The Hardest Step Is the First One

The fact that our environment typically shifts only gradually on a day-to-day basis can make the need for change hard to recognise. We have literally millions of habits – actions that require no conscious involvement – and they are hugely beneficial because they prevent the conscious mind from becoming overwhelmed. However, these habits can also prevent us from noticing if our activities are becoming ineffective.

Our tendency is to continue doing things that are not working because they are comfortable for us; meanwhile the situation that we are in becomes progressively worse.

It is similar to the example of what happens when a frog is placed in a pan of hot water. If the water is already boiling the frog instinctively leaps out. You and I do the same if we are placed in the path of imminent danger; we immediately seek an escape. However, if the water is initially cool but then heated slowly, the frog will not jump out and will boil to death. Similarly, we will tolerate a slow and steady increase in pain or the accumulation of unproductive habits, seemingly numbed to their effects, because of our natural desire to hold on to what we know. To change is perceived as a risk and is therefore to be avoided – I shall return to this theme again shortly.

> THE BIGGEST GAP BETWEEN REALITY AND PERCEPTION USUALLY COMES FROM THE POOREST PERFORMERS.

Without the ability to break this pattern we are basically powerless to improve our lives. Such an interruption can take place in three main ways: the situation eventually becomes unbearable, we experience some sort of disruptive event to shock us out of it, or we raise our level of awareness such that we can deliberately choose a better way. Then we can overcome the conditioning and set off in a completely new direction. Clearly, by far the best of these three mechanisms is to raise awareness. This enables a much quicker response and creates an initial impetus for change by enabling us to see the size of the gap between what we have and what we are capable of. Crucially, it also helps to create the belief that we can overcome whatever is blocking us.

A major problem that prevents the identification of this gap is that it is tough for people to be honest with themselves. This may be one reason that the words "brutal" and "honesty" are often seen in close proximity to one another. Honesty about where we are developmentally can be very painful since we can get into conflict with long-held beliefs that may be at the core of our identity. Also, we have a tendency to believe that we are average or above average. Given the definition of "average," logically we know this cannot be true for everyone but, nevertheless, there are very few people who are ready to rate themselves below average. We tell ourselves that other people are the problem and that they are deluding themselves, rather than acknowledging that we may actually be the source. Take the simple example of the survey that showed that 93% of people believe themselves to be above average drivers. I'm sure I need say no more! The result of this tendency is the creation of major blind spots – aspects of behaviour of which we are unaware that get in the way of high performance.

The natural behaviour of the subconscious mind is primarily to either deny such challenges or to project them onto others, while giving all of our attention to those things that support our self-image. As such we shield ourselves from any information that may interfere with our own self-perception, leaving us with limited ability to evaluate ourselves accurately. Ironically, **the biggest gap between reality and perception usually comes from the poorest performers**. They tend to most overestimate where they are (seeing themselves as above average) and what they can achieve.

For this reason, third-party feedback from a boss, subordinate, mentor, or coach is incredibly valuable. I have frequently been told by senior businessmen that they don't need a coach, whilst in the same conversation their blind spots have been highly evident.

Because of the power of the reticular activating system, our subconscious filter, we can completely overlook information that would give us clear feedback about our effectiveness and impact on other people, such as the way that other people respond to our behaviour.

At the same time, this same information may be totally obvious to others. Although this autonomous behaviour of the mind may protect us emotionally so that we may cope more easily with life, it is a huge hurdle to rapid growth. It is so difficult for individuals to recognise their blind spots that I believe everyone would benefit hugely from getting some form of expert advice in this area.

Even after blind spots have been identified, fear of letting go of what they know and the comfort of familiar patterns of behaviour will always work against people's ability to change. Many scholars have stated that there are really only two reasons why people change: the avoidance of pain or the desire for pleasure. Freud described the play-off between these two factors as "the pleasure principle," and it can explain why humans resist even positive change. We have a tendency to view anything unfamiliar as painful and anything familiar as pleasurable. Our natural survival mechanism dictates that we seek pleasure and avoid pain; therefore, we will have a tendency to avoid the unfamiliar. We seek to maintain the status quo.

Generally, the avoidance of pain provides a more powerful driver than the desire for pleasure, so it is often pain that provides the initial impetus for change. For example, we may become aware of a belief system that has created so many challenges for us that we cannot continue in the same way without facing the threat of the loss of something we value, such as a job, relationship, or physical asset. Such awareness can provide the catalyst for us to finally overcome our fear. When the fear of loss becomes larger than the fear of the unknown, we can and will discover the motivation necessary to change.

You do have a choice and it starts with a decision. Change always starts in the mind, which is the only thing over which you truly have control. Having identified the need to change, a clear decision is necessary that will enable you to work through the inevitable fear and doubt to practice a better way.

Practice, Practice, Practice

Once you make a decision to instil a new behaviour in your life, the behaviour needs to be practiced until it becomes habitual. This will overwrite old belief systems already in place and gradually install new ones. Our paradigms were typically installed over long periods of time, so persistence is required, but with determination this process brings assured results.

The fact that more effective behaviours must be underpinned by changes at the subconscious level explains why it is difficult to introduce changes of behaviour in the classroom. No matter how good the instruction may be, it primarily addresses the conscious mind. Although we may be able to understand a book from a single reading, perhaps even explain parts of it to someone else, the subconscious needs a great deal of practice at visualising and experiencing the concepts before modified behaviours will become automatic. In most learning environments it is not possible to effect the necessary changes to make any progress permanent. This exposes one of the greatest flaws in leadership development courses: the time frames involved in most of them are simply inadequate to effect a lasting transformation.

Practice is essential. **The more often that a new behaviour is exercised the more strongly the new neural circuits will develop** and the more automatic it will become. It is as though we are cutting a new path through the jungle. The first person along it has a very tough job, working hard every step of the way, but it becomes progressively easier for each successive trip. Our propensity to choose a new behaviour increases each time we exercise it.

One way to speed this process up tremendously is through the use of visualisation techniques. It has been proven that the subconscious mind experiences things we visualise in exactly the same way as if they were actually happening. So each time you visualise the attainment of a new behaviour or goal the subconscious mind experiences it as done and begins to change.

Athletes understand this process. They spend a lot of time practicing and very little time actually performing. This allows them to be their best. Unfortunately most executives attempt to be successful whilst approaching their role the other way around – they find it very difficult to find time to study and practice because they are too busy performing. Just as very few people ever really learn how to read well, because they stop learning once they are adequate at it, very often executives learn most of what they know about leading others early in their first leadership role. Initially they watched their peers or other leaders, but once they had learned enough to reach an acceptable level, the pressure of the job became too great and they no longer found the time to consciously think about the kind of leader they wanted to be. Their new behaviour patterns became habitual and thus were no longer examined. Henceforth they gain little conscious awareness of their weaknesses or opportunities for development and rarely, if ever, practice the skills necessary to become more effective.

> THE MORE OFTEN THAT A NEW BEHAVIOUR IS EXERCISED THE MORE STRONGLY THE NEW NEURAL CIRCUITS WILL DEVELOP.

In my coaching practice, I work with my clients to raise awareness (it all starts with awareness) of possible improvements in behaviours and then help them to identify simple exercises that they can incorporate in their normal business day. As long as they are prepared to put conscious effort into practicing these exercises and making some different choices sufficiently consistently for new behaviours to be established, rapid progress can be achieved.

Anyone Can Change

The old idea that the essence of our personality formed early in our childhood and that we are now stuck with it is simply another untrue belief system. Anyone can change if they choose to. It is not possible for anyone to hold you back or keep you down unless you allow them to.

You must decide what you want and that you are prepared to do what it takes to get it. Many people who never succeed in rising above the masses constantly ask themselves whether the reward will justify the work involved. They are seeking instant gratification, so their ongoing effort is highly conditional. In contrast, winners make a decision in advance that they are prepared to do what it takes to be successful, so their attitude to any activity that moves them towards their goals is completely different. They are committed.

It is helpful to recognise that breakthroughs in performance are really break-withs. What this means is that, though it can be intimidating, to make progress you must be prepared to let go of something that you know in order to replace it with something more effective. You must break away totally from old belief systems that don't serve – there can be no sitting on the fence – making a decision and committing yourself to a new course of action. Under these circumstances anyone can change.

Transformational Technique: Train Your Mind

The central theme of this chapter is that of learning to use your mind differently. The root cause of all of our results lies in the subconscious; therefore, this is where we must focus when we are seeking to improve our results. The route to do so is to take control of our use of the conscious part of our mind. In particular, we need to learn to think independently of the apparent feedback that we get from the external world and the "good opinions" of other people. Our perceptions, and those of others, are purely a reflection of the past and will tend to keep us stuck there. What we want is to break the thoughts-feelings-actions-results cycle by giving all of our attention to what we want to create moving forward.

An extremely powerful enabler in this process is what psychologists call metacognition: to learn to think about what you are thinking about. As you become conscious of your thoughts this self-awareness will enable regulation of your cognitive process to change those thoughts that don't serve you. However, remaining constantly vigilant to negative thoughts is hugely challenging, probably impossible; therefore it is fortunate that this is not necessary. Because our thoughts automatically express themselves as feelings, if we can instead become aware of when we are feeling bad this provides an immediate alert that we are engaged in destructive thinking.

It is a simple observation that no one ever improved their situation through worrying or focusing on the reasons that they could give themselves to explain why what they want is not possible for them. A heightened sensitivity to our emotions can be learned with relatively little effort, thus giving an early indication of the need to pay attention to our thoughts and return them to the positive.

Changing the way that you feel about your results to take total personal responsibility is incredibly enlightening. It places your power fully in your own hands. I recommend that you make a commitment to yourself that you will take full responsibility for your life and remain persistent to the task until you have completely integrated this new attitude into your belief systems. The increase in awareness that you gain will be transformational.

SHIFTING PERCEPTIONS

*I have yet to find a man, however exalted his station,
who did not do better work and put forth greater effort
under a spirit of approval than under
a spirit of criticism.*

~ Charles Schwab

Not only is awareness of yourself key in creating change in your life, your perception of others will also impact your choices of behaviour. A change in your awareness of why other people do what they do enables empathy, which is at the root of all relationships.

Lack of empathy is one of the most critical weaknesses that can undermine a leader. To be able to empathise with another person

LACK OF EMPATHY IS ONE OF THE MOST CRITICAL WEAKNESSES THAT CAN UNDERMINE A LEADER.

you have to put yourself into their circumstances, such that you can imagine their thoughts and emotions. Movie makers rely on this ability to create movies that inspire strong feelings in the audience. We have those emotions because we are able to imagine what it feels like to be in the same situations as those in the film – and since the subconscious has no ability to determine that what we are imagining is not real, we cry – or laugh – or get scared out of our wits.

As I introduced in Chapter 2, self-leadership plays a large part in your ability to lead. One of the most important aspects of this is your reaction to the behaviours of others. As you gain understanding of others and learn to empathise with their feelings, **your attitude toward them will change** and your behaviours will automatically follow. The potential impact that this could have on your leadership capability is huge.

Attitude – The Major Determinant of Success

Attitude is the composite of all of our thoughts, feelings and actions; in other words, all of the areas covered by the Stickperson described in Chapter 3. Above all else, attitude determines how successful we will be in life. It particularly affects whether we see the best or the worst in a situation, interpreting it as opportunity or threat, which then shapes our response and ultimately determines our results.

The most important aspect of our attitude in leadership relates to people. Just what do you really think of them? Success in business is much more about people than product. The relationships built through the course of a career are essential to the success of that career. It doesn't matter what industry we talk about; 85% of the skills needed at senior levels are people skills (as a reminder, even in the most technical jobs, such as research scientists, this figure is still 50%).

As with any other area of behaviour, attempting to create a lasting change in the way that we work with other people without addressing our underlying belief systems will have only limited effect. The most powerful lever that we can pull to improve our relationships is to change our beliefs about people and that comes from having greater awareness in relation to them.

Perspective Determines Action

As we have seen, when you change the way you look at things, the things that you look at will change. You literally filter the information from your senses differently and your behaviours shift accordingly. Your reactions and responses are determined by your subjective experience of what is happening to you.

This characteristic of the mind controls how you interact with people. For example, if someone on your team missed a deadline how would you interpret it: poor time management or commitment to quality? If he doesn't do a task that you have assigned, is he lazy or busy? If someone makes a decision without consulting you, is she overstepping the mark or showing initiative? This list could go on and on: a pushover or cooperative; a risk-taker or creative innovator; slow or thorough; lacking work-life balance or committed to the business. These are all examples of the use of the mental faculty of perception, which I covered in great detail in the last chapter, and which shapes our world.

Hopefully you now fully realise that the way you view any of these things is simply a result of your conditioning. Unfortunately, most people rarely stop to look at the degree to which **their own perspective** creates their experience. In failing to do this, they relinquish their capacity to truly influence their world and to take responsibility for their results.

One of the things that most affects perspective is the individual's mood, which can also set expectations. As demonstrated in Chapter 4, our neurology is constructed so that we filter everything to ensure that our experience is consistent with our belief systems. This means that mood will determine how experiences get filtered: when we are feeling positive, we are much more likely to evaluate people and events in a positive light.

One of the features of the physical world is that of polarity, which creates the appearance of opposites – we cannot have awareness of one side of the pair without also having awareness of its polar opposite. For example, if we could live on the surface of the sun we would have no word for light because we would never have been able to experience dark; therefore, no concept of light would be possible either. In fact, light and dark really exist on a continuum with only one variable, ranging from there being a lot of light or not very much of it. It is only when we observe how much light there is from a specific point along that continuum that other points appear light or dark relative to where we are. This idea was introduced in the previous chapter, and leads to the conclusion that nothing is good or bad, right or wrong, large or small, etc., until we make it so, relative to something else. So why is this important?

> YOU MUST FIRST THINK ABOUT WHAT YOU WANT FROM YOUR TEAM, AFTER WHICH IT IS ESSENTIAL THAT YOU EXPECT TO GET IT.

Whilst polarity is a construct of our mind that emerges from our perception of certain things, a by-product of it is vitally important because it points to the mechanism by which all advance arises. At one time all ships were built out of wood because people assumed that it was necessary to use a material that itself floated. To build ships out of steel it was necessary to establish how things float by understanding the law of buoyancy. This enabled people to become aware of the possibility of using materials of higher density than water.

Just as steel ships would never have been created by studying the fact that metals sink, no advance is ever possible from thinking about what we don't want. As a leader this is equally true of your team as it is for you individually. You must first think about what you want from them, after which **it is essential that you expect to get it.**

This type of advice, recommending an attitude of believing the best in others, is common. However, the explanation of why it is so important is less well understood, which may explain why it is such an uncommon practice in the workplace. As you know by now, action without belief is impossible, and belief without compelling evidence is unlikely for most people brought up in a scientific, proof-orientated world. Most people will "believe it only when they see it."

The reason your beliefs about others are so important is rooted in a strange and perhaps rather surprising phenomenon known as the Pygmalion effect, or self-fulfilling prophecy, so called after the Greek legend of King Pygmalion. The legend tells that the King sculpted a statue of his perfect woman then, by his effort and will, brought it to life. The term "Pygmalion effect" refers to the idea that when someone creates a belief in something that is not yet true, and then expects it with certainty, it will actually happen. In relation to people it suggests that we communicate our expectations of others to them, following which they conform and deliver results to match the expectation.

For any manager or leader of a company this is an important concept. If it is true, then any time you express lack of confidence in others it is likely that they will return it with mediocre performance, whereas if you believe in them and expect them to do well, they will live up to that expectation.

Scientific evidence for the Pygmalion effect is extensive. In what has become a classic in the sociology of education, published in 1968 under the title *Pygmalion in the Classroom,* Robert Rosenthal and Leonore Jacobson worked with the students from 18 classrooms at an elementary school. First, they gave all the students an intelligence test at the beginning of the school year. The two researchers had spent much of their careers in education and had become increasingly concerned that teachers' expectations of lower-class and minority children were contributing to the high rate of failure among these students. They took a group of students and selected 20% of them at random – without any regard to their intelligence test results – telling the teachers that these students could be expected to "bloom" or "spurt" in their academics that year. Any differences between these children and the rest of the class existed only in the minds of the teachers. At the end of the year, they came back and retested all the students. Those labeled as "bloomers" gained an average of 12 IQ points compared to a gain of 8 points for the remainder of the group. Further studies since then have repeated these results many times.

> WHAT WE EXPECT, ALL TOO OFTEN, IS EXACTLY WHAT WE GET.

Further compelling evidence of the Pygmalion effect has also been found in experiments with animals. For example, a group of psychology students were given rats to train in running mazes. Half of the students were told that their rats were genetically bred to run mazes quickly, while the other half were told that their rats were genetically inferior and would be slow learners. Actually, all of the rats were quite ordinary, neither bright nor dull. However, those rats believed to be bright improved daily in running the maze. They ran faster and more accurately. The "dull" rats refused to budge from the starting point 29% of the time, while the "bright" rats refused only 11% of the time.

Robert Tauber, a professor of education at The Behrend College of Pennsylvania State University at Erie, compiled over 700 doctoral dissertations and countless journal articles on stereotyping, perception of social differences, race, gender, ethnicity, body features, age, socioeconomic levels, special needs, and other personal and situational factors. What he showed was, **"What we expect, all too often, is exactly what we get."**

The process by which expectation gets converted to reality in the self-fulfilling prophecy has three main stages:

- We form certain expectations, or beliefs, about people or events based on our own, as yet unrealised, perceptions.

- Those expectations get communicated through cues because we behave in a way that we would not have done without the unrealised belief.

- People generally respond to these cues by adjusting their belief systems to match. Once this has happened a change in behaviours is automatic.

The result is that the original expectation becomes fact. To explain this more fully in the context of the Rosenthal/Jacobson study, the teachers had subtly and unconsciously encouraged the performance they expected to see. Not only did they spend more time with the students indicated as showing promise, they were also more enthusiastic about teaching them and unintentionally showed more warmth to them than to the other students. As a result, the "special" students felt more capable and intelligent and they performed accordingly.

By this principle we can see that what leaders expect from their team determines how they treat them and shapes, to a huge degree, the quality of their output. A study of 100 self-made millionaires found that one of the characteristics that they had in common was the desire and ability to see the good in others. They were people builders, not critics.

The Fundamental Question

Albert Einstein, the revered physicist, suggested that the most important question that we can ever ask ourselves is whether the inherent nature of the universe is friendly or hostile. As with anything else in our experience, our perspective on this question is simply an interpretation with its basis in factors of which we are unlikely to have much conscious awareness. In our mind we can create optimistic scenarios and we can also limit anything. **We have ultimate capability to view the world negatively or positively – that which we choose has a profound impact on how we behave.**

In my work with clients, one of the tools that I use to help to raise awareness of beliefs is the DiSC psychometric profiling instrument. This provides some very powerful insight into people's perspectives on this question.

DiSC is an extensively tested aid, proven by over 30 years of reliable application with more than 40 million users in over 50 countries and by extensive, ongoing research. The structure of the model consists of two major dimensions: the vertical dimension described in terms of **perceived power**, and the horizontal dimension **perceived favourability** of the environment, creating four primary styles as shown in Figure 5.1.

Figure 5.1 – The DiSC Model

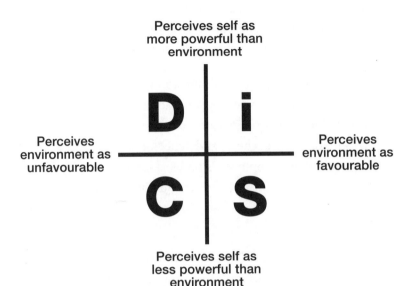

A summary of the preferred behaviour patterns and tendencies within each of the styles is as follows:

- **D**ominance: This dimension measures how one tends to overcome daily challenges and obstacles. "D's" are strong-willed, strong-minded people who like accepting challenges, taking action, and getting immediate results. Their emphasis is on shaping the environment by overcoming opposition.

- **I**nfluence: "i's" are "people people" who like participating on teams, sharing ideas, and energising and entertaining others. Their emphasis is on shaping the environment by influencing and persuading others.

- Steadiness: "S's" are helpful people who like working behind the scenes, performing in consistent and predictable ways, and are good listeners. Their emphasis is on cooperating with others within existing circumstances to carry out the task.

- Conscientiousness: This dimension measures how we respond to fear and our desire for accuracy and quality details. "C's" are sticklers for quality and like planning ahead, employing systematic approaches, and checking and rechecking for accuracy. Their emphasis is on working conscientiously within existing circumstances to ensure quality and accuracy.

The vertical axis is the "motor response to stimulus" axis. Both "D" and "i" styles tend to perceive that they are more powerful than the environment; that is, they can influence their surroundings. They are likely to increase their emotional response and physical presence in response to stimuli, becoming more assertive and proactive. On the other hand, "S" and "C" styles feel that they have little direct control over the environment and may decrease the strength of their responses to stimuli, becoming more adaptive and reactive.

> A POSITION OF POWER IS OF NO VALUE IF PEOPLE DO NOT FIRST BELIEVE IN THEMSELVES.

Eric Hoffer describes the impact of perceiving the self as less powerful than the environment in his book, *The True Believer*. In it he says, "Those who are awed by their surroundings do not think of change, no matter how miserable their condition. When our mode of life is so precarious as to make it patent that we cannot control the circumstances of our existence, we tend to stick to the proven and the familiar. We counteract a deep feeling of insecurity by making our existence a fixed routine. We hereby acquire the illusion that we have tamed the unpredictable." In other words, "S" and "C" types will tend to be particularly resistant to change and seek to operate within the existing environment.

Hoffer then explains that this will be the case even if people are in positions of power, saying, "Where power is not joined with faith in the future, it is used mainly to ward off the new and preserve the status quo." Hence, **a position of power is of no value if people do not first believe in themselves**.

The reason I noted Einstein's statement at the beginning of this discussion is because I want to highlight the significance of the horizontal dimension of this model: whether you perceive your environment to be favourable or unfavourable. This axis provides an indicator of the likely emotional response to stimuli. Because they consider the environment to be unfavourable, **"D's" and "C's" will tend to experience novel stimuli or unexpected events as antagonistic**. Anything new will be perceived as potentially conflicting with a "D's" sense of control or a "C's" sense of order and will be resisted. An "i" or "S," on the other hand, will tend to be receptive and accommodating. They will seek to incorporate changes into their world relatively harmoniously.

This is a critically important distinction. It means that the instinctive response of "D's" and "C's" in new situations is to be antagonised by people, perceiving them as adversaries. They will instinctively spar with them, trying to defend their position. Since most leaders have "D" as their dominant style (it does produce a very positive and powerful focus on delivering results), this points to an area where leaders may immediately look in order to enhance relationships with their staff. It also contributes to the explanation of why internal competition is so endemic in business. In contrast, "i's" and "S's" will instinctively see people as assets, looking for the best in them and helping them to see the best in themselves.

There is huge value in recognising that you will have a tendency to see people as either adversaries or assets. In the context of the Pygmalion effect, the implications for any leader with a bias strongly toward the D/C end of the axis are profound. No training course can teach them to behave differently while maintaining their congruence and integrity. They must change the core beliefs that determine their perception of the environment and the people in it. Surface level changes will not last and will convince no one.

The problem is that most of the communication that takes place between people happens at the subconscious level. Studies have found that in a normal face-to-face interaction, only a small percentage of the information exchanged happens as a result of the words that are used. Much more of the transfer is related to the tonality of the voice, while the largest element is likely physiological. Since much of the tonality and physiology will be controlled at a subconscious level, a management course that teaches how to communicate more effectively can only have a marginal effect unless beliefs are changed as well. In particular, the perception of the individual towards other people must be changed to one of positive expectation.

FOR ANYONE SEEKING TO CREATE GREAT RESULTS WITH OR THROUGH OTHER PEOPLE, THE STARTING POINT IS TO EXPECT THE BEST.

When striving to understand the process of communicating expectations, recognise that it is not so much about what a boss says but **the way in which he or she behaves** that makes the difference. Indifferent and noncommittal treatment of staff is the kind of behaviour that communicates low expectations and leads to poor performance. On the other hand, leaders who don the roles of "positive Pygmalions" and regularly set high but attainable expectations seem to be able to elicit the best performance from their subordinates.

You can help improve the performance of your employees by creating an accepting and encouraging social and emotional environment that includes warmth, attention, and positive, nonverbal communication. More interaction, praise, constructive feedback, and input can help the employee raise his or her performance level significantly. To put it simply, you create more effective employees just by believing in them and letting them know it. **For anyone seeking to create great results with or through other people, the starting point is to expect the best.**

Since expectation is heavily impacted by mood, if you do not manage your mood in a positive manner it is unlikely that you will be able to achieve the results that you desire. This is only one of the reasons why emotional self-leadership is so critical for leaders. Tuning into the emotions of the people around you will also give a good pointer to what type of results they are likely to create, both for themselves and with others.

People Can Only Do Their Best

In seeking to expect the best, it helps enormously to realise that people always do their best. This is one of the areas that gets most challenged when I work through it with my clients or friends. The argument will typically be that if you have done something in the past that you now recognise could have been done better, how can it be possible that you did your best? We hear this all the time from our friends and colleagues in statements such as, "I should have done better," implicitly bringing the hypothetical into a situation that occurred in the past. If examined it is easy to see that, being hypothetical, this must be fantasy. The learning that now makes a better course of action appear obvious was not available at the time and so could not be applied.

Take this more complicated situation with one of my clients, Sarah, who had failed to prepare adequately for an important meeting. Despite the fact that the meeting outcome was not badly affected, she felt she should have done better and had spent the time since being extremely self-critical. When we discussed this in the context that she was doing her best, she initially rejected the idea on the basis that she had known that she should have been doing more even prior to the meeting but had failed to do anything to change it.

An understanding of why her position was wrong can be derived from looking at her behaviour within the framework of the Stickperson. This makes it clear that knowing how to do better is not enough because **it is not your conscious knowledge that controls what you do**. Every action you take is controlled by the conditioning in your subconscious mind. No amount of thinking about doing something differently will have any impact until new conditioning has been installed because you are being controlled by your subconscious beliefs. Dr. David Hawkins described this as follows, "Personal past history represents the best that one could actually do then under given circumstances, which included one's perceptions and emotional mental states at the time. Mistakes are intrinsic to the learning process, which is the fate of the human condition itself."

Even if you think you know better, until that idea has been accepted by the subconscious it is literally impossible that you could act on it. You will not have the emotional resources to **do** what you **know**. So the root of Sarah's inability to take the action that she was aware of as having been necessary was not lack of knowledge but an ineffective subconscious belief. Because she did not understand the role of the subconscious mind in causing her actions she felt as though she had failed.

No one is wrong because of their subconscious beliefs, which they did not choose, any more than the hardware of the computer is wrong if it gets a virus. Earlier we looked extensively at the degree to which people actually choose their conditioning and discovered that **conditioning is something that happens to us** without our consent. If you are prepared to break the paradigms of your own conditioning and accept this concept then your whole perception will shift. The fact is that people can only ever do their best at every moment and as soon as they have learned how to do better, at the subconscious level, they will automatically do so.

Al Capone provides a great example of how someone can believe that they are doing well when almost everyone else would clearly see their limitations. He was at one time America's public enemy number one, a violent and indiscriminate gang leader who would put a bullet into anyone who got in his way. Yet he considered himself to be a public benefactor, unappreciated and misunderstood, as demonstrated by this statement, "I have spent the best years of my life giving people the lighter pleasures, helping them to have a good time, and all I get is abuse, the existence of a hunted man." He actually believed this. I expect that he would have been very comfortable with the idea that he was doing his best.

To see this for yourself, try this experiment: survey people at random and ask them if they seek to do a bad job when they go to work. If you are able to look deep enough to understand the emotional drivers that control their behaviours, what you will find is that they all want to do a great job; they simply may not currently be able to put their desire into action.

Other People Are Mirrors to Our Beliefs

In relationships, people see others as they see themselves. When I'm coaching, in order to understand people's self-image I always closely observe how they view others.

Ralph Waldo Emerson, the esteemed philosopher, once said, "People seem not to see that their opinion of the world is a confession of character." This means that whatever we are most critical of in other people is most often the thing that we least like about ourselves. Similarly, when someone is very critical of others, they almost always have a deep personal insecurity. Unfortunately, as a strategy for feeling better this particular approach will never work because it is impossible to truly feel good about undermining others. This is an ego trick, even though few people recognise it as such.

> WE TREAT OTHER PEOPLE ACCORDING TO THE WAY WE SEE OURSELVES.

This relationship between the opinion that we hold of the self and others is also true in the opposite sense. Anyone who has a positive self-image will look for the good in others. **We treat other people according to the way we see ourselves.**

The explanation for this feature of human nature is that people can only evaluate others, and their behaviours, according to their own model of the world (their internal representation of how things are). For example, they will perceive something that you do as lazy if they would consider themselves lazy for doing the same thing – they have internal rules to determine what constitutes laziness that are applied in all circumstances. You, on the other hand, might have found that

> YOU CANNOT BE RESPONSIBLE FOR WHAT HAPPENS TO YOU, BUT YOU CERTAINLY CAN CONTROL WHAT HAPPENS IN YOU AS A RESULT.

same behaviour to be the best way to release stress and unleash your creativity. As a consequence, many leaders unconsciously choose a team who are like them because they automatically interpret the behaviours of such people as desirable. The tighter their rules are about what constitutes acceptable behaviours, the more this will be the case and the more similar the members of their team will be. We are comfortable with sameness because it creates automatic rapport.

Gaining a deeper understanding of those who treat others, including yourself, harshly will be a tremendous help to you in empathising with the way that they think and thereby becoming less affected by their behaviours. You will come to recognise that such harshness or ill-temper, while it can arise from an inflated sense of self-importance, is more commonly the outward expression of deep discontent within themselves. It then becomes much easier to ensure that your self-image, that critical driver of your own results, reflects who you want to be, not how other people treat you. That could truly transform your performance.

A highly effective approach to improve self-leadership, based on this understanding, is to realise that you are not responsible for how people treat you, while at the same time taking full responsibility for how you respond to them. Once you realise that their words and actions aren't even about you but reflect what is going on in them, your empathy will immediately increase – you are aware of the root cause. To react to the behaviour, which isn't the real issue, can only damage your relationship.

As always, you are seeking to move from reacting to responding and thereby to master your environment. **You cannot be responsible for what happens to you, but you certainly can control what happens in you as a result.** As you increasingly learn to respond you create the opportunity to improve your results.

Start Caring

No one really listens to or cares what you know until they first feel that you care about who they are as a person. Again, this provides a terrific platform for rapport. Concern for others is at the heart of high-quality relationships. This concern cannot be faked. If you want to help people and have a positive impact on them, you cannot do so if your liking for them is not genuine or if you disparage them in any way. The more that leaders show that they are prepared to help others, such as by finding out what they want and helping them to get it, the greater ability they will have to influence those individuals.

A great attitude, and one that brings fantastic results, is to love and value people, to praise effort and to reward performance. Praise must be based on truth; otherwise it is just flattery, which convinces no one and damages relationships. This should not be a problem, though: if you look for the good in people you will always be able to find something praiseworthy. No matter how many mistakes people make, remember that it does not devalue their worth as a person. If you want great relationships, always find reasons to affirm someone first and avoid confrontation. Probably the most effective way to do this is to develop the ability to find the best in people, not the worst, by truly caring for them.

It has been taught that we should love people and use money – never the other way around. In my experience, too many leaders in business may not have realised the benefits to be gained from this approach and consistently switch the verbs – they use people and love money. In pursuit of money and increased shareholder value they often view employees and those around them as not only replaceable, but disposable (I once had a boss who took pleasure in telling us how many people he had fired). The fear-orientated environment that this creates will never inspire anyone to give fully of themselves.

Let's take a look at some alternative approaches to managing people that are rarely considered at work. First, acts of **kindness**. These have been proven to have a highly beneficial impact on everyone involved. Research has shown that it is not just the person who is the recipient of kindness that is affected, but also the doer and even anyone else who simply sees it. The most positive impact is often on the person doing the giving; this has been proven to create a massive positive shift in the biochemistry of the body. Unfortunately, few people are conditioned to behave in this way. Similarly, **compassion** is highly effective for creating harmonious solutions but is uncommon in the workplace. As discussed in Chapter 2, a compassionate response to other people's challenges will dramatically improve your ability to influence them.

None of this is very surprising in the context of the knowledge that we are emotional beings, controlled by the feelings in the subconscious mind. To ignore emotional routes to improved influence because they are outside the generally accepted norms is to limit the results that you could otherwise achieve.

The key to changing the way that you treat people once again lies in perception – the way that you think about others. It is much easier to be compassionate, for example, when we realise that everyone is doing their best from their own level of awareness.

You may remember Stephen Covey's story that I described in Chapter 2. Faced with disruptive children on the underground he became very irritated, until he understood the reason for their unruliness – they had recently lost their mother. In other words, **he needed to understand their story and consciously and subconsciously agree that it**

> YOU CAN MAKE THE CHOICE TO FEEL COMPASSION FOR OTHERS WITHOUT NEEDING TO KNOW OR VET THEIR STORY.

provided a valid "excuse" for their behaviour, in order to be able to change his perspective and feel compassion for them. I'm sure that had he found out that the reason for their behaviour was, for example, that they didn't like traveling by train, he would have found it much more difficult to shift his feelings in the same way. We probably almost all would.

The important thing to recognise here is that we all do this kind of thing all of the time. We project our values onto the world and judge other people's behaviour based on whether it is acceptable according to our own rules for meeting those values.

I'd like to propose to you a much more powerful attitude that becomes possible out of the awareness that everyone always does their best. If you recognise that no one else will ever conform exactly to your rules, because both you and they are unique, then it should also become clear that there will inevitably be times when what others do will appear to be wrong to you. However, knowing that they are doing their best provides the awareness that if they are struggling with their circumstances, and this shows up as "poor" behaviour, then they must also be suffering. **You can then make the choice to feel compassion for them without needing to know or vet their story.** This will enable you to access a range of responses that is currently outside your awareness.

Given the power of this approach, let's look more fully at the role of caring and emotions specifically in leadership.

Primal Leadership

We know that it is the subconscious mind that determines what we do, based on how we are feeling. In his book, *The New Leaders*, Daniel Goleman expresses the emotional task of the leader as being *primal*, in that he considers it to be the most important act of leadership. He states, "Leaders have always played a primordial emotional role. In the modern organisation, this primordial emotional task—though by now largely invisible—remains foremost among the many jobs of leadership: driving the collective emotions in a positive direction and clearing the smog created by toxic emotions."

When people feel positive it frees them to be their best. If people feel excited and motivated, their performance will improve, while any anxiety, anger, or dissatisfaction will rapidly cause them to lose focus and underperform. A leader is best able to create these positive emotions by empathising with others' situations and stepping into their shoes.

Emotions also affect teams as the moods of the people in the team rapidly align with each other. For example, in business meetings it has been found that this can happen in as little as two hours. The person who has the most effect on others is, perhaps unsurprisingly, the boss. Because of his or her greater influence, his or her mood will always have the greatest impact on the mood and subsequent performance of a team. Even if senior leaders don't have very much exposure to the business overall, because their mood impacts the people that work for them, the effects will inevitably work their way down the organisation to impact the whole company.

> ONE THING THAT CREATES AN ENORMOUS AMOUNT OF TOXIC EMOTION IS CRITICISM.

To get the best out of people, therefore, ways should be sought that allow them to enjoy the workplace. This may not be a common approach but the fact is that people do their best work when they enjoy it. **One thing that creates an enormous amount of toxic emotion is criticism.** It constantly amazes me how accepting we are of this behaviour, even though it does so much damage. And it is not just ignorance. We all know that the performance of a sports team can be uplifted or badly suppressed by whether the crowd gets behind it or is critical and negative. Perhaps it is simply that there is insufficient awareness of its impact in the emotional environment of the workplace for behaviours to change?

Whatever the reasons for our tolerance of this most damaging type of interaction, the benefits for anyone prepared to eliminate such behaviour from their repertoire will be huge. In studies, Daniel Goleman found that inept criticism by the boss is the major cause of conflict in the workplace. Furthermore, research by the California Task Force for Personal and Social Responsibility has concluded that only 20% of people can handle put-downs without emotional pain or psychological damage. Long before any of these studies, Dale Carnegie, author of the famous best-seller, *How to Win Friends and Influence People*, said, "Any fool can criticise, condemn and complain—and most fools do." This master of interpersonal relationships and human motivation did not describe people who like to use this approach as fools for no reason!

Everyone needs to start to realise that people are not creatures of logic but are driven by emotion. The pain that one can experience as a result of criticism can stir up resentments that will last for years. How often have you been in conversation with someone and they shared a negative comment the boss made to them perhaps years ago? In such circumstances it is possible to feel the sense of being wronged and the resentment that still lingers.

Part of the error that people make is to believe that in order to become a person of influence they must become an authority figure, correcting errors, uncovering weaknesses and blind spots, and giving "constructive criticism."

PEOPLE ARE NOT CREATURES OF LOGIC BUT ARE DRIVEN BY EMOTION.

Unfortunately few have learned the skills to coach and provide feedback in a constructive manner. This can be demonstrated by the fact that in the workplace, feedback is such a major cause of conflict, creating tension, hostility, and resentment. This costs leaders enormously in their relationships with their employees and greatly reduces their ability to influence and bring out the best in others.

John Knox, a Scottish reformer, summed this up when he said, "You cannot antagonise somebody and influence them at the same time." Any time someone is being antagonised they will move into resistance, seeking to find reasons to ignore what they are being told and defending their existing belief systems. As you are now aware, the resulting unpreparedness to change their belief systems then makes it impossible for change that could lead to higher performance. Whatever the intention of the leader in having the discussion, unless it was to bruise and injure, they will have failed.

It is also impossible to influence people while judging them. You must respect other people's models of the world. This does not mean that you need to agree with their ideas or adopt them. Just recognise that they are doing their best and make that okay. As soon as you judge someone, you set an expectation based on your previous experience and perception, and you bring the Pygmalion effect into play. It is inevitable that this will at times inhibit the creation of something new.

We have spent much time discussing self-leadership because it takes great character and self-control to be understanding and forgiving – but it produces incredible benefits. Without it you will never be strong in developing a key aspect of influence: rapport.

Rapport – The Foundation of Great Communications

Rapport is essential before anyone can be influenced. It can be defined as a relationship of responsiveness between people or groups and is a feeling of connectedness that is mandatory for effective relationships.

When you first meet people you will have no influence over them because rapport is missing. Establishing rapport may require specific focus to seek common ground when meeting someone for the first time or at the start of a meeting. Even then it must still be monitored at all times to ensure that it is not lost. **To have great communication, the parties involved must be in rapport at all times**: influence depends upon it. It is not complicated but it may take effort.

The immediate sign that rapport is missing is that there will be resistance from one or more parties, resulting in the complete loss or severe degradation of influence. People who are out of rapport will move toward judgment, becoming less receptive to what the other party may suggest.

The most effective way of building rapport is to behave as much as possible in the same manner as the other person, if possible expressing

A DEAF EAR IS THE FIRST SIGN OF A CLOSED MIND.

similar likes and dislikes. This is because most people like sameness: either people similar to them or who are as they would like to be. It requires great flexibility to be able to match the enormous variety of personal styles that exist. However, the less flexible you are the more people you will meet with whom you will struggle to establish rapport and who you will therefore be unable to influence effectively.

Sensory acuity and listening are vital skills for building rapport. Most people are very poor at listening, and again, this is one of the most critical skills for building great relationships. It is effective because of the feeling that it creates in the other person: that you are interested in, and care about, them. **When there is a breakdown in communications it is usually because people stop listening, not because they stop talking.**

This issue is of particular importance when people who gain seniority in a company develop a lack of patience in listening to the people under them – a characteristic that is markedly absent in the best leaders. **A deaf ear is the first sign of a closed mind.**

The key to great listening is to focus on the other person and notice what is going on for them. It is possible to capture a huge amount of information beyond the words that they actually use, but only if you are looking for it. With great listening you will make fewer mistakes, get access to better information, and improve your relationships.

There are several levels of listening ranging from the purely superficial to multi-sensory, deep listening. As you move through these levels, concentration increases, more and more of your attention becomes focused on the other person, you speak less, and you gain increasing amounts of information from what is not being said, such as through subtle nuances in their speech. To reach the highest levels of communications skills, sensory acuity is essential. I introduced this idea in Chapter 2. It is really part of deep listening, but it has been separated out for clarity.

Sensory acuity in the context of leadership refers to the ability to become acutely attuned to the verbal and non-verbal behaviours of others and, through refined distinctions, to be able to interpret what they are likely to be feeling. As we covered in Chapter 3, our conditioning, combined with the limitations of the conscious mind, dictate that we notice only a tiny part of the vast array of information that is available from the five senses. By learning to pay attention to much more of this information, you will gain the discriminating ability necessary to bring the full richness of the available detail to conscious awareness, which can lead to much more effective behaviours.

Some of the key areas where you can focus attention are physiological:

- Set of shoulders, tempo of hand movements, facial expression, angle of head, etc.

- Skin colour, skin tone, amount of shine

- Breathing (volume, speed, location)

- Lip size, the eyes (focused/unfocused, dilated/undilated)

- Pulse or tonality of voice (pressure of delivery, hard/soft, resonance, inflection, hesitation)

Highly developed sensory acuity together with the ability to interpret the changes that you see enables a large number of quality distinctions to be made in a given situation. It will give you immediate feedback as to whether what you are doing is likely to help you to achieve the outcome that you are looking for.

Everyone Responds Better to Appreciation

Too many of us take pleasure in discouraging others and pointing out their mistakes and failures. Although this is a natural feature of the human ego, it is one that can be overcome and the benefits to be gained by doing so are enormous.

Consider the application of this idea in career development sessions, annual employee reviews, or even simply in providing feedback. The standard approach in this type of meeting is to start with something positive, then to identify the deficiencies that form the main focus of the subsequent discussion and, almost as an afterthought, to finish on a positive. The problem with this, as so often occurs in any communications situation, is that the subconscious cues from the person "in charge" clearly indicate to the recipient what is considered to be most important – the flaws. So as soon as the conversation starts, albeit on a positive note, feelings of anxiety and defensiveness are automatically triggered.

When most people experience themselves becoming defensive it is deeply demotivating, so the impact will be quite the opposite of what is sought. The majority of them will become more cautious, less willing to learn, and more resistant to change. Finishing off the session with a positive note does not address this issue; the damage is already done. What people will remember from the conversation is not what was said but the things that created the strongest emotional response, which will primarily be dependent upon the true focus of the discussion. If you are doing a review or giving feedback and your focus is faults, then the recipient will feel it and respond accordingly. A focus on weaknesses does not encourage people and has little potential to help them to grow.

If we talk about property appreciating we mean that it is increasing in value. Conversely, depreciating means that it is decreasing in value. We should think about this in our relationships with people. Human assets can appreciate or depreciate in value depending on the approach of the leader. Are you appreciating or depreciating your team? The value that they will contribute will soon correspond. The most effective leaders are aware that one of their key tasks is to grow people, and they realise that the most effective way to do this is through encouragement and appreciation.

This concept offers a fantastic opportunity to gain a competitive advantage. In almost every business, every asset of the business depreciates in value and over a period of time it will need to be replaced. The cycle for this is highly variable in length but follows a consistent pattern: the asset depreciates and then there is a sudden investment over a short period of time, then the cycle of depreciation starts again. Clearly, **this approach will not work for people**, though it can be attempted through an aggressive recruitment policy to combat turnover!

> PEOPLE HAVE TO WANT TO DO THEIR JOB IF THEY ARE TO EXCEL.

Charles Schwab, an American industrialist who became a multimillionaire in the steel industry, said, "I have yet to find a man, however exalted his station, who did not do better work and put forth greater effort under a spirit of approval than under a spirit of criticism." Withholding critical comments is not enough. It is important to provide people with positive affirmation through praise or complements. Over a period of time, if this type of feedback is withheld, people's energy and commitment for what they are doing will gradually reduce, resulting in demotivated workers. Quite simply, people need praise to maintain high performance.

The reason for this stems from the very basic desire of human beings to achieve. In all but a few cases, where people have learned to be very highly internally motivated, they want to be appreciated for the contribution that they make, through their efforts and skills, to the success of the whole. Knowing that what you do is considered to be of value builds self-confidence and self-worth, which then stimulates a move to the next level of performance. This is the most positive of self-reinforcing cycles. Even if people do not show their desire for recognition it does not mean that they do not feel it.

Remember, the only people who can step up their performance effectively are those who feel positive about themselves, because performance is driven by self-image. You can begin by simply letting people know that their efforts are appreciated – they may have worked hard even if the result achieved was not good. If you look for something to appreciate you will never be disappointed. Thank people whenever you can and constantly give them credit for successes, praising them in front of others whenever possible – this is especially beneficial.

The key point to remember is that we are emotional, not logical beings. What we do is driven by the way that we feel, so **people have to want to do their job if they are to excel**. You can make someone do their work, but you cannot make them do it well. All too often motivation is ignored or taken for granted – after all, they are being paid and given the security of a job! The problem is that human motivators are always an inside job. No external motivation can get anyone to fully commit themselves to excelling at work.

Knowing what people need and value is the key to understanding how to motivate them. That which they value most deeply will move them most powerfully in their work, so by understanding them you can also influence them. As we discussed earlier, in order to influence someone else it is first necessary to understand how they influence themselves. Clearly, human beings are very complex and putting effort into exploring and understanding how individuals seek to meet their needs will never be time wasted.

Transformational Technique: Develop a Positive Attitude to Maximise Influence

Leadership, at its most powerful, is about using positive influence rather than force to get things done. Such influence can only be developed by understanding others more completely. With greater understanding their internal motivators can be stimulated, encouraging them to develop themselves and thereby enabling them to do their jobs better. This requires that people are recognised and treated as emotional beings, with feelings that determine how well they perform – even if the people concerned do not recognise the importance of their own feelings.

Developing leadership based on power as opposed to force depends on changing the nature of the interactions that you have with others; this is best done from a shift in perception about who they are and, particularly, why they do the things that they do. A change in your behaviours will then be automatic. I have found a combination of the following attitudes to be among the most effective in working with people: recognising that everyone does their best (including you) to reduce the natural tendency to judge them as good or bad; expecting positive outcomes from them to take advantage of the Pygmalion effect; caring about them and being extremely careful of the use of criticism so as to maximise rapport; and appreciating them whenever possible in order to increase the value of their contribution.

All of these approaches become more effective as your self-leadership skills progress, so this is a critical area of focus in personal development. As the boss, your mood and attitude set the stage for your entire team, so as you improve self-leadership, it will feed directly into tangible improvements in business performance.

Overall, a better understanding of others delivers benefits in two major areas: your ability to motivate them will increase and you will gain an increasing awareness that other people's behaviours, even if directed toward you, are actually not about you. You will then be able to respond from higher awareness, demonstrating excellent self-leadership, rather than reacting to what they do based purely on your conditioning. Shifting from reacting to being able to respond proactively will always improve results.

KNOW WHERE YOU ARE GOING

*The difference between great people and everyone else
is that great people create their lives actively, while
everyone else is created by their lives, passively
waiting to see where life takes them next.
The difference between the two is the difference
between living fully and just existing.*

~ Michael E. Gerber

All successful leaders have two
characteristics in common. The first is that they
know where they are going. Without vision they
will be unable even to lead themselves. Also, it
stands to reason that it is impossible to

persuade anyone else to do anything if you don't know what it is that you want them to do. Vision is one of those traits that no amount of money can buy. It has to come from within through developing the imagination and is realised by the development of clear goals. This is the focus of this chapter. The second characteristic of successful leaders is the ability to take others along with them. This requires influence and is covered in detail in the next chapter.

I mentioned above the need for a goal in self-leadership but why should it matter so much to know what you are aiming for? Many people who drift along with no clear idea of where they are going seem to do okay. But they don't really – at least not often. The problem is that with this approach there is an overwhelming tendency to give up when something happens that requires significant growth. As a result, people without goals generally face constant uncertainty and indecision.

Compare this approach with the attitude displayed by Helen Keller when she was asked, "Is there anything worse than being blind?" She replied, "Yes, the most pathetic person in the world is someone who has sight but no vision."

In my experience, when people are having problems making a decision it is usually because they don't have a clear enough vision of what they want in their lives. Imagine a situation where you are driving and reach a fork in the road. If you don't know where you are going it doesn't matter how well the alternatives are signposted; there would be no basis for a decision, and you would remain stuck at the fork, unsure of which way to go, or you'd take a route at random, just "hoping" that things would work out.

Now imagine the Olympics without gold medals, the pole vault without a bar, archery without a target, or a marathon without a finishing line. Where would the motivation for the participants to stretch and grow come from?

Unfortunately, these examples describe many people's lives. Without goals they lack meaning and tend to drift – there may be a great deal of activity but it will hold little interest, excitement, or fulfilment. You would not pay to watch a sport that fitted this description, so why would you choose to live your life in such a manner?

Let's take a look at how a well-defined goal affects our behaviours. Hopefully you now fully understand that your conscious awareness will be dominated by thoughts that are in harmony with your conditioning. Any others will be quickly rejected. This means that you will only recognise opportunities that present themselves to you if you have already programmed your Reticular Activating System (RAS), that incredible filter in your subconscious mind, to look for them. The RAS is constantly searching but will not

> THE MAIN FUNCTION OF GOALS IS NOT THE ACHIEVEMENT OF THE GOALS THEMSELVES BUT RATHER WHO YOU NEED TO BECOME IN ORDER TO ACHIEVE THEM.

raise to your awareness anything that you haven't already impressed onto it as being important to you. To focus the incredible power of the mind to get what you want you must be very clear in defining what you want and that means having goals.

Man who shoots at nothing hits every time.

~ **Confucius**

Most people don't have goals – it is estimated that only about 16% of people can clearly articulate what they want in their life and even less, only 3%, will have written it down. I believe that this indicates that, en masse, they simply don't recognise the value of a goal in helping them to be successful. Goals provide a clear basis for the decisions that will determine how successful you will be.

Oddly enough, many of the people who are the most stuck in their careers, or their lives, are those that are the most successful. Their problem is that they have become afraid of losing what they have achieved, whether this is possessions, money, title, reputation, or any other external measure of success. To replace this fear and overcome the block it is necessary for them to focus on the positive of what they desire instead of the threat of loss and this, once again, requires a goal.

In fact, we are natural goal achievers but much of the behaviour associated with this trait has been conditioned out of us – often by adults who taught us not to expect too much in life in case we should be disappointed, or because they considered it wrong to want too much for ourselves. We were born with an innate inner longing to stretch and grow. Babies have no need to be told to strive to crawl, walk, and explore their world. They don't have to learn any of these things – they will be carried anyway – but nevertheless they do. As time moves on, however, and we are subjected to outside influences, we get this natural trait trained out of us. We succumb to others' opinions as to what we should aspire and accept them as our own. From that point on we have limited ourselves.

To reactivate the natural capability that we had as babies we need to set goals. Goals bring the whole power of your mind into play in moving you toward what you want as well as keeping you moving and on track when the inevitable difficulties arise along the way.

At the same time, you should realise that **the main function of goals is not the achievement of the goals themselves but rather who you need to become in order to achieve them**. As Jim Rohn, a world-leading motivational speaker, author, and entrepreneur said, "The major reason for setting a goal is for what it makes of you to accomplish it. What it makes of you will always be of far greater value than what you get."

The Key Role of Purpose in Motivation

When you dance, your purpose is not to get to a certain place on the dance floor. It's to enjoy each step along the way.

~ Wayne Dyer

Unless you have already achieved everything that you want in life, and none of the many people that I have asked have ever said that this applies to them, you must learn. It is only through learning that we can raise our awareness to be able to create better results.

Perhaps the reason why so many people lose interest in goal setting is because when they achieve a goal, the feeling of satisfaction is so transitory that they perceive it is not worth the effort. A feeling of emptiness and lack of fulfilment

> YOU MUST CONNECT WITH YOUR DREAMS IF YOU ARE TO RELEASE YOUR EXCITEMENT AND PASSION FOR LIFE.

remain. What is missing for them is the direction and meaning provided by the context of a higher purpose. Unlike a goal, this purpose is not achievable but can be carried with us throughout our lives.

Let's go back to that image of the Olympics but this time with the competitors striving for medals. Why is it that we can be moved, sometimes to tears, by seeing someone take a gold medal? If it were the winning of the race that creates the emotion, then we could expect a similar response when watching every race. No – it is not the winning that brings a tear to the eye. What happens is that we are intuitively aware of what was required to achieve the feat: the courage, dedication, discipline, focus, and sacrifice involved. We thus recognise what the person had to **become** in the process of reaching such a pinnacle of human achievement and in doing so, we awaken that part of us that knows our true potential. As we tap into that awareness, we feel deeply moved, even ecstatic.

We can tap into this feeling through our own actions if we are aligned with a clear purpose for our life. Goals that are aligned with a purpose, stretching what we think we can accomplish, **provide the best reason to learn** and create a huge feeling of fulfilment that encourages the setting of even higher goals. This is the creative process in action and is the basis of all significant human progress.

You must connect with your dreams if you are to release your excitement and passion for life. One of the main differences between achievers and nonachievers is a sense of mission or purpose that gives meaning to what they do. The passion this creates arouses excitement in those that you lead and, once identified, defines the person that you would ideally like to be. It is purpose that enables you to become fully engaged and authentic.

I described earlier the compelling findings of Viktor Frankl in relation to the importance of meaning in our lives. By observation and through clinical evidence we find that when life loses its meaning, initially it may cause depression, but if severe enough it often ends in suicide. When we talk about finding meaning in life it is important that we realise that it must come from within. No one else can tell you what meaning you should have and no one can force you to accept their version of what your life should look like.

While we were young, and perhaps since, other people (our parents, teachers, bosses, spouses, etc.) will almost certainly have given us their version of who we should be. The model that they presented would always be one conforming to their values – but we are not them and we don't have their values, so their vision is highly unlikely to fulfill and motivate us. Until we work out who we want to be, we will almost certainly feel trapped.

Defining your purpose requires high self-awareness but if done effectively it will provide the deepest motivation. If, for example, your purpose is to make the lives of everyone that you come into contact with just a little bit better and you make your decisions on that basis, you will never lose meaning in your activities. By contrast, if you were to define your purpose as achieving fame or running a company, what would happen next once you had achieved it? The desire to run a company could be an effective goal but it would not be a good definition of purpose. The stories of people who apparently "have it all" descending into depression or turning to drugs to get their stimulation are manifold. It happens because they focus on external achievement, expecting this to bring them the happiness that they really desire. Once the goal is met, they find that the fulfillment from it is only temporary and they seek either comfort or numbness from other pursuits.

> THE PURPOSE YOU CHOOSE FOR YOUR LIFE MUST BE SOMETHING YOU REALLY WANT, NOT SOMETHING THAT YOU THINK YOU CAN DO.

The "how" of achieving a goal is not important until you know the "why" and that "why" is provided by your purpose. Your "why" is your ultimate motivation; it counteracts the fear and doubts that inevitably arise at some point as life's challenges unfold.

James Allen, the well-known philosophical writer, once said, "Until thought is linked with purpose there will be no intelligent accomplishment." One definition of "intelligent" is to learn about, understand, or deal with new or trying situations. Most people focus on "learn about and understand" in this definition, but to "deal with" the new or trying situations is at least as important to success. When I went through officer training in the Royal Air Force, one of the major competencies on which we were assessed was "effective intelligence" – they were not interested in what we knew unless we also had the ability to apply this knowledge to the numerous and varied challenges that they manufactured for us on an ongoing basis. So what James Allen may have been pointing to is that without purpose we will lack the ability to overcome challenges and will therefore fail.

Note that not all purposes are created equal in terms of their ability to provide drive and determination. When their greatest trials come, most people prove themselves capable of doing much more for others than they would do for themselves. A life purpose that has altruistic intent becomes amplified in the mind and can help someone to advance to unanticipated levels. Again, this can readily be seen in sports. Once a player takes his mind from the purpose of contributing to the team and switches to personal glory the team performance is weakened. The same is true in business. Leaders who support their employees and coworkers in helping them to achieve their best, by default also help themselves to achieve more than they could on their own. However, this effect will be limited if their personal achievement is their primary focus.

To be effective, **the purpose you choose for your life must be something you really want, not something that you think you can do**. One of the mistakes that can inhibit true expression is the tendency for people to choose a purpose or vision that they think they are worthy of rather than something that will bring out their greatness. As we have seen, the concept of self-worth is embedded in your existing beliefs and paradigms which are, by their very nature, self-limiting.

Once you know your life's purpose, you can start to identify your vision. The vision represents what you are seeking to do with your life, and goals are the progressive stepping stones along the way toward the vision. For example, if your purpose in life is to make business over the Internet more effective, then your vision could be the creation of a company that institutes revolutionary ideas in the way people perceive the Internet and interact across it. A goal that supports this vision and is in line with the purpose could be the creation within the company of a "think tank" of people creating ideas with this vision in mind.

To give your purpose the meaning that it needs to be effective it must be something that you are prepared to give your life for. Many people are shocked by this statement but only until they realise that all of us give our life for what we are doing, irrespective of whether it has much meaning. We simply do it one day at a time, which is the only way to move toward anything. So why not swap what you are doing now, if it doesn't have real meaning for you, for something of much deeper significance.

It is important to understand that goal setting and goal achieving are different activities: setting goals is an intellectual activity, while goal achieving is about mind-set, discipline, and process. Next, we will look at goal setting in more detail.

Defining Your Path

Most of us are highly aware of the things that we don't want in our lives. Yet, when pressed to come up with our one overriding purpose we are at a loss. Make no mistake, it is not an easy thing to decide why you were put on this earth and what you wish to accomplish. As my friend and colleague, Paul Martinelli, the President of LifeSuccess Consulting, likes to say, the two most important days of our lives are the day that we were born and the day when we realise why!

It will probably take thought, and perhaps even a few failed ventures, before you will become clear what it is that ignites the passion for life within you. In my own case, I explored a range of functional skillsets, including engineering, strategy work, and sales, across several different industries before I found out what I love to do. Now I feel certain that I will continue to do what I am doing now for the rest of my life.

Any goal we set must be aligned with our values. A value is essentially an emotion that reflects the degree to which we want something. Our highest values are the things that we seek to bring more of into our lives, while our lowest are the things that we will avoid at almost any cost. Values determine our perspective in deciding if something is good or bad, right or wrong.

An example of a value that many people seek to avoid and that can badly impede their ability to achieve their goals is rejection. This features especially highly for people who have a strong ego attachment to what other people think of them. The problem is that seeking to avoid rejection will also limit your success, particularly as a leader, because as you become more successful a higher percentage of people are likely to reject you. Ultimately, some people will reject you even if they have never met you, based solely on your position or the image that you project. Avoiding rejection will create a conflict between the goal and your values, which will tend to cause you to sabotage yourself.

If the goal of making a difference as a leader is important to you, then you will probably need to change some values to avoid being undermined by them. In this specific case you would need to recognise that, as I covered in the last chapter, other people's rejection of you actually has nothing to do with you. Their perceptions are always a reflection of their own belief systems, so in rejecting you they provide information about their own conditioning, such as their core beliefs about leaders or their limiting beliefs about their ability to do the same. The solution would be to let go of your concerns about what these people think of you, recognising their opinions as being outside your control, and find an alternative value that would serve you instead.

Effective Goal Setting

Never limit your view of life by any past experience.

~ Ernest Holmes

Even people that do set goals rarely maximise the process. Most only set goals that they know they can reach: we are programmed this way. Having learned early in life that not reaching goals carried a punitive result, we are generally very careful to set goals that are within our realm of perceived possibility. I believe that this is what Michelangelo was warning against when he said, "The greatest danger for most of us is not that our aim is too high and we miss, but that it is too low and we reach it."

Within the business world there is much promotion of the idea of SMART goals. This acronym has several definitions, but most often stands for:

Specific

Measurable

Attainable

Realistic

Timely

Although this method is widely taught and incorporated into corporate goal setting, it has a flaw that severely limits the possibility of true goal achievement. The problem lies in the third and fourth steps in this process, "Attainable" and "Realistic." Your idea of what is attainable and realistic will be limited by your past experience, so really **this model is based on what you know you can achieve rather than what is possible for you.** Only by looking at a different model of goal setting will your true potential be released.

I AM, I CAN Goals

An improved model for goal setting is the "I AM, I CAN" model described below. Its letters are a reminder that a goal will be most effective if it is:

Imaginative

Altruistic

Measurable

Inspiring

(Time) **C**onstrained

Audacious

Now

The most important element of effective goal setting is the use of the **Imagination**. Goal setting is not an intellectual process. You must be able to see into the future and envisage in your mind's eye that which has yet to be created. Everything that has been created by humankind, all of our advancement, started off as just a dream in someone's imagination.

To create such advancement you must forget precedent and start to visualise the future as you would like it to be. You must be able to visualise reaching the goal; actually see yourself, in your mind's eye, achieving the ultimate victory of its completion. Include as many details as you can to make it real. The subconscious mind cannot tell the difference between something that already exists in the physical world and something that you vividly imagine, so the more detail that you add the more you will create the behaviour necessary to achieve the goal. Because of the vital importance of the imagination to goal setting this aspect will be covered in much more detail below.

Goal setting for its own sake almost always ends in disappointment. Truly meaningful, **Altruistic** goals are essential to create something that is larger than yourself and to draw upon your full potential. When our motivation is unselfish and has the best intention for others at its heart it enables us to tap into previously hidden resources.

Goals must be **Measurable** so that you know when you have attained them. It is not enough to merely "do better." You must be able to track your progress and achievement and that means having a high degree of specificity about what success will look like. Ensure that nothing that you are seeking to achieve is contingent on something over which you have no control; for example, "My reputation among my peers is excellent..." would not be an effective goal because the way in which other people regard you is dependent upon their internal evaluation system. It is not possible to meaningfully measure your own progress if you have external dependencies that will affect your success.

Goals must also be highly **Inspirational** so that they will engage the emotions and create the necessary level of desire. In formulating goals to achieve this, ensure that the language used is expressive and creates a strong feeling of commitment and personal ownership. It doesn't matter who else supports the goal; if you don't desire it enough to commit to it yourself it will not serve its purpose. To inspire, goals must also be very specific. For example, to say that you want to be wealthy or slim is not enough. It is essential to state exactly how much money you want or precisely what weight you want to be. Specificity helps to increase your commitment and desire, much as the idea of going on a specific holiday that you particularly want is more exciting than just thinking about taking a few days off work. Emotional engagement happens once the brain has a clear picture it can work with, allowing connection to the goal at a deeper level and making it much more likely to be achieved.

We have all heard that tasks expand to fill the time available for them, and there is much anecdotal evidence that supports this statement. Tasks must have a time frame or there is no sense of urgency; the commitment is too vague and a feeling can be created that it is okay to put off starting. Effective goals are always "time **Constrained**" because putting a specific completion date on the goal gives a clear target to work toward. It makes the goal more real and clearly instructs the subconscious mind that you are serious.

The idea of creating **Audacious** goals is not new. It was presented in Jim Collins' book, *Good to Great*, where he coined the term "BHAGs" – Big Hairy Audacious Goals. There is no pleasure to be gained from playing small – and thinking big requires no more effort. The goal should be grand enough to both inspire and scare you at the same time and **must not be limited** to things you already know how to do. **No one ever achieved personal growth by doing something they already knew how to complete.**

A stretch goal can also motivate a group as a whole toward much greater achievement – but only if it is absolutely believed by the leadership. A good example of this is the way that Jack Welch, the chairman of General Electric, used BHAGs. Shortly after taking the helm he made a speech at the annual shareholders' meeting announcing that his goal for GE was to be number one or two in every market it was in. There was much scepticism at the time as GE was far behind the frontrunners in almost every business sector. However, the employees rallied behind his vision and GE achieved that goal. Another example was the way that Henry Ford instructed his engineers to build a V8 engine from a single block of metal. They told him repeatedly that it could not be done but he continued to send them away with instructions to do it anyway. Because he ignored what was considered to be realistic by his team, they eventually solved

> NO ONE EVER ACHIEVED PERSONAL GROWTH BY DOING SOMETHING THEY ALREADY KNEW HOW TO COMPLETE.

the problem. Had either of these men used the SMART model they may never have achieved their many successes. In both cases, because the leader of the company had the courage to set an audacious goal, they created the opportunity of achieving something significant – and in the end they did.

The final aspect of truly effective goal setting is to ensure that it is written, and visualised, as though it exists **Now**. Write your goals in the present tense from the perspective that they have already been achieved: "I am..." rather than "I will...," and ensure that they are always written in the positive, i.e., what you **have actually achieved**, rather than stating what you have stopped doing. For example, you should write, "I am a trim and healthy 75 kilos" rather than "I have lost 10 kilos." It is vital that you think of what you want as though it has already been done and avoid the negative of what you don't want.

To set this type of goal you must be able to see into the future – to envisage in your mind's eye that which has yet to be created. When I worked as a strategy consultant in the mobile phone industry during its early days, cell phones were used almost exclusively by businesses and usually required an extensive business case as justification for them. Very few people recognised the potential for almost everyone to have a mobile, but this is now the norm and it has changed our lives and the world we live in. For this to become possible, with service extended to the wider market, someone first had to conceive the idea.

Everything that has been created by human beings, all of our advancement, started off as just a dream in someone's imagination. Einstein carved into his desk, "imagination is more important than knowledge," and I believe that he was right. Knowledge relates to the past whereas imagination is about what could be in the future. Without imagination, excepting occasional accidental progress, there would be no advancement.

Imagination

Everyone has an incredible imagination. It will conjure up new images, ideas, and thoughts of incredible variety throughout our entire lives. Any time we are thinking of the future we are using our imagination, just as we are if we are thinking of the past and wishing it had turned out differently.

Whether we use our imagination to think of what we want or its opposite will determine how we feel. Fear and faith are really just opposite sides of the use of the imagination. Fear is what happens when the imagination is left undirected and shows that you believe that the focus of your worry may happen to you. Think about this; it is important. It is not possible to worry about something if you don't believe that its occurrence could happen to you. Faith, on the other hand, is what we get if we choose to direct our thoughts towards positive outcomes.

> MEMORY IS JUST THE PAST TENSE OF PERCEPTION.

Imagination is something that we are each born with and, along with creativity, is usually suppressed throughout our lives. We are taught from the earliest stages to conform to what others want rather than to imagine what we can accomplish. Think back to when you were first in school. We all learned to colour – but what was one of the main purposes of this activity? **To learn to colour inside the lines.** In other words, to conform. Once we mastered colouring inside the lines what were we then to do? **Make the flowers realistic.** We were taught to view what we see as reality rather than dream of what could be.

Walt Disney had an experience that clearly illustrates this point. When he was still very young, he was asked in school to colour a flower garden. When the teacher stopped to look at his picture she noted that his picture was not quite right because, "Flowers don't have faces on them." Walt confidently replied, "Mine do!" and today in Disneyland and Epcot they still do. He created his picture and held fast to his imaginative ideas throughout his entire life – creating things that have made a positive contribution to many lives in the process.

Walt Disney died a short time before the Epcot Center in Florida was opened. A journalist at the opening ceremony commented to Roy Disney, Walt's brother, that it was a shame that Walt was not there to see it. Roy replied, "He saw it first, that's why you are seeing it now."

If you are going to create any advancement you must forget precedent and start to visualise the future as you would like it to be. Your view of precedent is, after all, just a collection of memories, and memory is as selective as perception. In truth, all **memory is just the past tense of perception**: it is perception of the past as if it were occurring now. Therefore, since you now understand how our perception can only reflect our paradigms, the fact that memories will be equally distorted should be relatively obvious.

I suggest that you use your imagination to create goals in every area of your life, including health, relationships, personal/spiritual development, career, and finances. This will add meaning, excitement, and texture to your life. Remember, if you don't know where you are going, and you can only get this from the imagination or by following someone else, you will undoubtedly end up somewhere but it may not be a place that you would ideally choose.

Finally, I recommend that you **write your goals down**. Every expert agrees that this will dramatically increase your chances of success; a goal that is not written is only a wish. Carry a summary of your goals on a goal card in your pocket or in your handbag and review it frequently. Each time you do so your subconscious mind will have the idea of what you want reinforced upon it. When you review it, get into an attitude of thankfulness, as though the goal is already achieved. This will accelerate the process of reaching it.

The Motivation of Pain versus Pleasure

It has been theorised for thousands of years that at the most basic level there are just two human behavioural motivations: the desire to move toward pleasure and the need to avoid pain. This concept was introduced in Chapter 4. The choice of words is important here. It is the **need** to avoid pain versus the **desire** to gain pleasure because for most people, pain wins every time; people will do much more to avoid it than they ever will to gain pleasure. Think of it this way: how many people go to great lengths to shuffle around their debts rather than focus on their ability to bring in more income? How many stay in a bad relationship to avoid the pain of a breakup? How many choose to continue doing things that damage their health to avoid the pain that they associate with implementing change?

In fact, it is likely that both pleasure and pain are the result of just one thing – the use of the intellectual faculty of imagination. Nevertheless, an awareness of the pain versus pleasure concept can still be very useful in helping to understand why we behave as we do and how it may be possible to make changes.

In Chapter 4 we covered extensively the way in which the choice about what we link pain and pleasure to (i.e., our perception), determines our destiny. Because most people will do much more to avoid pain than they will do to gain pleasure, it is often in seeking to avoid pain that they gain the initial motivation to make changes in their lives. On the other hand, when things are going well people will usually seek to minimise change because of the fear of losing what they have attained; letting go of the known becomes the major factor that holds them back.

Figure 6.1 – The Emotional Roller Coaster of Pain Oriented Motivation

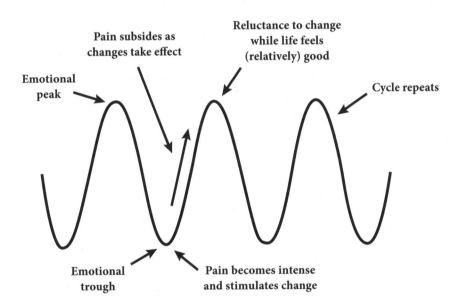

As illustrated in Figure 6.1, the problem with this strategy is that it causes oscillation between emotional peaks and troughs of roughly similar intensity, while the average quality of the lives of those involved improves only gradually (if at all). They go back and forth between the desire to create change and losing their drive to take action once things seem to be going better. As things start to slide backward they start to fear losing what they have and the pain ramps up until it hits a threshold where change becomes a must. They then take action to eliminate a part of the problem and the intensity of the pain is dissipated, so the drive to create change is lessened and the motivation needed to find a long-term resolution to the problem disappears. As the pain that was driving them diminishes, they gradually revert to their old behaviour and the old problem returns. They are gripped by their conditioning, unable to sustain progress.

The Terror Barrier – Change Takes Courage

If we are to break out of the oscillations created by the need to avoid pain it is essential to practice ongoing learning so that we continue to move forward. If we are not learning, because of the ever-present nature of change, we can only be going backward. As Abraham Maslow, the psychologist best known for his proposal of the hierarchy of human needs, said, "You will either step forward into growth or you will step back into safety." The thing that prevents us from moving forward is the Terror Barrier.

I learned the model of the Terror Barrier from Bob Proctor and have since seen how the awareness it delivers helps many clients to overcome blocks to their success. It is most easily explained by examining four levels of thinking:

Level 1 is Bondage: This is the comfort zone, where people's thinking is in harmony with their existing conditioning. You must realise, though, that we can feel comfortable even when things are going badly. This is why people will go to work to do a job that they hate and worry that they may lose it, hang on to a failing relationship, or even continue with poor health habits even after they have been told that their habits are killing them.

Level 2 is Reason: People start to entertain a new idea, but haven't really taken it seriously so they don't begin to impress it upon the subconscious mind. Since no action is possible without the involvement of the subconscious mind they cannot change their behaviours.

Level 3 is Terror: A new idea is impressed upon the subconscious mind but because it is out of harmony with the existing conditioning, we experience a feeling of discomfort. We have moved out of our comfort zone and pretty quickly we begin to experience fear and doubt. This is when Maslow's statement about stepping forward into growth or back into safety comes into full effect.

When people feel fear, they naturally assume that it means that they cannot do whatever they were thinking of and fall back to the primal fight-or-flight response, metaphorically (or literally) running away. This feeling can be made to disappear either by changing your thinking or by altering your paradigm. The easy way is to change the thought and bring it back into harmony with their conditioning, and in the process return to their comfort zone at Level 1. However, because people don't understand what just happened, they then rationalise all the reasons why their new idea would not have been any good anyway. Unfortunately, quitting feels good for a short period, but then it sucks forever!

The things that most stop us from getting what we most want in life are the reasons we give ourselves, which are really excuses, for why we can't be successful. We then back up these excuses with any justification, no matter how feeble, that will allow us to believe our own lies. Hence the reason why it is said that rationalising why we cannot do what we want is like "rationing lies" to the subconscious mind. It always ends up with us back in mental bondage.

The major problem with Level 1 is that while stuck there it is impossible to grow because absolutely no learning can take place. Furthermore, since the world is constantly changing, if people are not responding to the change, whilst it may feel comfortable for now, it really means that they have a problem coming. The old expression, "If you always do what you've always done, you'll always get what you've always got," is not true. Unfortunately for those who take this approach, persisting with the same old ways of doing things while the world continues to change, virtually guarantees that their results will decline.

> YOU MUST NOT LIMIT YOURSELF WHEN SETTING A GOAL BY GIVING ANY ATTENTION TO "HOW" IT WILL BE DONE.

A ship in harbour is safe, but that is not what ships are built for.

~ John Shedd

Level 4 is Freedom: To free ourselves from our comfort zone we must break through the Terror Barrier and realise that the uncomfortable feelings associated with new thoughts is nothing more than feedback that we are doing something unfamiliar. It is critical to recognise that fear does not mean you cannot do something – it is simply the natural consequence of thinking new thoughts. If you stay with the thought over time your conditioning will be altered to match it.

This makes it possible to take that step forward into growth and enables fear to be recontextualised into something to be celebrated as an indication that we are growing. We need to do uncomfortable things now in order to have what we want in the future. By setting a goal that is sufficiently exciting to overcome the fear you will quickly learn that this feeling is not something to be avoided and, pretty soon, you will have a different interpretation and experience of it.

Through this process you will also ensure that your primary motivation is toward pleasure, rather than the avoidance of pain. This will enable you to break out from the endless oscillations shown in Figure 6.1, where successive peaks are of similar height, to put your life on an upward track of progressive growth and development.

Learning – The Foundation of Goal Achievement

We discussed earlier the error that many people make in goal setting: that of believing that they must already know how to achieve that goal when they start. **You must not limit yourself when setting a goal by giving any attention to "how" it will be done.** The purpose of a goal is to help you to grow, which requires that you learn. If you are not learning then you are going backward; hence, a commitment to lifelong learning is one of the key traits of successful people.

Unfortunately, most people approach learning incorrectly. They think that the outcome is to improve with every trial or event. **This is impossible.** Any time you take on something new, by definition you will have to do things that you have not done before so the results will not always be as expected. Also, the environment is in a constant state of flux. The combination of these two factors makes it inevitable that **at times you will fail**.

Although this is self-evident, most people attempt to live seeking to avoid failure. Fear of failure and its corollary, the search for perfection, are huge factors in shaping their behaviours. If they dominate your thinking you will probably have a tendency toward procrastination and a track record of giving up on many occasions when you failed, rather than learning from the experience and trying again.

If that has been your approach to learning then it is essential that you adopt a new strategy with a completely different approach to "failure." An effective learning process involves several steps:

1. Decide what you want – this is the goal-setting process.

2. Take action to move toward your goal.

3. Notice the results of your efforts.

4. Evaluate your results against the desired outcomes and refine your actions.

5. Repeat steps 2-4 until success has been achieved.

Take Action

We have already covered Step 1 of this process in some detail. The next stage in making anything happen requires that you take action – **there is no alternative but to try** something.

In personal development circles there is common reference to the quote, "Do, or do not. There is no 'try,'" from the fictional character Yoda in *Star Wars*. I believe that this is frequently misunderstood. I agree that there can be no "try" in place of total commitment to the ultimate goal, but **trying is essential within the process of goal achieving**. It is the essence of persistence, which Napoleon Hill in his book, *Think and Grow Rich*, found to be so vital to success that he devoted a whole chapter to it. Tony Buzan, the author best known as the creator of mind maps, describes persistence as "the engine of learning and intelligence":

two factors that we have discussed extensively in relation to purpose and goals. If we are to find ways to do anything that we have not done before we must experiment and persist until we have been successful.

If winning requires experimentation, then we must also make room to take risks. That can be difficult for many of us who were conditioned as children with beliefs such as "better safe than sorry" but this must be overcome. The truth is, if you play it safe you will be sorry because this approach also makes it impossible to win.

I love this quote from the actor and comedian, Flip Wilson, "The less we risk, the more we lose when we win." It really sums up the essence of the largely unrecognised risk involved in setting low goals. If you aim low you may get the limited satisfaction of hitting your goal but part of you will always know that you are kidding yourself. As I described in the Introduction, we experience the full flush of success only when striving for something that is sufficiently large that the odds seemed stacked against us. It is this that provides the need for us to grow and defines us as goal achievers in its true sense.

If you are still not convinced on this point ask yourself this: is it possible to win if you know that you cannot lose? This is the boundary condition that will inevitably be reached if goals are made sufficiently easy. Usually in my seminars I find a few people who answer yes to this question initially, at which point I ask them to consider for how long they would watch a sports team playing with no opposition. How much glory, how much celebration, would there be if they were to score? Such activity would be no more than a training session and no one ever won anything in training. **Low goals with minimal risk serve no useful purpose.**

No one ever stretched to become the most that they could be without failing, sometimes on multiple occasions. Look at the following example of the failures of President Abraham Lincoln who:

- Failed in business at age 21

- Was defeated in a legislative race at age 22

- Failed again in business at age 24

- Overcame the death of his sweetheart at age 26

- Had a nervous breakdown at age 27

- Lost a congressional race at age 34

- Lost a congressional race at age 36

- Lost a senatorial race at age 45

- Failed in an effort to become vice-president at age 47

- Lost a senatorial race at age 49

- Was elected president of the United States at age 52

Lincoln failed many times on his way to success and learned something each and every time. It was this learning that eventually allowed him to succeed in attaining the highest office in the United States, and moreover, to be ranked by scholars among the top three U.S. presidents, with the majority of those surveyed placing him first.

There is a book about his ascent to the presidency by Doris Kearns Goodwin called *A Team of Rivals*. It describes the background and motivation of those who opposed Lincoln, many of whom eventually became his cabinet members. Lincoln found, as most great leaders do, that the best environment for growth is not to be surrounded by those who think as you do, but instead involves being confronted on a daily basis by those who would question and offer alternative solutions to issues. He discovered that in order to be successful he had to create an environment in which each of his rivals could be successful as well, and to achieve this, he moved his cabinet away from a competitive environment and into a creative one. His actions, understanding, and willingness to

> THE MOST IMPORTANT THING WITH LEARNING IS TO SEEK TO LEARN WITH EVERY ATTEMPT.

learn with each failure brought an entire nation together after one of the most brutal civil wars in history. It is the mark of a phenomenal leader that he was not afraid to fail – and fail publicly. This gave him massive freedom to take the action that he deemed necessary.

Notice Your Results and Refine Actions

Each time you take action toward your goal you will get a result and this result will provide information about how much progress was achieved. The brain will do this automatically but, because its evaluation will be coloured by conditioning, it is often worth getting external input from third parties as well. Ideally this process is called feedback, though some people prefer to call it "success" or "failure."

We will rarely achieve any new objective the first time we try, so we need to compare our performance against our goal, make any changes to our approach that may be necessary, and **then try again**. If we keep the focus on the goal, identifying shortfalls and taking new actions on an iterative basis, it is inevitable that we will move toward it. All that is necessary is to work on each new idea in turn. When the Wright brothers built the first aircraft I'm quite sure that they didn't start with a blueprint. Only once they had come up with the aerofoil design for the wing would they have been able to even contemplate how to control it in flight. We are goal-achieving mechanisms, so once your subconscious has locked onto the goal it will find a way to deliver.

The most important thing with learning is to recognise that it is a process, not an outcome, and **seek to learn with every attempt**. Thomas Edison is quoted as saying it would take a matter of a few weeks to invent the lightbulb. In reality, it would take him almost two years of failed attempts before he would find success. It is said he tried over 6,000 different carbonised plant fibres, looking for a carbon filament for the bulb. When he was asked by a friend whether he ever became disillusioned with failing he replied, "I've never failed. I've just learned a thousand ways not to build a lightbulb." He viewed it as a multi-step process and obviously had to fail many times to find the right way. This is why Thomas Watson, the founder of IBM, was correct when he suggested, "If you want to succeed double your failure rate."

I believe the best definition of success that I have seen is that developed by Earl Nightingale, one of the founders of the personal development industry and the first person to record a spoken word album that sold a million copies. He described it as "the progressive realisation of a worthy ideal." In this context you will once again see that your perception (i.e., your interpretation of your results, is critically important). If you realise that you learn more on days when things are not going well, and can contextualise the process within this definition of success, then you will see that you are more successful when you fail badly, provided you learn effectively in the process. This is the fastest way to move yourself toward your goal.

Believe It

*If I have the belief I can do it, I shall surely
acquire the capacity to do it even if I may
not have it at the beginning.*

~ **Mahatma Gandhi**

The deciding factor in success is that you must have belief, and this means ensuring that the relevant conditioning is supportive of the goal. The problem is really twofold: how to get the new, innovative thoughts into your mind, and how to get the old ones out. There is no chance that you will change your performance until what you want is part of your new identity.

To make this happen it is essential that you are able to see yourself in possession of your goal and to hold that focus until the subconscious mind has been reprogrammed. By believing and visualising success, seeing yourself as though it has already been done, you will impress that image upon your mind and engage the full power of the Reticular Activating System to search for opportunities to achieve it. This is why the use of a goal card, which constantly reminds you of your goal, is so valuable. Because the subconscious cannot recognise the difference between something that is vividly imagined and something that is actually happening, each time you visualise your goal you diminish the effect of the Terror Barrier, replacing old beliefs with new, empowering ones.

Start Here, Now

I hope that you are now convinced that having clear goals is essential, which is why it is one of the characteristics of leaders. All leaders who have great impact are very clear where they are going.

I heard the story of somebody approaching a seminar leader and telling him that if he followed the leader's instructions and strived to reach his goals, he would be 68 by the time he achieved them. The leader's response was, "Well how old will you be if you don't go for them?" It is always possible to come up with reasons why we cannot do what we really want: we are too old, too young, too inexperienced, not well enough educated; we don't have enough money, don't get the support that we need from our boss ... This list could be endless.

However, these are not the real causes of our inability to achieve. They are not even be-causes, as many people often prefer to think of them in these circumstances. They are actually just our paradigms speaking. If you are prepared to look, you will always be able to find someone else who has done what you want to do, overcoming very similar obstacles to your own in the process.

"A journey of a thousand miles begins with a single step" is arguably the best known teaching from the Tao Te Ching. As you begin to take action and change the way you look at things, you will gain a new perspective and the problems that you face will diminish. The essential element is to start. Whatever you have been doing, remember that you have been giving your life for it – one day at a time. Start now to determine your purpose and set some clear, written goals. Make sure that what you are giving your life for is worthy of you.

Transformational Technique:
Define Your Purpose and Set Clear Goals

If you are to unlock the whole power of your mind it is vital that you focus clearly on well-defined goals. This is a characteristic of all great achievers; they know where they are going and are determined that they will get there. Write your goals down using the "I AM, I CAN" principles that I've outlined to ensure that they are as effective as possible. In particular, make sure that you do not know how to achieve them before you start, which would prevent the goal from delivering its principle purpose of requiring you to grow in order to achieve it. And never allow fear to influence what you choose to do.

In order to provide context for your goals it is crucial to understand your purpose. Purpose is that vital element that can never be reached but instead provides the "why" behind everything that you do. It is this understanding that ensures that you can draw upon the persistence necessary to overcome obstacles along the way.

As you set your goals, be sure that you focus on what really matters to you and what you value, not on what others might think. There is no fulfilment in allowing others to determine what you should do with your life. As you work toward these goals remember that learning is a process that involves successes and failures. The most important aspect is that you continue to try, ensuring that you learn from all of your results and using your experience to become more effective on the next attempt.

As you achieve each of your goals simply set the next one. This is the creative process in action.

LEADERSHIP STEMS FROM WHO YOU ARE

We must be the change we wish to see in the world.

~ Mahatma Gandhi

Successful leadership must operate from the principles that produce success, not just be an imitation of the actions of successful leaders. This requires that we become like they are, not only in action, but also in thought. In other words, the starting point for leadership is the set of internal beliefs, values, and rules that shape our interaction with the world. This provides the basis for influencing people at a deep level such that they will be prepared to follow.

As I mentioned in the introduction to the previous chapter, the ability to take others along with them is the second characteristic of all successful leaders.

Developing Influence

Influence can be defined as, "A power affecting a person, thing, or course of events, especially one that operates without any direct or apparent effort." In the context of leadership I like to think of it as getting people to do what you want by being nice. Although the use of force does create limited influence by stimulating some behaviour change in others, it never engages the hearts and minds and is a poor substitute for what is possible as you develop more of who you are. We have already established that the only way that people will do a good job is if they want to. It is a personal choice, which will never happen through the use of force. Thus, it is virtually impossible to lead successfully without well-developed influencing skills.

One of my clients once asked me how hard it is to become an influencer of people. My response was, "That depends how good you want to be." In the areas of technical and functional skills, where it would not be unusual to find people who have devoted many years of effort to their development, it is difficult to be recognised as being outstanding. However, because few people have put much effort into developing their influencing skills, the level of expertise of the average person is relatively low. Therefore, much less effort would be required in this area to rise, for example, from average ability to the top 10%. An improvement of this nature would greatly increase your chances of excellent results. Furthermore, as with all other leadership competencies, influence can be learned, so it is realistic to determine to be outstanding in this area.

John F. Kennedy learned the skill of influence. As a young man he lived very much in the shadow of Joseph P. Kennedy, his older brother.

However, he developed the skills necessary to become the youngest president to take office at the time, as well as the first Catholic elected to the office. Despite the fact that he faced staunch opposition in the House and Senate, because of his skills of influence he was able to dream the biggest dreams, such as the launch of the space program. He was also able to influence Americans to take responsibility for their lives and the state of their country with the words, "Ask not what your country can do for you, but what you can do for your country." Kennedy's impact is still felt today through the generations that were affected by his incredible ability to influence the minds and hearts of those he led.

We Reproduce That Which We Are

Before you can inspire with emotion you must be swamped with it yourself. Before you can move their tears, your own must flow. To convince them, you must yourself believe.

~ Winston Churchill

Influence comes from the life we live and how we manage ourselves on a daily basis. Only to a limited degree does it come from the position that we hold, our qualifications, or how we present a speech or express ourselves in a meeting. **Influence has everything to do with who we are, not who we say we are – or even who we think we are.** We teach what we know, yet it is what we **are** that we reproduce; therefore, whatever behaviours a leader displays will be modeled in his or her followers, whether for good or bad.

Anyone with children can clearly see this in action. You can talk to them all day about the need to be kind and thoughtful of others, but if you treat them in any other way, or if they see you mistreating others, this is the behaviour they will reproduce. Similarly, if you constantly talk about integrity, yet lie, cheat, and do everything you can to deceive others when it suits you, then so will those around you. Children behave like their parents and employees generally migrate to behaving like their boss. Whether leaders display courage, conformity, or indeed cowardice, their followers will do the same.

It is essential that as a leader you are seen to give what you want to get and model in yourself first the qualities you wish to see in others. There is no other way of creating the behaviours you seek. For example, if you want your team to be loyal, you must first show loyalty, or to have a staff with strong integrity you must first demonstrate integrity.

Character – The Core of Leadership

When a leader has significant weaknesses, such as a tendency to step in and control or criticise, such flaws will usually be amplified as that individual becomes more senior in rank or influence. Therefore it is essential to remove such weaknesses by developing the internal strength necessary to improve your self-leadership and hold yourself to a higher standard.

This internal strength may be called **character**. It particularly comes to the fore when things are not going well or some unexpected event is encountered. Like so many areas of life, it is easy to be good-natured when times are easy; hence, the reason that it is said that character is not so much created by circumstances as it is revealed by them.

A review of many of the writings on leadership will quickly establish that one of the areas that most of the researchers, analysts, and commentators agree on is that not only is character essential, it is at the core of leadership. General Norman Schwarzkopf, commander of the Coalition Forces in the Gulf War of 1991, said, "Leadership is a potent combination of strategy and character but if you must be without one, be without strategy."

So what is this quality referred to as character? Definitions vary but almost all have their foundations in qualities of moral or ethical strength. Some examples of high character behaviours or attributes are:

- Impeccability with your word, never falling short of doing what you say you will do

- Modeling what you expect of others

- Preparedness to be honest and open about your flaws

- Basing your decisions on the needs of the organisation, not on your personal agenda

- Approachability and willingness to receive feedback with an open mind

- Treating everyone in the same way and exemplifying humility

- Demonstrating support for others and working collaboratively

- Demonstrating persistence in the face of difficulties

- Preparedness to make the tough choices, especially where personal reputation or popularity could be at stake

- The ability to manage your own emotional state as the environment around you changes

Character in and of itself is not enough to be a great leader, but leaders do not become great without it. It is essential to survival, at this level, to be able to control how you respond to the uncontrollable events that happen to you. No leader will ever be without challenges for long and it is character that enables them to deal with them.

Let's look at some of the elements required to develop a strong character.

Integrity – The Cornerstone of Character

Given the challenges of integrity at the corporate level that have become public knowledge in recent years, the need for improved standards of moral and ethical behaviour has become intense. There is a widespread sense of lack of integrity at top levels, stimulated by the issue of executive pay as well as the uncovering of unethical behaviour by the press.

In his book, *The Seven Habits of Highly Effective People*, Stephen R. Covey writes about the importance of integrity in creating success: "If I try to use human influence strategies and tactics of how to get other people to do what I want, to work better, to be more motivated, to like me and each other—while my character is fundamentally flawed, marked by duplicity and insincerity—then, in the long run, I cannot be successful. My duplicity will breed distrust, and everything I do—even using so-called good human relations techniques—will be perceived as manipulative... if there is little or no trust, there is no foundation for permanent success."

IT IS NOT POSSIBLE TO "TALK THE TALK" WITHOUT "WALKING THE WALK."

Leaders must hold themselves to higher standards than they expect of others. There is no other foundation so essential to success or worthy of your focus for development. **It is not possible to "talk the talk" without "walking the walk"** consistently and in all areas of your life. It is really quite simple – if people feel that they cannot completely trust you in all areas they will not be able to trust you in any area. As Albert Einstein said, "Whoever is careless with the truth in small matters cannot be trusted with important matters." It is a natural assumption for others to infer that how you act in one instance will be carried over into others. This is why the revelation of even a single indiscretion by a leader can cast doubt over every accomplishment that leader has achieved, no matter how honestly gained. We assume that how they do anything is how they do everything – and it's very difficult to convince us otherwise.

Those that pretend to be something that they are not, or who seek to encourage others to do things that they do not model themselves, cannot be authentic. They will live with the uncomfortable knowledge that their duplicity could be found out at any moment, thus creating insecurity, limiting their own sense of worth, and suppressing their own capabilities.

The simplest model that I know to really understand this point is the Johari Window, a tool created by Joseph Luft and Harry Ingham in 1955. It can be used to help people better understand their interpersonal communication and relationships.

Figure 7.1 – The Johari Window

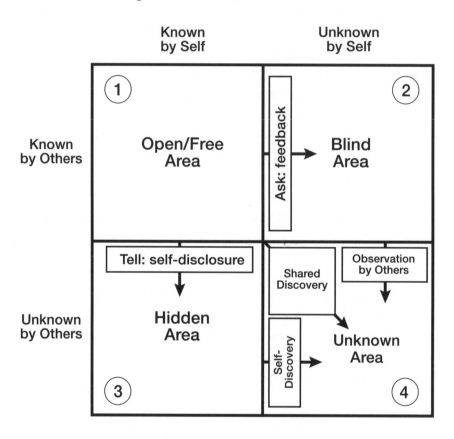

In this model, each person is considered to be represented by a window with four panes or quadrants. Looking at the window from my perspective:

- The "open" quadrant represents things that I know about myself and that others know about me. This can include not only factual information but also my feelings, motives, behaviours, wants, needs, and desires. This window will get bigger as others get to know me better, and as I become more self-aware of things about me already known by others.

- The "blind" quadrant represents things that others know about me but that I am unaware of, such as the quality of my eye contact during conversation. These are blind spots and are common to everyone. Much of personal development is about identifying and overcoming blind spots. Feedback and/or improved self-awareness are required to reduce the size of this pane.

- The "hidden" quadrant represents things that I know about myself that others do not know. There are vast amounts of information contained in this quadrant, and my ability to be congruent in words and actions depends upon how I feel you would react to knowing these things. Reducing the size of this pane is called "self-disclosure."

- The "unknown" quadrant represents things that neither I know about myself nor you know about me. A lot of conditioning and many belief systems that may not become obvious until I'm placed in new situations reside in this quadrant. So do aspects of my capability of which no one is yet aware.

In general, the more information that can be moved into the "open" quadrant the better. This requires a give-and-take process between ourselves and the people we interact with. As our level of confidence and self-esteem develops, it becomes easier to actively invite others to comment on blind spots. It also becomes more comfortable to be honest about weaknesses and behaviours that previously we would have preferred to keep hidden.

No matter what anyone else thinks about us or what position we hold in our company, ultimately, security comes from within. It stems from the knowledge that we are living up to a set of principles and values that are worthy of us and that we have nothing to fear from our "hidden" information becoming public. People whose public and private behaviours are very different should not be confused with people of real character. Honesty, consideration of others, and a commitment to ethical principles cannot be done on a part-time basis. They are an expression of who you are.

The importance of collapsing the "hidden" area of the window is huge – you will have challenges in behaving congruently to the exact degree that you continue to seek to ensure that aspects of yourself remain unknown to others. As a leader you must step up and set yourself a higher standard: this is the route to higher performance and greater fulfillment.

Integrity in Action

Integrity requires that you behave in an ethical way and do what you say you will do, all the time – there is no room for flexibility. John Maxwell, the best-selling author of over 50 books, states that integrity is a commitment to character over personal gain, to people over things, to service over power, to principle over convenience, and to the long view over the immediate. I'm sure that he is referring to power in the context of exercising control over others, and I think this message is absolutely spot on. People with integrity have nothing to hide or fear – they have the ground rules to allow them to make the essential choice between what they want to do and what they ought to do. This enables them to deal with the constant challenge of it being much easier to give good advice than to follow it. We gain credibility when the principles by which we live match our talk and when both add value to others.

Having integrity means fully living life according to your values and thereby avoiding some of the pitfalls that confront us all. For example, with integrity you will never get drawn into office politics to get ahead. People will experience you as being genuine because you have no need to pretend to be anything other than who you are. Everything that you say and do will be fully congruent, all the time.

Ralph Waldo Emerson, the American essayist, poet, and philosopher said, "What you are shouts so loud in my ears I cannot hear what you say." He was referring to the fact that **behaviours speak louder than words**. It is not what people say that matters, because their behaviour will always indicate what is going on inside. People are able to sense another's underlying attitude

> INTEGRITY REQUIRES THAT YOU BEHAVE IN AN ETHICAL WAY AND DO WHAT YOU SAY YOU WILL DO, ALL THE TIME.

irrespective of what they say or do because the choices that they make almost always reflect their true character. Consequently, leaders must be totally authentic in words and actions if they are to generate trust.

If you choose to attempt to teach people to behave in a way that you do not live by yourself your authenticity and integrity will constantly be challenged. It is critical to step up and live your principles. As John Maxwell says, "It may be a harder way to teach, but it is a much easier way to learn," and one of your most important tasks as a leader is to help people to learn. If they are not learning it is literally impossible for their performance to improve.

Once you have high integrity you will not only seek total honesty, with yourself and others, by telling the truth but you will also leave the right impression upon those who witness your daily actions. So often we see people trying to avoid the obvious lie and shape the impression that they leave through the use of misleading, incomplete, or inaccurate information.

Anyone who reaches the stage of personal development that allows them to act with integrity will experience a huge sense of relief. For one thing, it becomes much easier to remember what you have told people if it is the truth! This openness about your thoughts, feelings, and actions projects authenticity and creates the sense of a leader that can be trusted.

Note that integrity does not mean being right all the time. We already know that this is not possible for anyone – mistakes are inevitable. **Being wrong has nothing to do with integrity.** All except the most intolerant people will forgive the occasional honest mistake, especially if they can see that your response to it is positive.

What people will find difficult to forgive are breaches of character or integrity that call your trustworthiness into question, such as anything that has a bad intention behind it. Even small lapses of this nature can have a huge impact. Once lost, the confidence of your team will be very difficult to regain. As Mahatma Gandhi said, "The moment there is suspicion about a person's motives, everything he does becomes tainted." For this reason we should examine the role of trust in greater detail.

Trust and Leadership

Technique and technology are important, but adding trust is the issue of the decade.

~ **Tom Peters**

Trust is generated according to your character and the way that you treat people, essentially through the example that you set. If you want to increase your influence you must gain people's trust.

In the first chapter of his book, *The Speed of Trust*, Stephen M. R. Covey (the son of Stephen R. Covey and CEO of CoveyLink Worldwide) describes trust and its impact like this: "Simply put, trust means *confidence*. The opposite of trust—distrust—is *suspicion*. When you trust people, you have confidence in them—in their integrity and in their abilities. When you distrust people, you are suspicious of them—of their integrity, their agenda, their capabilities, or their track record."

Trust is vital to every relationship in any aspect of life. Where it is present it is possible to build strong relationships; without it there will always be defensiveness and a lack of willingness to commit one's all. Leaders of businesses must create great relationships with staff, customers, owners, and the public. Without trust no satisfactory relationship will ever exist.

When it comes to generating trust it is not your position, the size of your office, the value of your home, or how much you earn that matters, nor is it that your title may be Chairman of the Board or that your family has a villa in Antigua. People really don't care: none of that means anything to them. What they care about is what kind of person you are.

One of the behaviours that most undermines trust is the choice to be disloyal to people when they are not present. This usually takes the form of gossiping and has become so common in the workplace and such a part of the cultural norms of some companies that they don't even notice.

> ONE OF THE BEHAVIOURS THAT MOST UNDERMINES TRUST IS THE CHOICE TO BE DISLOYAL TO PEOPLE WHEN THEY ARE NOT PRESENT.

Hopefully, increased awareness of the negative impact of this behaviour, particularly because of the immense amount of distrust it engenders, will stimulate some change.

I remember several occasions where bosses of mine "shared" with me criticisms or concerns they had about the performance of other members of the team. There was a part of me that felt pleased to be taken into their confidence, but then I thought of what would happen if I disappointed them. I realised that they were just as likely to share my errors or weaknesses in the same way. I now questioned how many of the things that they said to my face I could really feel confidence in. They lost my trust.

In another favourite trust-destroyer someone will typically start with the line, "I was told not to tell anyone, but…," followed by their justification for breaching the confidence that was shared with them. This is an attempt to build favour by taking someone into their confidence, but it displays a complete lack of trustworthiness. Every time you talk behind someone's back in a way that you would not be prepared to talk to them directly you risk undermining you own integrity. The best thing to do is to stop, immediately.

> TO TRUST OTHERS IT IS FIRST NECESSARY TO TRUST ONESELF.

Ultimately high morale stems from trust in the leader. George MacDonald, the Victorian writer, said, "To be trusted is a greater compliment than to be loved." When people feel trusted it paves the way to building a highly positive environment, but **to trust others it is first necessary to trust oneself**, and this means having self-confidence. People who have difficulty believing in themselves always find it difficult to extend this belief to others.

Self-Confidence

A smooth sea never made a skilled sailor.

~ **English Proverb**

As we discovered when we looked at the role of the subconscious mind in determining how people act, it is impossible to behave in a way that is inconsistent with the self-image. People need to be confident in their own skin if they are to project confidence to others – not trying to live a pretence that they are something that they are not. We have seen that when pretending they can never be authentic and everyone picks it up at some level through the subconscious communication that underlies all interactions. The listener will get the feeling that whoever they are with is not being fully honest and start to ask themselves why. Moreover, people will be hesitant and cautious when they detect that the leader is not genuine or "faking it." Therefore, confidence, trust, and integrity always go hand-in-hand.

It is important to realise that confidence has nothing to do with the absence of problems. In fact, problems are circumstances that highlight the amount of confidence that a person truly has. Those who are pretending to be strong leaders, but who really lack confidence, will tend to panic and overreact during a crisis. Those who have strong confidence are much more likely to be able to remain calm, and that calm will encourage others to follow during a crisis rather than question the judgment of their leadership. Confidence allows leaders to make difficult choices that are then accepted because of the level of trust they have gained through the authenticity of their daily actions.

The ability to remain calm and to function at a high level depends upon a strong belief in one's ability to deal with problems. This gets communicated as confidence.

A leader who believes in himself will also believe in others. This is because strong self-confidence allows a leader to support and encourage others to be the best that they can be, without feeling the need to maintain and prove their own superiority. Belief in oneself is at the core of establishing a creative environment rather than a competitive one. The greater the ability of a leader, the greater their confidence is likely to be.

If the appearance of confidence strays into arrogance or controlling behaviour, this is likely to be based in insecurity. Some examples of how this reveals itself in the workplace are:

- A desire to take the credit

- Seeking to win rather than create synergy

- Talking frequently about past successes

- Passing the buck when things go wrong, rather than accept responsibility

- Cutting down, ridiculing, or belittling others

On your journey of increasing self-awareness I encourage you to ask yourself whether you have a tendency to display these traits. If so, then some effort to develop your own self-confidence is likely to hugely benefit your leadership ability.

Stress

One of the most obvious signs of a lack of self-confidence is stress. If I am stressed it points to an underlying belief that my personal resources are inadequate to deal with the situation that I am facing. Quite simply, it arises when we run out of choices of options and behaviours that we believe will achieve the outcome that we want.

Whatever its source, the pressure of stress allows negative emotions to take over in immediate, powerful, and intensely subjective ways. Stress causes most people to work harder but achieve less, leading to chronic underperformance. Much of the coaching that I do simply helps people to identify new choices that they were not aware of before we started. They still have access to everything that they could do before the coaching session but, due to their conditioning or as a result of the stress itself, they were unable to see additional options. As we probe to understand more fully how they limit themselves, they learn how to identify additional choices on their own, which builds self-reliance.

A powerful example of this occurred when one of my clients, Graham, perceived that his new boss didn't understand his work, was leading ineffectively, and was taking the credit for things that he (Graham) had done. His response to this had been to become very resistant to doing what was asked of him. Arguments with his boss were common, resulting in him being excluded from meetings and a complete loss of influence. Furthermore, he was incredibly stressed because he understood the impact that this situation was having on his career

STRESS ARISES AS A RESULT OF THE INTERPRETATION THAT YOU GIVE TO A PARTICULAR SITUATION.

but did not know how to change it. Through discussion he became aware of some different approaches to managing upward and how he could view what was happening in a much more positive light. He began focusing on delivering what his boss required and trusting that other leaders of the business would still be aware of his contribution. Rapidly, as his actions changed, the antagonism that had been present subsided and he regained his influence. It took only a couple of months for him to completely turn around a difficult situation that was threatening his career, simply through an increase in awareness of new choices.

You can see from this example that **stress arises as a result of the interpretation that you give to a particular situation**. Its source is in the mind, never in the external environment. For evidence of this, think about a recent work situation in which you or someone else was stressed, but other coworkers were barely bothered. They responded differently because their mental interpretation of the situation was different. They didn't experience a different situation; they just gave it a different meaning.

An example of this would be if you were to interpret that pressure was being placed on you from bosses, "causing" you to lie awake at night worrying about your job, but you notice colleagues in a similar situation joking and laughing as usual. They probably don't care any less about the work or their job; they just choose not to be pressurised. It is a demonstrable truth that there is no pressure in the world, just people feeling pressure because of their interpretation. If things are happening that you cannot control, the best approach is to seek to work with it rather than attempting to force the circumstances to change.

When you get the desire to control things outside yourself it will always create stress – for you and probably the people around you. Even if this desire comes from overuse of strengths, such as the ability to see a solution quickly and a passion to resolve the problem, its effect is still negative.

In my experience, people adopt a controlling or dictatorial style because they don't know how to get what they want and empower others at the same time. In other words, these approaches are indicators of a weakness in leadership skill. If they knew a better way they would choose it; nevertheless, the cost of this lack of awareness is high because of the negative impact that it has on those around them.

The most effective way to remove stress is to let go of the need to control because **you experience stress to the exact degree that you seek to change the people and things in your life**. If you are able to accept them just as they are you will find that it is impossible to experience disharmony. Trying to force change in anything is a cause of constant stress because the use of force always creates opposition.

Consider the example of Patrick, a client who had succeeded in alienating senior people in several parts of his organisation because of his tendency to push his team too hard and his lack of awareness of his impact on others. He had reached the point where he was struggling to find a position in the organisation because many people considered him unemployable, his reaction to which was to attempt to force people to listen. He had become aggressive and judgmental, seeing everything that happened

> YOU EXPERIENCE STRESS TO THE EXACT DEGREE THAT YOU SEEK TO CHANGE THE PEOPLE AND THINGS IN YOUR LIFE.

to him as an attack and reacting in kind. Once he was able to perceive things differently and recognise that none of the events that he was so unhappy about were really as he had interpreted them, he was able to relax and allow the natural course of events to unfold. His influence increased, tension disappeared, and very quickly people who had previously been unprepared to help began to support him. His change of attitude allowed him to see the world differently and changed the outcome dramatically. He soon had the role of his choice.

As you grow your self-confidence, so you will increase your ability to let go of stress because you will feel less need to attempt to control your environment, knowing instead that you have the capability to deal with anything that arises.

Perfectionism

Perfectionism also points to lack of self-belief and while some people may consider perfectionism a good thing, you should not allow yourself to be misled. It will always create artificial limitations. If you are a perfectionist it is likely that you will be affected in the following ways:

- It will set up the fear of failure before you even start a task. Because you will constantly think that everything you do has to be perfect, you will attempt to avoid doing anything, or at least anything challenging. You may do a lot of planning and thinking, or you may not even get that far. If you are setting an objective to be perfect then it is guaranteed that you will be disappointed, and the subconscious mind will always seek to avoid disappointment as it associates this with pain. Under these conditions you will sabotage yourself, failing to take the necessary action and creating procrastination and delays.

- It will never optimise results. I do believe that there are times when a perfectionist can produce very good results; for example, when the pressure of a deadline and the fear of nondelivery become greater than the fear of failing to achieve internal standards, but this is likely to be at the cost of other things that could have been achieved instead or at the same time. Much time is usually wasted in getting started and, bearing in mind the Pareto principle, which says that 80% of the value comes from 20% of the effort, striving for perfection will never be the most effective use of time.

- On top of the difficulty of getting going, even when you do eventually start you may get so over-inspired that you start thinking about all the many, many things you could do as well.

They all seem to need to be researched in detail and structured into the final piece. This is called analysis paralysis.

- You regularly find that you are an expert in what everyone else is doing and you take great pleasure in telling them. This is never appreciated.

- It makes you miserable. No one believes in perfectionism, so trying to live up to it creates defences and causes you to become extremely uptight. There is a perpetual worry about what other people are thinking because of the certain knowledge that, since you are not perfect, they are bound to find something to criticise. So you work incredibly hard to keep parts of yourself hidden, not just from others but also from yourself (what Jung described as the "shadow") and in the process, destroy your authenticity.

- When you get to the point that the job just has to be done and no excuse can delay it any longer, you end up working ridiculous hours to hit the deadline. Very likely you will then internally try to excuse yourself for having produced something less than perfect by rationalising that you didn't have the time, but you won't really believe it, which further undermines your confidence.

The Root of Perfectionism

Perfectionism is driven from insecurity. It comes from a desire to prove yourself, often due in part to linking your identity to what you do. This is an ego trick. It offers no prospect of fulfillment and there is really nothing good that comes from it, which is why Tony Robbins describes perfection as the lowest standard in the world. There is a fabulous quote by Dr. David Burns, Professor of Psychiatry and Behavioral Sciences at the Stanford University School of Medicine, which encapsulates this idea. He says, "Aim for success not perfection ... Remember that fear always lurks behind perfectionism. Confronting your fears and allowing yourself the right to be human can, paradoxically, make you a far happier and more productive person."

Perfectionism can be understood better in the context of the two basic forces that motivate human behaviour that were discussed earlier: the need to avoid pain and the desire to gain pleasure. One of the main sources of such pain is fear of criticism. As well as the criticism that people feel they receive from others, they also have to deal with the incredibly powerful inner critic that nags away inside their own minds. This critic is particularly damaging, killing off many ideas before they are even properly formed. I'm sure that everyone will be able to recognise this pattern of thought, where an idea comes up that stretches the comfort zone and then all of the reasons (or excuses) why it is not a good one rapidly leap to mind and the idea is slaughtered in infancy. It is the Terror Barrier kicking into action and must be overcome if you are to achieve more than minor, incremental improvements.

> ONE OF THE MAIN SOURCES OF PAIN IS FEAR OF CRITICISM.

The fear of criticism acts in direct opposition to the desire for success, setting up conflict within the mind. Since perfectionists have already set themselves up to fail from the start, because of their impossible standards, the fear will usually win.

The answer to overcoming perfectionism is to swap perfection for excellence. The dictionary defines excellence as relating to any activity in which one is outstanding. Notice that it makes no reference of a need to be perfect. Life should be fun. It is when you let down the defences so that your true self can emerge. In the process your integrity and authenticity will automatically improve as well. The effort that you put into letting go of your perfectionism will pay huge dividends to your self-confidence.

The Confidence to Create Change

Confidence breeds the courage to create change, and it requires much courage to be different. It has been said that, in the context of the modern world, the opposite of courage is not cowardice but conformity. Conformity is the enemy of success for it blocks forward progress, requiring that you remain within the bounds of accepted norms. We have already established that if you want to be successful you cannot do it by following what most other people are doing. It doesn't matter how far you go back through history; the masses have always been heading in the wrong direction. You need to have the self-confidence to forge a new course, and this requires the courage to be different. Significant progress, whether for an individual or a business, always comes as the result of someone's preparedness to make courageous decisions. Only the self-confident individual is capable of doing this.

Such self-confidence has become the hallmark of Sir Richard Branson. Despite the fact that he dropped out of school at age 15, his dyslexia having resulted in poor academic performance, he has built a business empire with over 350 companies and accumulated a net worth of more than £4 billion. Many of his ventures, such as his airline and mobile phone companies, took on major incumbent operators with considerable domination of their sectors. Many external observers would have felt such ventures to be ill-considered. However, he has proven over and over again that his vision and entrepreneurial flair can turn even the most unlikely opportunity into a success.

This sort of confidence can only come from within. A leadership position or title does not give anyone courage, but one may gain a leadership position from having courage. We know that leadership always starts with the individual, and a leader may not require a formal position or title to lead others. In fact, some of the most courageous leaders are those who rise up from the ranks of the masses to assume a leadership position, especially in times of crisis.

In my opinion, the ultimate example of this is Mahatma Gandhi. He had no title, no office, no rank or privileges, no armies, and no formal authority of any kind. Yet he was able to hold massive influence over important leaders and political movements as well as hundreds of millions of people in India; this influence continues today through studies of his life and teachings. It took considerable courage to stand up to the regimes in South Africa and India but he was prepared to die, if necessary, for what he believed in. The clarity of his vision combined with his ability to inspire others to follow enabled him to achieve what many would have thought to be impossible.

Courage from a leader inspires courage and commitment from followers, provided that they are given permission to take risks. Leaders must both model courage and be supportive of followers, irrespective of the outcome, if they are to be able to draw courage from others. The alternative is a company dominated by fear, where no one takes action until they know that it has "sign-off" from above. Creativity in such companies is dead.

Handling Criticism

Criticism is something we can avoid easily by saying nothing, doing nothing, and being nothing.

~ **Aristotle**

All leaders will be criticised. Their actions will be second guessed, broken apart, and analyzed in the smallest detail. As a leader you will never please everyone and will need to deal with the many people who utterly refuse to celebrate the success of anyone else because of their own limitations. We see this frequently, for example, in the treatment by the press and the public of international athletes. These are people who have the focus and dedication to make the sacrifices necessary to get to the top, yet if they stumble when they finally reach the pinnacle of their sport, they are ridiculed for any momentary lapses or inadequacies. A great example of this is Tim Henman, whose failure to win Wimbledon, despite having come so close so many times, is frequently portrayed in the U.K. as a failure. He attracts much criticism – the fact that he stayed close to the top of the world rankings for so many years is soon discounted by those who prefer to watch from the stands or their armchairs at home. They cheer when their idols win, enjoying the feel-good emotions that they experience, but bring them down when they lose. They are merely spectators – and spectators can never understand what it means to be a player.

We also see this behaviour directed at our statesmen and politicians and at famous names from the entertainment industry. There is a feeding frenzy by the media, supported by the millions that buy their papers and magazines or watch their programmes to uncover the next "shocking" story about their private lives. The people who join in with this kind of criticism don't realise that they're displaying a belief in their own inadequacy, or that seeking to bring down anyone who rises above them will never make them feel better. They are spectators as well, but this time in life, and their behaviours are purely an expression of their own limitations and insecurity.

> EGOTISM DICTATES THAT YOUR CREATIVITY WILL RARELY BE UNRESERVEDLY ADMIRED BY THOSE THAT DON'T HAVE IT.

I don't believe that this can be summed up much better than the way that Theodore Roosevelt captured it in his 1910 speech in Paris: "It is not the critic who counts; not the man who points out how the strong man stumbles, or where the doer of deeds could have done them better. The credit belongs to the man who is actually in the arena, whose face in marred by dust and sweat and blood; who strives valiantly; who errs, who comes short again and again, because there is no effort without error and shortcoming; but who does actually strive to do the deeds; who knows great enthusiasms, the great devotions; who spends himself in a worthy cause; who at the best knows in the end the triumph of high achievement, and who at the worst, if he fails, at least fails while daring greatly, so that his place shall never be with those cold and timid souls who neither know victory nor defeat."

Egotism dictates that your creativity will rarely be unreservedly admired by those that don't have it. Once again, this has nothing to do with you and everything to do with the detractors. For anyone who lacks creativity this particular ability is likely to appear to be impractical daydreaming. Often they will seek to shape the innovator to fit their own model of the world; then if they fail, rather than accept that their worldview may be wrong, they will probably seek to undermine the credibility of the person concerned.

A Rough Road?

If you are going to live at a higher plane than others you must learn to deal with such criticism. You will need to use your imagination; you will have to set yourself apart as being different and you will have high-profile failures from time to time. As Tony Robbins points out, "If you are going to become a successful leader, then even people who have never met you are going to reject you." The most important aspect of attitude necessary to deal with criticism is not to take it personally. As you come to understand the behaviours of others and recognise that, as Wayne Dyer says, "Anyone who judges others doesn't define the other person, they define themselves," you can rise above their criticism.

We can isolate ourselves even more from the negativity of others by understanding that anyone behaving in this manner is actually suffering, thus allowing us to empathise and have compassion for their position. As you hopefully now recognise, the power of compassion to create positive outcomes is enormous. By raising our awareness of why others behave as they do, our own self-leadership will improve and we will be able to remain calm and comfortable even when facing serious challenges.

It also helps enormously not to take yourself too seriously. So much unnecessary upset comes when people feel that they have been insulted, when tolerance or a sense of humour would actually serve them much better. There is an old Zen story that illustrates this point well:

> *There once lived a great warrior. Though quite old, he was still able to defeat any challenger. His reputation extended far and wide throughout the land and many students gathered to study under him.*
>
> *One day an infamous young warrior arrived at the village. He was determined to be the first man to defeat the great master. Along with his strength, he had an uncanny ability to spot and exploit any weakness in an opponent. He would wait for his opponent to make the first move, thus revealing a weakness, and then would strike with merciless force and lightning speed. No one had ever lasted with him in a match beyond the first move.*
>
> *Much against the advice of his concerned students, the old master gladly accepted the young warrior's challenge. As the two squared off for battle, the young warrior hurled insults at the old master. He threw dirt and spit in the master's face. For hours he continued the verbal assault with every curse*

and insult known to mankind. Through it all the old warrior merely stood there motionless and calm. Finally, the young warrior exhausted himself. Knowing he was defeated, he left feeling shamed.

Somewhat disappointed that he did not fight the insolent youth, the students gathered around the old master and questioned him. "How could you endure such an indignity? How did you drive him away?"

The master replied, "If someone comes to give you a gift and you do not receive it, to whom does the gift belong?"

The master knew, as his students did not, that peace of mind is something over which you can develop conscious control. By refusing to accept the young warrior's insults (his "gift") or reveal any weakness, he exposed the warrior's own weakness and thus defeated him.

With understanding of how our thinking works, you can now see that you have the ability to determine your attitude and that no one can insult you or negatively affect your mental state without your permission.

Adaptability

As you gain confidence, let go of the need to control, and increase your ability to cope with criticism, so your adaptability will also improve. Adaptability refers to the flexibility to deal with changes in circumstances and make the best of them, and is a vital trait of leaders. Working against it is our natural tendency to hang on with great tenacity to that which we know, not realising that **true freedom comes in letting go.**

A good example of an adaptable mind-set is provided by the story of Gandhi's lost shoe. As Gandhi stepped aboard a train one day, one of his shoes slipped off and landed on the track. He was unable to retrieve it as the train started rolling. To the amazement of his companions, Gandhi calmly took off his other shoe and threw it back along the track to land close to the first shoe. Asked by a fellow passenger why he did that, Gandhi replied, "the poor man who finds the shoe lying on the track will now have a pair he can use." Not only was Gandhi adaptable to his situation, he benefited others in the process.

> TRUE FREEDOM COMES IN LETTING GO.

Flexibility is incredibly valuable in building effective relationships within the workforce, one of the main responsibilities of a leader. To excel as a leader you must hold yourself to a higher standard than those you lead and part of that means never expecting them to change so that you can remain the same. Any time you give up working on finding a way to work better with your team you have failed them as the leader.

Humility

It may not be immediately obvious, but personal humility solves many of the challenges that are inherent to leadership. By not having to stand out for the benefit of the ego it frees you to be authentic and selfless. Humility allows leaders to maximise the ability of their team to meet their own basic human need for significance because they are not driven by it themselves and do not require the limelight to feel important.

Ken Blanchard, the author and developer of the situational leadership model, once said, "People with humility don't think less of themselves, they just think about themselves less." A leader who allows others to shine and who takes a genuine interest in their well-being will engage the hearts of those he leads, not just their heads. If you are to do this you must leave your ego at the door and understand that true leadership is about service to your team.

In his outstanding book, *Good to Great*, Jim Collins provides powerful evidence of the ability of this approach to produce bottom-line results. The book summarises the findings of a large research effort, undertaken by a select pool of graduate students at Stanford University, to identify companies that made the leap from good to great and which of their characteristics made this possible. Initially, he gave his research team specific instructions to ignore the role of leadership, feeling that this was too much of a simplistic approach. However, the data was clear that there were too many consistent features of these companies that could not be explained in any other way and a description of "Level 5 Leadership" emerged.

> NONE OF THE GOOD-TO-GREAT CEOS EVER SOUGHT THE LIMELIGHT.

In relation to the nature of the leadership of these companies Collins relates, "We were surprised, shocked really, to discover the type of leadership required for turning a good company into a great one. Compared to high-profile leaders with big personalities who make headlines and become celebrities, the good-to-great leaders seem to have come from Mars. Self-effacing, quiet, reserved, even shy—these leaders are a paradoxical blend of personal humility and professional will."

The second of these areas, professional will, equates to having the mindset of a goal achiever – knowing where you are going and having a commitment to get there no matter what. The first point, personal humility, is more difficult, because while most people would profess to understand it, few would be able to explain its importance, and even fewer actually display its qualities on a consistent basis.

This is a huge blind spot for the majority of leaders. In Jim Collins' study he discovered that **none of the good-to-great CEOs ever sought the limelight**; indeed, they typically avoided it. When their company performance was recognised they always sought to give the credit to others. By contrast, in the comparison companies that were used in the study, in over two-thirds of cases there was "the presence of a gargantuan personal ego that contributed to the demise or continued mediocrity of the company." Clearly there is no place for the leader who is seeking a means to pump up his or her personal ego in a company that is striving to raise itself out of the pack.

Interestingly, **genius has also always been associated with great humility**. Successful people who allow their ego to become inflated and take the credit for what they have done often find that "success" ruins their life. The papers are littered with stories of famous people having serial marriages, succumbing to addictions, or having lives otherwise filled with misery.

Truly successful people do not typically encounter this challenge. Their motivation is the inner satisfaction that comes from their work, which is much more powerful than any externally generated recognition. **They aspire to reach the very high standards that they have set for themselves**; the fulfillment that comes from progress toward these aspirations is enough because it plays to their deepest and most powerful human needs. Those that do get publicly recognised always express thanks for their gift, attributing it as not being of their personal making and never seeking to take the credit. They are never arrogant because they genuinely don't consider themselves to be better than others, even if they are better at some things, and as a result they treat everyone with respect and dignity, as an equal.

The ability to admit mistakes and accept the consequences without seeking to blame others is another important feature of humility, and another characteristic of Jim Collins' Level 5 Leaders. A powerful ego will never allow the public acknowledgement of weakness necessary for this to happen.

Be the Change

If you are to become a better leader it is indisputable that you must be willing to grow. The most powerful basis for such growth comes from the motivation of leading "on purpose." When leaders have a deeper meaning for their leadership, a clear purpose, they aren't motivated by external recognition or rewards; they are motivated from within. This gives them the greatest chance of achieving success in their careers and for their company. It provides the moral fortitude to stay focused on what is most important and to never trade long-term goals for short-term gain.

Leadership also means taking others with you, which is impossible unless you develop the leadership skills and capabilities to do so. On the one hand, you cannot lead someone effectively if they have greater leadership capabilities than you do, and on the other, if you are not prepared to grow then you will shy away from helping others to do so for fear of making yourself obsolete. **A high level of personal dedication to growth is essential to maximise leadership potential.**

In seeking growth, one of the most powerful tools available to you is perspective. Leadership is about relationships and most problems in relationships can be resolved when we change our internal perspective such that we can see others differently. As John Maxwell once said, "It is not possible to resolve another person's hurt until we have first discovered the cure and accepted the treatment ourselves."

First there is having, like having an important-sounding title, then there is doing, but most importantly there is being. To really create change you must first "be" the change you wish to see. Your mood will spread, so if you are not inspiring people through your positive nature, whatever you do instead will also be contagious. Therefore, emotional self-control and self-leadership are essential. Without that platform you will have limited ability to help others.

I recommend that you reflect on who you are and how you are doing on a regular basis. Ask yourself questions such as:

- Am I the kind of leader that I would follow?

- What is my impact on the people around me?

- What do I really think of others and what are my expectations of them?

- How well did I handle myself in that situation and how could it have been improved?

- Where am I avoiding being honest with myself?

To become your best you should be asking yourself questions of this nature frequently, being willing to be deeply honest in your introspection and prepared to make any changes necessary.

Having identified areas of potential growth, you must then change the way that you think. For example, if you want to improve self-confidence, start to focus on what has gone well in the past and build great expectations through goal setting for the future. Refuse to entertain the memories of what you think might not have gone well – remember, memory is just the past tense of perception and is therefore purely an interpretation that can serve you or hold you back. Just as your interpretation of current circumstances can be changed, you can also change the way you think of things that happened in the past such that the memory of them becomes positive. As soon as you can change your meaning around what happened, the emotions will also change, along with any related future actions.

There is nothing that happened in your life that is beyond this approach. Take someone who had been bullied by a previous boss and as a result has taken on the belief that they are easily pushed around, and moreover, still has a great deal of resentment relating to the events and the person. Each time they relive any of the negative situations with that boss they reinforce the limitations that it has created in their current behaviours. By thinking about the event differently, perhaps recognising that the boss was actually suffering internally and the bullying was an expression of his own self-doubt, or becoming grateful for the personal lesson about how to avoid allowing something similar to happen again, the memory can be re-contextualised and the emotional charge reduced or removed. It then loses its ability to continue to control you into the future.

Remember, no one can control your thoughts unless you allow them to do so, but if you harbour negativity about others you are allowing them to control you. Ask yourself whether what you are thinking about will move you forward and if it won't, find a way to change it.

Transformational Technique:
Build Character, Not Reputation

The only way to increase your influence in the world is to develop who you are as a person, thus enabling you to fundamentally change the way that others perceive you. This requires an internal growth process based on ethical principles that demands ongoing effort focused on values and action. As you progress you will increase your ability to engage the hearts and minds of those you lead, giving you more influence and true power than any position or impressive credentials ever could. Remember: you cannot lead anyone without their consent or force them to do a great job against their will.

No matter how carefully you manage outward appearances, if your foundations are weak the flaws will always be revealed at some point, normally when you would least want them to be – when the pressure is greatest. At such times stress, since it will tend to make you more reactive, will often bring to the surface deep aspects of your conditioning that you would usually be successful in controlling. You simply can't hide your true self, and whether you gain credit or lose it in such circumstances will be based on your actions.

You must be able to be authentic, letting your actions speak for who you are. When talking to others stop trying to impress them by talking about your accomplishments and remember that, like children, people will copy what you do, not what you say. Therefore, you must develop the attitude and behaviours that you wish to encourage – things like integrity, self-confidence, and flexibility. These form the basis of your character, and although character will not make you as a leader, lack of it will certainly damage you.

*The signs of outstanding
leadership appear primarily
among the followers.*

~ Max De Pree

PART 3

BUSINESS
TRANSFORMATION

8

LEAD THE PEOPLE, NOT THE BUSINESS

If you treat people as they are, you will be instrumental in keeping them as they are. If you treat them as they could be you will help them become what they ought to be.

~ Johann Wolfgang von Goethe

Many believe that business is about the provision of a product, a commodity, or a service. In reality business is about people; those you lead and work with and those that supply you or buy your product. None of these people do anything because the business requires it. They will only commit themselves to it if what is required of them is in line with their own thinking and if what they do is appreciated. Leaders must be able to inspire this commitment in others and, in the process, create change by moving them toward new actions.

IT IS ESSENTIAL THAT A LEADER SEEKS TO UNDERSTAND THE MOST EFFECTIVE MOTIVATIONAL APPROACHES FROM THE PERSPECTIVE OF OTHERS.

To influence others to change it is first necessary to understand how they influence themselves. If you think back to the explanation of the Stickperson you will recognise that it is **the invisible that creates the visible**; thoughts were the initiating events that led to the creation of every aspect of the modern world and all future progress will also be as a direct result of them. We must identify the thought processes that drive people to do what they do (or do not do), recognising that whatever they choose to engage in, they always do so for a reason.

One of the biggest mistakes many people make is to try to use the same strategy to motivate others as they would for themselves, looking at the situation purely from their own perspective. But we are each unique and as such are certain to have different needs and values, so **it is essential that a leader seeks to understand the most effective motivational approaches from the perspective of others.**

Having understood their needs, influencing others must be done with integrity; for example, asking whether what you seek is in their best interest or your own. The ability to influence anyone comes from relating to them, not ruling them, and forcing someone to do something if they have not yet been convinced it is a good idea, is not persuasion but intimidation.

Your greatest successes will always be linked to persuading people from their own perspective. Once they adopt an idea as their own, they will pursue it without continued motivation from you: their own inspiration will carry them forward. Any time someone hasn't yet accepted your proposed solution, if you are able to reach an understanding of their individual concerns then you have a much better chance of influencing them.

Everyone is motivated by their own needs and expectations. As in a negotiation, the starting point in creating alignment and buy-in is to find something that both parties agree on: an area of common ground or a common purpose. This means gaining awareness of the other party's belief systems, setting up the possibility of a win-win outcome, and limiting the likelihood of an adversarial situation developing. It also enables you to allay their specific concerns. Quite simply, you must start by finding out what they want, which

> YOU WILL GET THE BEST RESULTS IF YOU START FROM WHERE OTHER PEOPLE ARE AND LEAD THEM GRADUALLY TO WHERE YOU WANT THEM TO GO.

is impossible to do if your focus is on what the business needs from them. If you openly and willingly seek to find a win-win solution that allows you to give them what they want whilst also serving the needs of the business, their attitude will change and they will become more open and receptive.

You will get the best results if you start from where they are and lead them gradually to where you want them to go. In the short term a desired result may be produced by commanding compliance, using coercion to gain agreement, or raising the prospect of negative consequences for failing to conform. However these approaches will never optimise the long-term result and will do much damage to the relationship in the process.

Leadership Types

There are as many variants of leadership as there are people; this reflects the unique nature of every individual. As a result, the study of leadership has been studied extensively and there have been many attempts at a definition that captures its essence, for example:

- Stephen Covey: "Leadership is communicating peoples' worth and potential so clearly that they are inspired to see it in themselves."

- John Kotter: "Leadership is coping with change."

- Tony Robbins: "Leadership is the ability to significantly influence the thoughts, feelings, actions and behaviours of those you lead."

- Warren Bennis: "Leaders are people who do the right things."

- Ken Blanchard: "Leadership is an influence process."

- John Maxwell: "Leadership is influence."

An understanding of what great leadership entails is not new. The philosopher Lao-tsu made the following observation 2,500 years ago:

A leader is best when people barely know he exists, not so good, when people obey and acclaim him, worse when they despise him. But of a good leader, who talks little, when his work is done, his aim fulfilled, they will say, "We did it ourselves."

These words of advice are as applicable today as they were all those years ago.

Whatever leadership means to you, one thing is certain: there is a big difference between supplying someone with the tools necessary to do their job, which is management not leadership, and providing them the encouragement and opportunity to grow and be successful.

With awareness it is obvious that leadership works through people and culture – not hierarchy and systems. However, over time it is common for policies and processes to be developed to control the few, which then have an unfortunate effect on the culture of the organisation, dampening the spirit of the many and making relationship building difficult. This happens because people have forgotten the need to influence and sought instead to

> WITH AWARENESS IT IS OBVIOUS THAT LEADERSHIP WORKS THROUGH PEOPLE AND CULTURE – NOT HIERARCHY AND SYSTEMS.

control. By looking at the approach of leaders in relation to how likely they are to seek control we can identify them as falling into one of four types, as identified in the following simple model from Tony Robbins.

Type 1: Title

Many people still operate in a controlling fashion, using their position or title as leverage to get things done. They expect others to follow and demand it when they don't. When a baby's needs are not met it throws a temper tantrum, becoming red in the face and screaming until someone does what it wants. Sadly there are still many leaders that like to operate in this manner. It does nothing for anyone and will never deliver high performance.

Leaders that have a tendency to behave in this way have been able to get away with it because it can create results of a sort – so many are prepared to tolerate it and too few are aware how much more is possible. However, this approach is very limiting and where leaders rely on the power of their position to get others to follow, they will be followed only as far as their stated authority dictates and no further. In this situation, employees will do only what they have to do, when they have to do it. They will never go above and beyond and so will profoundly inhibit their potential. This approach is not leadership – it is dictatorship.

Type 2: Barter

Leaders at the level of "Barter" take some time to learn about their team but everything is conditional: an "If you do this then I'll do that" type of approach. What this means is that they are always measuring to ensure that people are conforming to their rules. Unfortunately, anyone who always measures everything will quickly find reasons to be disappointed in what others are giving. They see everything as a series of isolated incidents, so one bad outcome is enough to lead them to the conclusion that they are giving more than they are getting back and to stop them from further giving. This inevitably creates a breakdown in the relationship.

I find it bizarre that some companies seem to pride themselves on this attitude. They will say, "You're only as good as your last job" in a way that suggests that this is an approach to be proud of. What it really shows is a complete lack of understanding of people, and, more specifically, of the human learning process. As we have already discussed, it is impossible for anyone to develop in a straight line or to take on new challenges without the certainty that they will make some mistakes.

People who think this way seldom develop deep relationships that last over time because an event will always occur sooner or later that they consider to have been below the standards expected (their standards). When this happens they will either withdraw, expecting the other person to make amends, or migrate back to the dictatorial style of Type 1 and demand more effort. Either way, the negativity that they will communicate makes it very difficult for most people to respond. This approach is not leadership either – it is trading.

Type 3: People-Centred

People-centred leadership is the first level at which people really start to think of others rather than themselves. Fred Smith stated, "Leadership is getting people to work for you when they are not obligated"; in other words, recognising that they have the freedom to choose what they do or do not do. You can, to a degree, get people to conform using regulations, but the relationship that you hold with them has much more power to influence their behaviours. This type of leadership allows the followers to choose, guaranteeing the self-motivation of all who decide to go with the leader.

To truly lead others you will need to develop the power of influence. Through the use of influence, people will extend themselves to bring out capabilities and levels of resourcefulness that they may not even have been aware that they have. This is critical because leaders do not, and cannot, run the company by themselves – the help of others is essential, just as the captain of a ship may decide which direction to head but it is the crew that makes it happen. This may sound obvious but I think many leaders behave as though they think they are single-handedly running their company or team. You only have to look at how little effort they expend in building a culture where people are aligned and motivated.

As a leader you need your team but that is not enough: it is also vital to have its trust, loyalty, and commitment. In short, a team must be inspired. When we look at inspiration we find that it originates from within – hence the importance of helping people to discover and believe in their true potential. We can move people most when we speak authentically from our own values and experiences; this happens as we become more self-aware and improve our self-leadership. The people-centred leader understands all of this and has begun to develop the skills necessary to motivate people much more powerfully than, for example, by offering them money or title.

Type 4: The Servant Leader

We covered in detail in the last chapter that, **at the highest level, one of the most critical attributes of leadership is the ability to engage the hearts as well as the minds of followers**. This is achieved not by force but by focusing on service to tap into the deepest motivators of human behaviour. Two of the greatest examples of this type of leader are Mahatma Gandhi and Nelson Mandela, both of whom were prepared to remain committed to their purpose even when they suffered pain – because it was the right thing to do. In the process they mobilised huge numbers of people to put aside short-term personal gain and to follow them.

> AS A SERVANT LEADER YOUR GOAL IS NOT TO GET PEOPLE TO THINK MORE HIGHLY OF YOU BUT TO GET THEM TO THINK MORE HIGHLY OF THEMSELVES.

As a servant leader your goal is not to get people to think more highly of you but to get them to think more highly of themselves. Improved results will then follow automatically because of their change in self-image.

To reach this point, attitude is vital. Many leaders take themselves way too seriously and are overly concerned about their self-image and how they are perceived. It is easy for us to become overly concerned with our reputation and lose focus on our character. Servant leadership is never motivated by a desire to control, what other people think, or meeting the needs of the ego. Neither is it influenced by how important the people being dealt with are considered to be. Everyone receives the same treatment, driven by a genuine caring about the welfare of others.

This level of leadership is a natural extension of the model that was developed in Chapter 2, as shown in Figure 8.1.

Figure 8.1 – Servant Leadership in Context

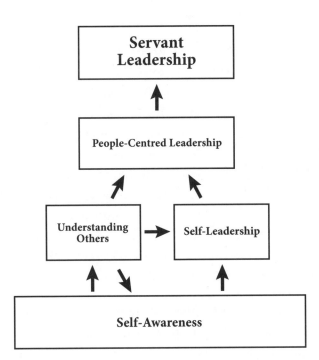

The extent of our influence will be directly linked to the authenticity with which we demonstrate that we are willing to serve, genuinely wanting others to win and constantly seeking the win-win solution. Servant leadership completely changes the working environment because in becoming a servant, **a leader must shift focus from caring primarily about business to caring for people.** This is exceedingly rare in today's competitive environment.

Developing Others

As a leader, your responsibility is the development of others. You will never be strong in this area if you are worried that they may challenge your position or weaken your authority. Strong self-confidence must be present in any high-quality leader.

As we have already covered, to make the most significant impact possible on others, first find out what they want and then help them to get it. To bring out the true potential in each of your employees you are going to need to have a high awareness of human potential and focus on bringing it out in them. You might think of it in relation to the well-known quote by John F. Kennedy, which I've taken the liberty of modifying slightly to fit the situation: "Ask not how your employees can serve you, but how you can serve your employees." Deep relationships of mutual concern and respect will automatically follow.

> PEOPLE NEED TO HEAR THAT A LEADER BELIEVES IN THEM AND WANTS THEM TO SUCCEED.

The best leaders bring others along by seeing in them something that they were unable to see in themselves, and by believing in it long enough so that the other person is able to believe in it, too. **People need to hear that a leader believes in them and wants them to succeed.** It is impossible to do this too much. Once people recognise and understand that a leader wants them to succeed and is committed to helping them, through regular reinforcement they will begin to believe that they can achieve what they have been asked to do.

This awareness is incredibly powerful because it takes so little effort to help others to feel important. Small gestures done with sincerity, such as a simple "thank you" or remembering to ask about their children by name, can have a huge impact. It doesn't have to take much time, nor must it cost money. As long as the motivation is genuinely caring it will have an impact in the heart of the employee.

It is essential that you imagine your employees performing at a higher level than they are doing now. To highlight the quote at the opening of this chapter, Goethe knew this when he said, "If you treat people as they are, you will be instrumental in keeping them as they are. If you treat them as they could be you will help them become what they ought to be." This is the Pygmalion effect in action: people will tend to meet your expectations, whether they are high or low. It is plain to see where leaders should focus their efforts if they wish to have a transformational influence on each and every person.

You will get a far better return on the effort you put into making others feel good about themselves than you will in trying to convince them to feel good about you. It's a win-win situation anyway, because if you succeed in making them feel better about themselves, they will also think better about you! Often, all it takes to transform the attitude, and subsequently the performance and results, of a person is to convey a strong belief in them. This in turn will generate a high level of trust between you and that employee.

> YOU WILL GET A FAR BETTER RETURN ON THE EFFORT YOU PUT INTO MAKING OTHERS FEEL GOOD ABOUT THEMSELVES THAN YOU WILL IN TRYING TO CONVINCE THEM TO FEEL GOOD ABOUT YOU.

Contrast the service-oriented leader with the leader whose mindset is to look for weakness. Experience has demonstrated to me how difficult it can be for the employees of such leaders. In one situation that stands out very clearly. I was asked to coach Peter, who was failing to meet his boss's expectations. Unfortunately the boss in question was unwilling to make time to become personally involved in the process, either to change his own perspective or to understand how he might have contributed to the breakdowns in their relationship. Despite extensive, deliberate, and committed efforts by Peter, and much recognition of personal change by other people, his boss was still looking for his weaknesses – his opinion was already formed, and he had no intention of changing it. Consequently all of Peter's efforts were wasted, and he ended up leaving the business.

If you are in a situation where you have limiting beliefs about the capabilities of a member of your team, recognise that in most cases your attitude will be enough to create the outcome you expect. If you do not make the decision to think differently it is unlikely that any effort from the employee concerned will make much difference.

"The Golden Rule"

One simple ethical guideline has been endorsed by many teachers and been influential among people in very diverse cultures for millennia. It is arguably the most essential basis for the modern concept of human rights and provides a basis for the resolution of all ethical dilemmas. Known as "The Golden Rule," it takes the form of a single question: "How would I like to be treated in this situation?" It always provides a strong foundation for dealing with any situation if you are able to put yourself in someone else's shoes and answer this question with honesty, because such honesty will create empathy.

When I'm working with my clients, this question alone is often enough to achieve a breakthrough in their understanding of how to deal with some tough interpersonal challenges. By looking at a situation from someone else's point of view, they are almost always able to identify both new choices and blind spots in their own thinking that were limiting their options.

Think about this: how could you justify seeking better treatment from others than you are prepared to give them? Whatever criteria you may choose would inevitably open up the conclusion that if there are some people that you could justify treating badly, then there must be others from whom you would consider similar treatment of you to be acceptable. John Maxwell, in his book, *Ethics 101*, summarises it this way: "It eventually becomes like a game of king of the hill. Did you play that as a kid? One person climbs up onto a hill of dirt and tries to stay there while everyone else tries to knock him off. The only way to win is to be the biggest bully and even if you *do* win, you get pretty beat up in the process."

We learn this thinking as children. At that time if we wished to be well received by our parents, for example, it was often not necessary to do something of merit ourselves. Instead, we probably found that if we could get our siblings into trouble, we had a good chance of looking good by comparison. The problem is that this sets up an environment where someone has to lose in order for us to win. People who retain this view into adulthood are poisonous personalities. Ultimately they see everyone else as a threat to be dealt with or a challenge to be conquered.

Steps to Bring Out the Best

There are some simple actions that you can take to bring the best out in others:

Appreciate Them

Imagine this situation: You've worked several late nights to get a report done for your boss that he needs for the next board meeting. When you hand it to him he says … nothing. How likely are you to do the same thing again? We were deeply conditioned through school to believe that appreciation had to be earned by doing well, so most people are reluctant to give appreciation before set goals have been achieved. Everywhere you look, people really only get appreciated for what they do – after they do it!

If you appreciate people for who they are first, you will tap into a much more powerful motivator – the internal one that is the source of true satisfaction – and in doing so you will release more of their true potential. To underestimate the value of a person is a bad mistake driven from low awareness. There is always an inherent value in everyone that goes much deeper than their current activities. If you can help them to recognise this in themselves everyone wins.

Encourage Them

The best relationships are always between people who help each other, providing support and encouragement. No one ever felt good because they were told that they weren't able to do something. Under these circumstances poor performance is the norm.

Seek to Understand and Listen

Seeking to understand is so important that if forms the basis of one of the habits in Stephen Covey's *Seven Habits of Highly Effective People*. He describes it as the single most important principle that he has learned in the field of interpersonal relations, and four chapters of this book are dedicated to help readers to understand it. Understanding primarily comes from one source, and that is study. If you want to understand people better you must study them. The other element, listening, is critical because of the effect that it has in empowering the other person; many of my clients have commented that one of the aspects of having a coach that they most enjoy is the feeling of being very deeply listened to. We do not lose our connection with others when we stop talking, but when we stop listening.

Give Frequent and Congruent Public Shows of Confidence

I can think of no better way to illustrate the power of this principle than to talk about one of the outstanding leaders that I had the privilege to work with and learn from. Jim Sloane joined Deloitte Consulting to run the telecoms industry sector in the U.K. at a time when that sector was experiencing significant challenges. We were a quarter of the way through the year and had achieved around 7% of our annual target, with few new opportunities in the pipeline to indicate that things were likely to get any better. However, by the end of the year we had achieved 150% of our target and this transformation of results was maintained over the following years. At the time he joined, Jim had only a minor relationship with a company that was to become his major client, but by the time he was promoted to the global board of Deloitte Consulting only three years later, it was one of the firm's top five clients worldwide.

How did Jim achieve this feat? Of course, Jim is outstanding in a number of areas, but in my opinion the major contribution to his success was the way that the team transformed under his leadership. At every meeting he would highlight the outstanding performance of members of his team and express his confidence in them. This was especially the case, it seemed, if they were currently experiencing challenges. Catalysed by this public support and Jim's obvious belief that they could succeed, he ended up with a very highly motivated team and a rapidly growing order book.

Praise Effort and Reward Performance

Often these two areas get blended together; people don't get praised unless they get good results, irrespective of how much effort they have put in. This approach will never bring out the best. When you praise someone they will seek to replicate that behaviour, so you should focus on whatever you want to encourage more of. However, ensure that your praise is always based on truth – feeble flattery will never impress anyone and it may well have the opposite effect to that which was intended.

To maximise the benefit to be gained from praise, it must be kept separate from rewards. Where an expectation is established that compensation goes hand in hand with praise, the positive impact of the praise will be lessened.

Use Coaching Rather Than Criticism

Leaders must move people from dependence to independence. Historically, many bosses disempowered their staff through micromanagement and prevented them from making decisions, and in the process stifled innovation and growth. With coaching, people can be led to take responsibility for their part in moving their company toward its goals. Anyone can be a critic and unfortunately many bosses are. In my seminars I sometimes ask who knows of a statue to a critic – so far no one has been able to identify one. For certain, they are fairly few and far between, with good reason: almost all advances are as a result of the efforts of people who are creators and builders. The destruction of ideas and enthusiasm that critics are responsible for is a very high price to pay for their potential small contribution in terms of helping to avoid making mistakes. Coaching, on the other hand, builds people's confidence in their own abilities. As such it provides the optimal means of releasing any dependence that staff may have on their leader and of positively influencing their future level of achievement.

Leadership Flexibility

To the man who only has a hammer in the toolkit,
every problem looks like a nail.

~ Abraham Maslow

Different aspects of a leader's job require different skills. A one-dimensional approach can never work in all situations, so it is critical to develop a range of styles as well as the awareness to know when to use them.

Creativity and flexibility are essential for developing the adaptability necessary to optimise approach and to find empowering solutions for the daily issues and events that arise. In fact, one of the foundational principles of Neuro-Linguistic Programming (NLP), which can be defined as the study of how to accelerate the achievement of excellence, suggests that the person

> AS A LEADER IT IS YOUR JOB TO MAKE THE RELATIONSHIP WORK, NOT THE OTHER WAY AROUND.

with the most behavioural flexibility will ultimately determine the outcome. Therefore, as a leader you must be able to find more ways to help someone to change than that person has of holding on to their old behaviour.

In practice, this is often not what happens. A major error that I have seen over and over again is leaders who expected others to modify their behaviours to adapt to them: they were heavily dependent on a single style. Often such leaders seem to believe that because they are the boss, others should be the ones to modify their style to be able to work effectively with them. The error in this approach is that even the simplest personality models have at least a dozen major types, so a one-size-fits-all approach to relationship building will only be effective for a small percentage of the audience. Leaders capable of adopting only a restricted range of styles will find themselves regularly creating conflict situations that require the use of force of character or position if the conflict is to be overcome. This will never allow anyone to get the best out of the people that work with them.

To be effective, every leader must develop behavioural flexibility and adjust their approach to the needs of the person or group that they are dealing with by selecting the style that will be most effective in any given set of circumstance. This is especially important in situations where you are working with people junior to yourself. Since flexibility of approach is a core leadership skill, to do otherwise is to expect a higher level of leadership from them than you are demonstrating yourself. **As a leader it is your job to make the relationship work, not the other way around.** Where relationships break down, you empower yourself to go to a new level by accepting responsibility for the situation.

We can see from this that the greater the degree to which leaders develop and display flexibility, the more effective they are likely to become. When working with others, frustration and anger most often surface when people reach the end of their range of behaviours, or have exhausted the choices that they are aware of for dealing with the situation they are facing. Once again, this is an issue of awareness. If leaders were aware of how to get what they wanted without negative emotions developing they would do so, but their lack of knowledge of how to influence positively leaves them with no further options.

A recent example of a situation faced by one of my clients illustrates this very well. Jane became very angry when a colleague on the board of her company discussed with one of her team a possible career opportunity without mentioning it to her and, as a result of not knowing the individual's situation, badly upset the person concerned. She consciously used her anger to influence both the colleague concerned and the managing director, who had had full knowledge of the situation, to force an apology and to do everything that they could to recover the situation. Because she achieved her desired outcome, Jane felt very happy to have used anger in this way – to her, at the time, the end justified the means. However, following our discussion she realised that she had adopted this very aggressive approach only because she did not have the awareness of how to achieve the same outcome in a more positive fashion.

Although such use of anger may be understandable, **if it is wrong to get other people to do what you want using physical force, then it must also be wrong to do so using emotional force**. This constitutes manipulation and intimidation and can really only be classed as bullying, especially if a more senior person uses it as a tool in order to attempt to control their staff. In the end it provides no effective motivation.

As such, I believe that there is no "appropriate" use of anger in the workplace. It arises as a result of personal weakness and the outcome in anything other than the very short term is almost always negative. For this reason it is important not to deal with confrontation while you are angry. Instead you should strive to keep any confrontation at a non-personal level and make sure that no grudges are harboured.

Any time that you allow fear-based conditioning to govern your actions you will become hostile to those around you. Your perceptions will get distorted, and you will find yourself in a reactive rather than a responsive mode, controlled by your conditioning and your environment as opposed to shaping things the way that you want them to be. Access to your purely cognitive functions will be restricted and the fight-or-flight mechanism will start to kick in.

No one ever performs well in this state. Rapport is lost and the biggest bully comes out on top, albeit temporarily. If you do this, the person on the receiving end of your loss of control will probably be upset by it, and ultimately your ability to influence them (i.e., to lead them), may suffer permanent damage.

To overcome your own anger, the key is to focus on the fact that the negativity is caused by a situation in which you feel you have run out of options. When most people run out of options their natural reaction is to focus on the problem that they are facing; however, **no one ever found a solution by focusing on the problem**. This was beautifully summarised by Thomas Troward in *The Doré Lectures*

> LEADERSHIP AND LEARNING ARE INEXTRICABLY LINKED.

when he said, "The law of floatation was not discovered by contemplating the sinking of things, but by contemplating the floating of things which floated naturally, and then intelligently asking why they did so." So it is for us. Any time we experience problems in relationships with others, it is vital to stay focused on looking for a solution, not on the problem, and to do everything we can to avoid making it personal.

Leadership and Change

Creating change is the highest expression of leadership, so if you want to examine your effectiveness as a leader this is the place to start. If, through evaluation, you realise that you are not a change agent then you should probably be classed as a manager, not a leader.

In his international best-seller, *The Fifth Discipline Fieldbook*, Peter Senge says, "You can always sense the presence or absence of leadership when ... a field of competence and learning exists—enhancing and reinforcing people's efforts." **Leadership and learning are inextricably**

linked. To change a company you will need to influence change in others and also to change yourself, and that means everyone must learn new and different techniques.

As previously discussed, the starting point for any change initiative is the leader: **you will need to be the change that you want to see** and become an active learner. This means:

- Being prepared to step outside your comfort zone

- Examining your humility to determine whether you really have the "certain degree of confidence" needed to learn

- Ensuring that you have developed the resilience and self-confidence necessary to deal with failures

Clearly, few people are comfortable with the idea of failure, but as a leader this prospect may be an even more difficult issue for you. Change is impossible without risking failures, because any time you attempt something new it is impossible to be certain in advance that it will be successful, and such failures can badly damage reputations. On the other hand, if you do not risk anything then you will be stuck in your comfort zone while the world around you continues to change. Under such circumstances ultimate failure is inevitable.

One of the benefits of working with a coach or mentor is that this provides the opportunity to learn, away from external pressures and with honest and constructive feedback that is less likely to be offered by colleagues and those reporting to you. Feedback is a vital element in raising your awareness of your true effectiveness. You must become aware when your results fall short of your goals so that you can adjust your approach. Unfortunately, most people find it awkward and uncomfortable to give feedback for any of the following reasons:

- Fear of repercussions

- Wanting to appear to be a great team player

- Wanting to please the boss

- A desire to be seen as being consistent with the division or company message

- It feels uncomfortable because we don't want to hurt other people's feelings

- Lack of knowledge of how to give feedback in a constructive way

The ultimate result of shielding men from the effects of folly is to fill the world with fools.

~ Herbert Spencer

YOU HAVE THE POWER TO CHANGE YOUR LIFE.

This issue of people receiving limited or poor feedback is at its most serious when it relates to the personal performance of a leader. In Michael Watkins book, *The First 90 Days*, he describes how easy it is to unintentionally discourage people from sharing critical information, resulting in the leader becoming isolated and consequently leading to uninformed decision making. This then damages credibility and further reinforces the isolation.

To avoid this issue, you must deliberately seek to be closely connected to the people around you and encourage feedback, but very few leaders do. According to Daniel Goleman, the problem is generally not that leaders are so vain that they believe that they are infallible. It is because **they do not believe that they can change**. Clearly **this perception is absolutely wrong** – anyone can change, but as with all other aspects of behaviour the first requirement is to believe that you can. One of my greatest hopes for you as you read this book is that **you will come to realise that you have the power to change your life**. You already have everything that you need to make this happen; you simply need to start to use your mind differently.

In contrast to the norm, the best leaders actively seek honest feedback to get a more accurate picture of what is going on, both in terms of their own behaviours and within the business. To allow this to happen, so that people are not discouraged from giving further feedback in the future, they have also learned to receive it in an open, friendly, and nondefensive manner. Note that this will be more difficult for anyone who believes the world to be intrinsically hostile, providing another example of the fundamental impact that your perceptions will have on your results.

Leaders who have become good at receiving feedback know that without it, their personal development will be restricted and they will not have the information necessary to make good business decisions. They also know that how they change in response to the feedback is as important as how they behave in the moment. If someone has braved the fears and discomfort of providing feedback and you fail to demonstrate that you are prepared to take action on it, their willingness to do the same thing in the future is likely to be minimal. Just as you must believe that you can change to get the benefit of feedback, you should very visibly demonstrate that you will respond so that other people can also share that same conviction. If you do otherwise they will rapidly lose the desire to overcome their own discomfort and the feedback will dry up.

If you want to become a powerful leader and continue to develop, you must be able to change. This will require you to get out of your comfort zone and welcome feedback. And as you show your willingness to learn, you unconsciously give others permission to do the same.

It Takes One to Make One

As you grow as a leader you will pass on your enhanced skills to others – **possibly the best measure of a leader over time is how many leaders he or she has created**. No company can be effective if leadership only exists at the top.

Developing others requires senior leaders to demonstrate flexibility and to have access to a range of styles that they can adopt according to the circumstances that they are facing. Among the numerous styles possible, research shows that **to have and to communicate a clear vision** and **to be an effective coach** are probably the two most important. The first of these, vision, is absolutely vital for a leader because it provides direction and unites a company by encouraging its employees to work

> IF YOU CHOOSE TO GIVE YOUR AUTHORITY AND INFLUENCE TO OTHERS, SO YOUR AUTHORITY AND INFLUENCE WILL ALSO INCREASE.

as a team and pull in the same direction. The overriding value of the second style, coaching, is that it enables the leader to create new leaders throughout the organisation by helping others to learn. Equipping others to do a tough job is much harder than shepherding them through it or doing it for them but, over time, provides much greater strength and advancement of the company than a more directive style. Coaching is the optimal means by which this can be achieved.

Ultimately, the overall level of success of the company is highly dependent upon the people that make it up. John Paul Getty said, "It doesn't make much difference how much other knowledge or experience an executive possesses; if he is unable to achieve results through people, he is worthless as an executive." As your confidence increases, provided it is combined with humility, so the confidence of the people around you will also increase. **By switching from directing to guiding and supporting; in other words, by becoming a servant leader, you become a more powerful role model.** In the process, you will also gain enhanced relationships and coaching skills to help others to develop alongside you and allow them to shine.

Paradoxically, **if you choose to give your authority and influence to others, so your authority and influence will also increase**.

Transformational Technique: Serve People and Build Leaders

The vehicle by which all of the results of a business get delivered is the people in it. Therefore, there can be no more effective approach to maximising performance than to seek the most effective methods of inspiring them to want to do the very best that they can for the business. In particular, the business needs leaders throughout if it is to become a highly responsive and creative organisation equipped to flourish in the marketplace. Leadership cannot be delegated but its growth can be encouraged. One of the best ways to do this is to model that which you wish to help grow in others.

The most important element in inspiring others is the way that you treat them. I recommend that you always remember "The Golden Rule" and treat others the way that you would like to be treated yourself.

Take the attitude that the ends never justify the means, even in pressure situations, if those means have a negative impact on others, and ensure your standards in this area are beyond reproach.

It is a paradox of human psychology that while people remember criticism they respond to praise. If you criticise you will create defensiveness and make it highly unlikely that you will achieve your outcome of stimulating positive change. Encouraging and appreciating others will bring out more of their potential, whereas if you handle them badly, their results will be correspondingly poor.

If you are to become more effective yourself and behave in a way that exemplifies leadership, you will need to maximise your ability to learn: solving increasingly complex problems requires your level of awareness to increase. Therefore, I suggest that you become highly proactive in the way that you approach feedback so that you can get high-quality information to guide your change efforts. Keep your focus on seeking solutions and ensure that the experience that people have of you is always empowering.

In the new world, where companies are required to respond to market changes at an increasing pace, employees must come first, with leaders seeking to serve and support rather than control.

THE LEARNING ORGANISATION

*I came to see, in my time at IBM, that culture isn't
just one aspect of the game – it is the game.*

~ Lou Gerstner

Lou Gerstner's appointment as the CEO of
IBM in March 1993 could not have happened at
a more difficult time. The company, which he
has described as "arguably the most successful
business organisation ever created in the '50s,
'60s and '70s," and which had virtually invented
business computing, had just 100 days left
before the cash would run out. By the time he
stepped down in 2002, IBM was once again the
biggest name in its industry.

Initially, Gerstner did not believe that he was the right person for the job because he thought the problem was primarily technical. **What he discovered, though, was a cultural issue**; a company that had, as he put it, "got stuck in the old way of thinking. And the world changed and IBM didn't."

Most people readily talk about culture but few really understand its potential to insidiously undermine all efforts of leaders to improve corporate results. It shows up in both visible and invisible ways. Culture determines how people think, act, and view the world around them. It is created naturally and automatically every time people come together with a shared purpose. Culture is powerful and invisible and its effects are far-reaching: it determines everything from a company's dress code to the work environment, to the rules for getting ahead and getting promoted.

To achieve a significant improvement in corporate results it is always necessary to change the culture, and the starting point for effective change in any area is always a greater understanding of it. Hence, this is where we begin.

One way of understanding the nature of corporate culture more fully is to recognise that in many ways, a business exhibits the same features as the mind of an individual, allowing us to draw a parallel to the Stickperson.

The "Stick Company"

Much as a person can be considered to be made up of three parts, a conscious mind, a subconscious mind, and the body, so the "stick company" also exhibits three very similar components.

The part of the company that equates to the conscious mind is where people are aware of why things happen the way that they do.

The many aspects that are measured and monitored, which operational managers and executives use as inputs to their decision-making processes, all fit into this region. So does corporate governance. For example, information about the sales pipeline may be evaluated for indications about likely end-of-year performance, or levels of customer satisfaction tracked to identify product or service issues. Choices are then made about which events or indicators the company must react to and in what way. These decisions, and the information that they are based on, are transparent and understandable to the people involved.

Such aspects of company behaviour, which form part of overall conscious awareness, are written into the structures, policies, processes, and procedures of the business in order to provide coherence and drive repeatability. An example of this that has now been adopted on a widespread basis is quality processes such as the ISO 9000 regulations. These are standardised with the goal of ensuring that even people outside the business are able to understand what they mean and are designed to control the actions of the organisation.

Unfortunately, driving performance with this approach cannot work because the conscious elements of the organisation do not have the power to determine what results will be achieved, much as the conscious mind of an individual is not responsible for the results that the person gets. If leaders fail to understand where the true power lies, believing that their success can be attributed to the visible aspects of behaviour, the company will fail to achieve its potential and could have some very difficult times.

Lou Gerstner classes such approaches under a term he calls the "success syndrome." He says, "[IBM] got stuck because it fell victim to what I call the success syndrome. The more successful enterprises are the more they try to replicate, duplicate and codify what makes them great. And suddenly they're inward thinking. They're thinking, 'how can we continue to do what we've done in the past?', without understanding that what made them successful was to take risks, to change and adapt and to be responsive." This is a great example of what Arnold Toynbee, the great historian, was talking about when he said that "nothing fails like success" in summarising the history of society and institutions. The difficulty in sustaining high performance over the long term is caused by a failure to understand the real driver behind corporate results.

The part of the organisation that is primarily responsible for results is much less visible and tangible than its structure and processes. This part is the "subconscious" of the company and is made up of the culture and norms that determine whether the company will be a high-performing team or a loose collection of people working together. These powerful, invisible forces form "ground rules" that, though not formally written down, exist as a set of shared habits and beliefs that dictate what is considered acceptable behaviour by individuals, and which traits will be most highly valued. They determine the standards that will be upheld, provide the foundation for all actions and decisions within a team, department, or organisation, and are often expressed as "the way we do things around here."

THE GLUE OF A TEAM THAT COMMITS ITS MEMBERS TO AN ORGANISATION IS THE EMOTIONS THAT THEY FEEL.

Just as the average person will lack awareness of their conditioning or how it was created, so organisations tend to be unaware of the characteristics of the automatic interactions that take place every day. These aspects of an organisation's culture may be more apparent to an external observer than an internal practitioner. Much as it was once universally accepted that the Earth was at the centre of the solar system, flaws in behaviour are very difficult to recognise once accepted within the company. People no longer stop and think that there might be a better way because they become conditioned to the status quo.

The collection of beliefs, expectations, and values shared by an organisation's members are transmitted from one generation of employees to another. For example, I once worked in a company where, at that time, it had become such common practice to cancel people's holidays to meet pressing deadlines that no one at the top seemed to question it. Many people would challenge this practice as unreasonable when they joined but then later come to accept it as part of what it took to work there. Ultimately, if they stayed to become one of the leaders of the business, they were likely to forget their initial reservations and become part of the problem by perpetuating the behaviour. Meanwhile, it was the families and the marital relationships of the employees that suffered.

We can even become immune to extremes in behaviour and eventually accept them as the norm, as evidenced by examples such as the multi-billion-dollar accounting frauds at Enron and WorldCom, or the fact that megalomaniac dictators, such as Hitler and Stalin, can get whole countries to follow them. Unfortunately, if a lie is repeated often enough people will start to believe it. Whatever the culture and established norms of a business, people automatically pick them up and behave in accordance with them. They then apply the filters of that perspective to every problem that they face, thus losing creativity. Strategies from the past will be dug up and reused so that, while people may believe that they are "thinking" about each problem, in reality, innovation will be limited and they will tend to come up with similar solutions, even when circumstances have changed. This is part of the reason why new hires from outside the company or industry can have such a large impact: they actually see the problems and opportunities differently.

Much as it is our feelings that determine how we behave, so the mood of a company (i.e., how people feel about working there), will determine the collective reactions of its employees. This factor is often underestimated by leaders, even though studies have found that it accounts for around 20-30% of business performance. **The glue of a team that commits its members to an organisation is the emotions that they feel.**

This is an area where leaders have no control, only influence. It is only through their own example, and the rules they choose to live by, that they can mould the culture that drives the company. Hence the reason why the recommendations of the previous chapter are so important.

Thus, we can see that an organisation's culture is effectively its members' collective mental models, which become aligned over time to match those of its leaders. If you want to make significant, non-linear changes in the effectiveness of your organisation then you must investigate its culture and work at the level of its paradigms or beliefs about itself. This will not be easy. As I discussed in detail earlier in this book, a flawed paradigm cannot even be recognised by the people involved in it, and most people naturally resist changing their minds about anything. Take, for example, the first flight of the Wright brothers: it was another five years before the general public was prepared to believe that they had actually done it.

NEW IDEAS MUST BE INTRODUCED WITH GREAT CARE IF THEY ARE NOT TO SUFFER A STILLBIRTH.

The Corporate Terror Barrier

*In every work of genius we recognise our
own rejected thoughts.*

~ Ralph Waldo Emerson

**Like the individual seeking to change their conditioning, a
company seeking to make cultural changes also faces considerable
difficulties from its own version of the Terror Barrier.** The norms, or
informal expectations of the group about what is considered acceptable,
become "accepted wisdom." Then, just as the public were resistant to
believe in the Wright brothers' flight, any idea that challenges these norms
is easily rejected. We see this on regular display in meetings, where a very
common response to any new idea is for someone to immediately give
all of the reasons why it won't work. It is totally acceptable for someone
to "play devil's advocate" so **new ideas must be introduced with great
care if they are not to suffer a stillbirth.**

People who work within an organisation hold an image of what
the company stands for and what is possible for it to accomplish. This
becomes the corporate self-image that determines which new ideas are
accepted and how quickly. Initially such ideas may be resisted in a very
gentle and covert manner: the corporate equivalent of Level 2 thinking,
Reason. However, once it looks as though the idea is beginning to gain

support, and the further it diverges from the corporate image, the more powerfully individuals or groups are likely to react against it. Sometimes, they will be prepared to go to extreme lengths to block the initiative.

This can be counteracted through deliberate action by the company, working at the level of its norms and paradigms. For example, I heard about one company that countered the tendency for people to argue against new ideas by establishing a practice that whenever anyone suggested something new, the next person to speak was required to say something supportive. Though simple, this was incredibly powerful because of its impact in breaking habitual patterns of resistance and of quietening the voice of the critic, thus giving time for new ideas to gain traction and helping to make them less readily rejected.

A major challenge for companies in changing their culture and norms is that **the traditional corporate hierarchy, though effective for setting direction, is ineffective for inspiring people or moving them to action and independence**. As Stephen Covey describes in detail in *The 8th Habit*, most companies are still run in the industrial age model, by people calling themselves boss and with subordinates who wait to be told what to do before taking action. People are not typically given the challenge that they need to grow because of their codependent relationship with their bosses, a relationship in which they are controlled and where they have accepted that they should be. Consequently, they do not come forward with their own creative ideas for resolving problems. This conclusion was supported by a recent survey by Mercer Human Resources, which found that less than half of the employees surveyed felt encouraged to come up with new and better ways of doing things.

Thus, there is a crushing cycle of dependency, where bosses take the credit when things go well, and the people that do the work exist in a state of chronic demotivation. The bosses feel justified in directing every action of the employees because they don't see examples of initiative or independent action; meanwhile, the employees have little desire to do their best as they get scant recognition for their efforts.

Compare this with the approach of the very best leaders described by Jim Collins in *Good to Great*, where he uses the metaphor of mirrors and windows to describe the behaviour of a Level 5 Leader. Such a leader **looks "through the window"** and seeks first to give credit to the employees when things go well, knowing that this creates the best and most enduring returns for their business. As we have already seen, employees who are deeply appreciated and credited with success will strive to live up to that acknowledgement. At the same time, a Level 5 Leader understands the need to shield employees when things go wrong. By taking responsibility for errors and mistakes, **looking "in the mirror"** and seeking to identify what he or she might have done better, such a leader prevents the creative spirit of others from being undermined. The employees already know who is or isn't at fault without it being revealed to the world. When they perceive that they are being shielded or protected, they will strive to earn that protection and in turn do the best job possible.

My first experience of being dealt with in this way was during my first tour in the Royal Air Force. I was responsible for all of the communication systems and navigation aids for a flying station, and we were due to make a change to one of the operational frequencies used for communicating with aircraft. I gave instructions to my team to make the change over a weekend and all seemed to have gone smoothly.

Everything changed on Monday morning when I was asked to immediately go and see my boss, Squadron Leader Dave Eighteen. He had just received a very irate call from the Senior Air Traffic Control Officer because, incredibly, we had neglected to notify Air Traffic Control that the change had been completed. The smartest thing I did that day was to opt for the no excuses policy, accepting full responsibility and apologising immediately. Perhaps because of this, and perhaps because Dave was such an outstanding leader, I did not receive the dressing down that I expected. We merely discussed how we could make sure that such a mistake was not made again in the future. That day, Dave really won my commitment, and his style and approach have inspired me ever since.

When I got back to my unit I asked to speak to my Warrant Officer. He was a highly experienced professional (he had been in the RAF for 10 years longer than I had been alive at the time) who, though he notionally reported to me, had unwritten responsibility for making sure that I did not make any critical mistakes. As I told him what had happened, without any accusation or blame, much as Dave had done with me just a few minutes earlier, there was a significant cementing of our relationship. Over the next few days I felt this extend to the members of my 35-strong team. I apparently became very popular with the men that worked for me, despite the enforced distance that was required because of my status as a commissioned officer. My interpretation of this reaction remains the same now as it was then: that I gained huge respect because I was prepared to take the heat for a situation in which I could easily have chosen to pass the blame to someone else further down the line.

If companies are to be successful in moving through their Terror Barrier, they must find a way to allow employees to fully express themselves and their ideas and be prepared to make changes without the fear of failure. The alternative is to remain highly vulnerable to the "success syndrome" and become an organisation constrained by its rules and regulations.

Flexibility in Organisations

Many organisations have very clearly defined policies and procedures that employees are required to fit into, and these tend to become more legalistic over time. This creates a major issue because, while such policies may make the management of large numbers of employees easier, they also stifle creativity. Instead, flexibility is required that sustains the corporate identity and at the same time allows new ideas to be generated.

In her breakthrough book, *Leadership and the New Science*, Margaret J. Wheatley uses the following metaphor of a stream to illustrate the importance of focusing on a goal rather than adherence to a precise plan for achieving it. Water always flows downhill in response to the pull of gravity, until it ultimately reaches the ocean. Anything that it needs to do along the way, such as cascading down rapids or forming large lakes, is inconsequential to the ultimate outcome. Hence, rivers can be very broad and slow-flowing, like the Amazon, or cut deeply into the rock, like the Colorado; it is of no consequence to the river on the way to its objective. "Organisations," she says, "lack this kind of faith, faith that they can accomplish their purposes in varied ways and that they do best when they focus on intent and vision, letting forms emerge and disappear." She then demonstrates how some of the latest scientific evidence reveals that "*disorder* can be a source of new *order*, and that growth appears from disequilibrium, not balance. The things we fear most in organisations—disruptions, confusion, chaos—need not be interpreted as signs that we are about to be destroyed. Instead, these conditions are necessary to awaken creativity."

> FAILURE TO LET GO OF THE KNOWN IS ONE OF THE MAJOR CAUSES OF STAGNATION FOR A COMPANY.

Failure to let go of the known is one of the major causes of stagnation for a company in exactly the same way it is for an individual. Unlocking the creativity of the organisation is the key to future success, and this can only be done through a different approach to the employees. It requires that the culturally accepted norms are understood, unpicked, and then reformed to allow leadership to be exercised by any employee that can be encouraged to do so. As we saw in the previous chapter, the organisation must make leadership development part of its culture such that a critical mass of leaders can be created throughout the business.

Focusing on people will have far more impact than a reengineering of the business and will create long-term strength because **people are your business**. Just as an audience reflects back the level of passion and enthusiasm of a speaker, so those leaders that see employees as disposable are likely to find the employees treating the company the same way.

Breaking an existing paradigm can be even harder for a company than for an individual. As we each know in our own lives, most people are only motivated to change when things are bad. This is true at work or at home. So many people, because of their lack of belief in their own capabilities, spend a great deal of time trying to hang on to what they have – even if what they have isn't really what they want. I can think of many people from my time working for large corporations who used to come to work to do a job that they didn't enjoy and still worry about getting fired. There are few people who feel truly empowered to attempt to do or have what they really want.

To break this pattern and foster change, the company must create an environment that minimises the stress that employees feel when they need to step outside their comfort zone to try something new.

Goals Are Transformational

Just as a clear goal is one of the most powerful tools for changing behaviours for an individual, so it is for a company. A corporate entity without a clear purpose, vision, and goals will often find its people dissatisfied and demotivated, drifting with no clear sense of direction. Meanwhile, there is considerable evidence that organisations with clear goals dramatically outperform those without them. So the definition of corporate goals is not just an exercise in goal setting, but a practical means by which to boost productivity.

Goals are also critical to the cohesion and commitment of a team. Goals keep people focused, channeling their efforts and, provided they have buy-in, will motivate the team to work much harder than they would do otherwise.

Contrast the sports team that is still in contention for a major title with one that is already out of the running – it will almost always have the edge over the one that is out of the running because of the focus and desire created by the goal. Similarly, within a company, to wholly engage each member of the team it is important to have a common goal and make sure that they believe in it.

Research by Accenture found that businesses that sustain success focus on surpassing themselves, not on beating the competition. In other words, they work in a creative mode, not a reactive one. Also, these companies typically only compare themselves to the best in the industry, not those closest in relation to their size or previous performance. Many companies unknowingly limit their own success by classifying their performance in relation to their size and closest competitors. This is known as the comparison paradox. **By improving enough to beat your closest competitor it is easy to perceive that**

you are making significant gains, when in truth you are making the smallest gain possible while still improving. By choosing to focus on being the best, regardless of size or current position, you allow for the maximum creativity and advancement.

Many companies have attempted to communicate purpose or direction through their mission statements. Unfortunately, though well-meaning, such statements generally have little value in driving behaviours because they are too far removed from the needs of the individual. They lack relevance and must be brought down to the level of the work units so that people can feel a strong association with what they are collectively trying to do. The role of the leader in this process is to make sure that the goal is clearly communicated so that people understand its relevance to them and are inspired to strive for it.

> LEADERSHIP DEVELOPMENT IS FUNDAMENTALLY DIFFERENT TO CAREER PLANNING AND MUST TAKE INTO ACCOUNT THE PURPOSE, VISION, AND GOALS OF THE INDIVIDUAL.

Current personal planning and development processes generally fail to capitalise on this core motivator of people. **Leadership development is fundamentally different to career planning and must take into account the purpose, vision, and goals of the individual.** The development of leadership competencies is unique to every individual; no two leaders have precisely the same set of natural ability, interests, skills, or styles. However, as Zenger and Folkman showed in *The Extraordinary Leader*, this does not imply that anyone is limited. They showed that every leadership competence can be learned and that strength is only required in a few competency areas, provided that these areas are well spread across the spectrum of those required. They also identified that "one of the major failings in leadership development programs has been the tendency to aim too low ... There is no reason to accept mediocrity in leadership any more than in software programming, customer service, or selling."

Focus on Strengths Not Weaknesses

There is nothing more transformational in a company than developing the leadership skills of its employees. To build true leaders it is essential to build on areas of strength for each person, unlike the common approach that seeks to identify "development areas" (i.e., weaknesses). Focusing on weaknesses will always hold the likelihood of being deeply demotivating, once the reasons why people have these weaknesses in the first place is understood.

Weaknesses usually develop in areas in which people don't like to get involved or because they have little natural ability, or both. Either way, to ask them to do more of the very things that they are uncomfortable with cannot be the best way to motivate them and help them to develop. Once they have reached an **adequate** level this is usually seen as mission accomplished.

No one ever became great by aiming for the "middle ground." The motivation to be outstanding comes from encouraging people to do **even better** the things that they like doing and already do well.

A further benefit of building on strengths is that the consequential increase in self-esteem and confidence can positively impact some areas of weakness, even without the conscious awareness in the individual of what is happening. Provided there are no "fatal flaws," which would totally undermine someone's ability to be successful, **developing strengths can be the best way of mitigating weaknesses.**

Recognise the Individual

*There will never be a really free and enlightened State
until the State comes to recognise the individual
as a higher and independent power, from which
all its own power and authority are derived
and treats him accordingly.*

~ Mahatma Gandhi

I recently read an article that made this statement, "In the past I've seen people treat their job like a cat that finds a nice warm cosy place to nap. It may feel great in the short term, but taking a longer view: These individuals will one day find themselves unemployable and on the scrap heap, lacking current skills and with a recent career history of mediocre job performance." I believe that, although some employees undoubtedly adopt this attitude, many organisations are co-conspirators in the perpetuation of the situation, thus highlighting a major opportunity for getting more out of the workforce. I fully agree that every individual should take full responsibility for their own growth and development – that is what the core of this book is about – but this statement places the organisations that they work for in the role of casual observers. There is so much to be gained by taking a far more proactive approach to unlocking the true potential of your people.

> TO TAP INTO THEIR INSPIRATION, EVERYONE MUST HAVE GOALS THAT THEY OWN.

In working with my clients I have found that career planning cycles are very often rote exercises: many people involved in them lack the necessary expertise and also, on occasion, the time or inclination to complete the job well. I have rarely spoken to a leader who has told me that they take individual **wants** into account. This creates no excitement for the people involved. Instead of discovering what will enable their people to feel fulfilled at work, the entire focus is on the needs of the business.

Without tapping into what people want and how to help them get it, leaders and managers are forced to fall back on the transitory and limiting motivation of external motivators, such as salary or a promotion to stimulate performance. In fact, a recent survey of U.K. workers found that only about a third of them place priority on these factors. For the others, satisfaction was more heavily based on aspects such as environment, challenge, colleagues, and development opportunities. Perhaps if there is a lack of understanding of this issue it gives some insight into why another survey found that less than two-thirds of employees are satisfied with their job. The possibility of progression or pay rises is inadequate to stimulate personal growth and development.

When people are coerced rather than inspired they lose touch with their passion and spend the day going through the motions. It is easy to tell when someone is in this category because retirement will be a major goal for them and they will immediately be able to tell you when they hope to achieve it!

To tap into their inspiration, everyone must have goals that they own. These goals give them meaning in their work, and it is the meaning that people attach to what they are doing that shapes their perception. This then underpins their attitude and subsequently determines the quality of their results.

The following well-known but powerful story illustrates the importance of the way the people perceive their work: "One day three stonemasons were asked to describe what they were doing in their work. The first replied that he was building a wall. The second replied that he was earning money to keep his family fed and warm. The third replied that he was building a cathedral that would be enjoyed by generations to come." All three were engaged in the same activity but each had a markedly different perspective on the meaningfulness of their work and as a result, experienced different levels of fulfillment, with the third stonemason benefiting much more than the other two. For an activity to feel meaningful to us it must engage the sense of being involved in something much bigger than ourselves: something that is worthwhile and whose purpose we are caught up in, something that we can own and bring to life. This is almost always where I start when coaching anyone with motivation issues. First we seek to establish a real meaning for the person in going to work.

It is vitally important that corporate employees have a personal motivation for what they are doing. When I left the Royal Air Force and was searching for my next job, I met several people for whom the fact that I had been an officer in the military detracted from their assessment of me. They perceived that I would not have needed to learn how to get people to do things because I could give them orders to get my objectives met. What this missed was that, in terms of motivation, the military is no different from any other organisation: getting the best out of people still requires influence. **Perhaps we did have a greater ability to force someone to do their job but they still had to want to do it if they were to do it well.**

Enhancing performance requires that people learn and change, which is uncomfortable because they must move outside their comfort zone and cross their Terror Barrier. To develop a competency because a personal development plan says that the job requires it is never enough. If people become aware of a gap between the work they are being asked to do and what they personally want, as no one has taken responsibility for aligning the two, they will either become highly despondent or leave.

Occasionally I've had the conversation with a boss that starts with something like, "What if people work out what they want and they end up leaving because they decide they don't want to work for us?" This has never yet happened with someone that I have coached; once people work out what they want, they are generally able to find a way to get it where they are. However, I accept that it is possible, and my view is that in such circumstances I would have provided a service to the company. Why would anyone want to keep people who are not motivated to perform at a high level and whose goals do not align with the company's purpose? This thought process is similar to that of a manager asking the old question, "What happens if I train them and they leave?" to which the most appropriate response is, "What happens if you don't train them and they stay?"

The starting point in getting the best out of others, therefore, is to find out what they want. Once this is known, find a way to align it with what the company needs – if this is not possible then it may be time to accept that they are in the wrong organisation. It is much better to allow a person not committed to the company goals to move on than continue taking up valuable headcount and space. Everyone should know precisely what they need to do for the company to be successful and they should also be excited to do it.

Whenever a company does put in the effort to find out what someone wants and then provides opportunities to get it, huge motivation and commitment is created. Learning is then maximised and the people asset value of the company can increase dramatically.

Focus on the Whole Person

Even with clear goals, development plans can still fail. There are numerous reasons for this, and gaining a good understanding of why we do what we do, for example by studying the ideas around the Stickperson, enables an effective process to be put in place.

One of the most popular methods of facilitating people development is through training courses. The problem is that they really don't deliver on their own; courses rarely create long-term change because they don't address the whole person. Overall, studies have shown that less than 10% of the people who attend training get significant benefit over time. For some participants there may be an immediate improvement due to the external motivation provided by the training. However, because the impact of conditioning is not taken into account, any gain generally disappears within three to six months as participants fall back into the comfort of their old habits and paradigms. As we have clearly seen **knowledge is not power. It is only the application of knowledge that is of value,** and ensuring its effective application requires a different and more comprehensive approach than that which is normally found.

> KNOWLEDGE IS NOT POWER. IT IS ONLY THE APPLICATION OF KNOWLEDGE THAT IS OF VALUE.

The application, on a sustainable basis, of new knowledge from a training course requires changes in the subconscious mind. But, most training courses are aimed at the conscious mind, and although we can sometimes learn by exposure to information on a single occasion, it is very rare. Learning at the level of the subconscious, which is where all enduring change must take place, needs much practice and repetition over time to allow the replacement of ingrained habits and beliefs. No brief course or seminar will achieve this goal. Unless new habits can be installed there will be no sustained performance improvement.

Create a Learning Environment

To get people to reinforce desired behaviours until they become habitual the environment must be supportive. Any fear that they hold will suppress their ability to move to a new paradigm. We have touched on subconscious fears frequently throughout this book, necessarily so because they are such a big factor in what holds people back: fear of rejection, of public speaking, of making a fool of themselves, of growing old, of not having enough, or a multitude of other social factors. We need only examine the enormous range of phobic responses to observe that fear does not have to have any basis in reality either. Like everything else, it is just an interpretation of an event or circumstance.

Fear is the major cause of stress, which is widely acknowledged to be the cause of 80% of disease. Some sources would say that the figure is even higher. The issue is that **it is incredibly easy for any company to create an environment that stimulates fear**. For example, if there is intolerance of mistakes or differences, or if criticism is considered to be acceptable, it will often stimulate this reaction. In Chapter 5, I discussed the enormous significance of whether people consider their environment to be friendly or hostile and how this is clearly measured by the DiSC profiling tool.

> PEOPLE NEED TO BE GIVEN PERMISSION TO TAKE RISKS: IT IS LITERALLY IMPOSSIBLE TO MAKE PROGRESS WITHOUT THEM.

My experience of working with these profiles is that most people in business are operating from a perspective where they expect other people and situations to be antagonistic. These people are likely to be guarded against a range of anticipated risks, and moreover, to lack authenticity. They will also have a tendency toward negative traits such as being judgmental, controlling, or egotistical.

For an organisation to provide an environment that stimulates growth it must recognise that when people do new things mistakes are inevitable. They are a natural and inevitable part of the learning process, essential for any progress to be made. Therefore, people will make a larger number of mistakes the more new things they try. If this is not tolerated and supported, even encouraged, it will not be long before they seek instead to play it safe – to avoid losing what they have rather than try to make things better. Playing it safe directly obstructs creativity and achievement.

People need to be given permission to take risks: it is literally impossible to make progress without them. This does not mean that the company's future should be randomly staked on any new idea but, equally, to attempt to prevent risk must result in stagnation. As Roberto Goizueta said when CEO at Coca Cola Inc., "We become uncompetitive by not being tolerant of mistakes … you can stumble only if you're moving."

This issue is important because so few people are aware of it. I recently saw a great example of how **not** to behave at a large FTSE 100 company, from a senior executive who might have been expected to know better. The results that were being achieved from one of its strategic acquisitions were very poor, and the decision was made to pull out of this business. A letter was sent out to a large group of the leaders of the business directing that such mistakes must be avoided in future. This statement shows naiveté, since it has no validity without the assumptions that the people involved in the decision at the time could somehow have done better and that it is possible to avoid mistakes. We know both of these assumptions to be wrong. If they had known how to do better they would have done so and the avoidance of mistakes is impossible.

If we are moving, no amount of practice, planning, or preparation will allow us to avoid the occasional stumble. Therefore, the inevitable result of attempts to get others to "do better" or instructions to avoid mistakes will create situations where people will begin to play not to lose. The impact will be to cause ideas to be suppressed, ideas that represent the future growth, innovation, and value creation of the company. It is never possible to be certain that anything new will work before it has actually been tried, just as it is impossible to know how you will reach a goal before you actually get there. Life has a habit of putting unexpected challenges in the way and trying is one of the essential steps in the learning process.

Letters such as the one described above will stifle creativity, lower morale, and actually reveal the insecurities of the writer. Critically, they also block the ability of a company to learn the real lessons that would propel it to greater strength in the future because of the implicit tone of blame, which then creates defensiveness.

It is easy to set up a culture of defensiveness. When things go wrong some companies go on a hunt for someone to blame, while others seek to identify the lessons that can be learned, how the failure could be turned into success, or where there may have been successes hidden within the apparent failure. Whenever there is a tendency to look for someone to blame when mistakes are made, it keeps companies looking into the past rather than focusing on making improvements in the future. This behaviour is likely to be so embedded in the culture of the company that it may not even be recognised by the leaders, as was the case in the company from which the example above was taken.

Learning and high performance happens most freely where people feel safe and liked. Well-understood physiological explanations exist as to why we learn less effectively when we are under stress – it is not my intention to cover them here. However, this is an important factor to keep in mind when seeking to establish a learning environment. W. Edwards Deming, founder of the Quality Movement, observed that fear was one of the greatest destroyers of energy, morale, and profit, and that its elimination was one of the greatest spurs to company and organisational success.

Doing anything new always involves an element of discomfort as people move into the area of being consciously incompetent and challenge their Terror Barrier. However, organisations must seek to limit the stress involved. When people are not stressed their mental ability improves: they are better able to solve problems, their attitude toward others creates a more convivial and rewarding environment for everyone, and they have more energy and optimism. As a result, they can be much more effective in their work.

The Collaborative Mindset

It is amazing what you can accomplish if you do not care who gets the credit.

~ Harry S. Truman

Teamwork is always at the heart of high performance. However, it can be a perplexing topic because even though true individual success is virtually unknown – pretty much everyone gets support and help from others – a high level of teamwork is rarely found in today's workplace. This is often especially true at the senior levels of an organisation where there tends to be more ambition. Patrick Lencioni, author of *The Trouble with Teamwork* and *The Five Dysfunctions of a Team*, states, "I have found that only a small minority of companies truly understand and embrace teamwork, even though, according to their Web sites, more than one in three of the *Fortune* 500 publicly declares it to be a core value."

There are many models available that describe the development stages of teams but the one that I have found the most useful, because of its beautiful simplicity and clarity in expressing some of the limitations created by internal competition, comes from the excellent book, *Coaching for Performance*, by Sir John Whitmore, one of the pioneers of the coaching industry. The model is shown in Figure 9.1, which also captures its relationship with Bruce Tuckman's well-known forming-storming-norming-performing model to aid understanding.

Figure 9.1 – Levels of Team Development

Team Development Stage		Characteristics
COOPERATION (performing)	Interdependent	Energy directed outward to common goals / Highly cooperative by retaining dynamic tension
(norming)		
ASSERTION (storming)	Independent	Energy focused on internal competition / Exceptional individual performances, maybe at expense of others
INCLUSION (forming)	Dependent	Energy turned inward within team members / Need for acceptance and fear of rejection are strong

Level 1, **Inclusion**, occurs when a team is created or for an individual, when they join an established team. At this stage, people will typically feel somewhat isolated, and there is a strong drive to be accepted by the other team members. Very often they will compromise their own ideals, including conforming with others or behaving in ways that may not be natural for them, in order to meet their emotional needs. At this level, if an individual on the team is successful, it is likely that other members of the team will feel threatened. Because of these strong emotional drivers, people cannot perform at their best.

A team will move into Level 2, **Assertion**, once the majority of its members feel included. The hierarchy of the team becomes established and the principle driving force is internal competition as people seek to get to the top. Although the team lacks cohesion, people's desire to prove themselves can lead to high productivity from some of the members, albeit often at the expense of others. There are likely to be considerable challenges to the leadership, and individual successes are likely to be received with some jealousy by the rest of the team. Conversely, individual failures will be secretly welcomed, even celebrated. Because of the possibility for exceptional individual performances at this stage, one of the challenges associated with it may be to recognise the greater potential that exists.

Finally, a team may move to Level 3, **Cooperation**. This is when real creativity becomes possible. Once here members will be highly supportive of each other and will truly welcome each other's successes. There will be a high level of enthusiasm, commitment, and motivation toward external goals, and because of the supportive and trusting nature of the environment, people are free to be at their most creative. At the same time, to avoid becoming overly comfortable, dynamic tension will be retained by allowing for dissent.

From a lower level of awareness this dynamic tension may be recognised as confrontation, which most people dislike and seek to avoid. However, in a strong team confrontation is to be encouraged, provided that positive norms are established around the way that it is done. This is how the value contributions and diverse opinions of the group will often surface. It only undermines the high-level functioning of the team when it is done as an attack on

> BECOME CURIOUS, NOT CRITICAL OF CONFRONTATION, SO THAT UNDERSTANDING MAY BE GAINED AS TO ITS ROOT CAUSE.

the person. If someone makes a suggestion that is not agreed with, any rejection of it must not be directed at the individual. This doesn't just affect the person whose idea it was, but also dissuades other members from speaking up with their own contributions. It may close them down from further participation.

This is not to say you shouldn't give individual feedback. When we don't give feedback we do people a disservice; feedback provides critical information that is needed as part of the learning process. It is our responsibility to ensure that it is handled in a constructive manner so that people's self-image is enhanced, not damaged, by it.

The more common response to confrontation is defensiveness, which never produces good results. I believe that if confrontation does arise the most effective approach is to **become curious, not critical of it, so that understanding may be gained as to its root cause**. Curiosity stimulates questions to be asked that enhance understanding and lead to higher awareness. Since results are an expression of awareness, for individuals or teams, then curiosity becomes an enabler to higher performance.

High-quality leadership and well-developed group emotional intelligence is required for confrontation to occur while ensuring the ongoing harmony of the team. The development of a coaching approach, using questions in a nonjudgmental style, is highly effective for this kind of interaction. The team will then be able to unlock the power of collective decision making, which will be much greater than that of even a very bright individual.

Unless teams are able to reach the cooperative stage, allowing creativity to be unleashed, much of their energy will be wasted internally. It is impossible to imagine a sports team doing well with this approach. In every high-performing sports team the members know exactly what their job is and they do it, even if it is not the most glamorous or highest profile role. Great individual performances mean little if the team does not win and may even be considered to be negative. Everyone needs to be aligned behind the success of the team.

> EVERYONE GAINS FROM HIGHER LEVELS OF COLLABORATION.

Because genuine cooperation is very unusual in business, very few teams get above Level 2, which drains their energy and limits their success. In work, it seems much more difficult for people to appreciate and accept that if they put the team first they will all benefit in the long run. Perhaps this is partly because we were conditioned at school to believe that collaboration was bad – there it was called cheating! As a result there is internal competition, which shows up as people wanting to be seen to have the best ideas, produce the best results, be smarter than everyone else, etc. This always detracts focus from the efforts of the company to become stronger and therefore impacts performance in the marketplace.

In this context business is just like sport: **everyone gains from higher levels of collaboration**. To reach the top, members of teams must develop a great attitude in relation to each other and their objectives.

There are many teams full of talented individuals that never amount to much. Like an orchestra that has no role for any player, irrespective of individual ability, who is unable to coordinate with the other musicians, businesses would benefit from adopting a similar attitude. Rewards need to be restructured such that each member can clearly see how putting the team first will maximise their own success.

The more talented the team members, the more difficult this may be to achieve because they will often believe that they can succeed best by competing – they expect to be able to win anyway. This is a defining characteristic of the "D's" in the DiSC model described in Chapter 5, which is the primary style of most of the leaders that I have worked with. Talented individuals, therefore, are more likely to feel that they would lose out if everyone else were to perform better.

Under the constraints that many businesses have to work with, this fear may often have some validity. Perhaps the biggest issue arises because the rewards process has, in effect, become one of dividing up a fixed-size pie, whether this is in relation to salaries, bonuses, or even the identification of high-potential employees. It is normal, in such cases, that the allocation of rewards is very much a comparative process that considers the relative performance of the individuals in relation to each other. Then, for the stars to be rewarded more highly,

> AS LONG AS FEELINGS OF SCARCITY ARE ALLOWED TO PERPETUATE, COMPETITION WILL PERSIST AND THE ACHIEVEMENT OF HIGHER LEVELS OF PERFORMANCE WILL REMAIN ELUSIVE.

other members must receive less. Because of this, the scarcity mentality that most people are conditioned with from birth becomes embedded in the company, and a strong win/lose culture is unavoidable. This inevitably leads to those affected remaining at Level 2, constrained to a competitive approach that limits the creativity of the team.

Similar motivators are also likely to be at play between different groups within your organisation. Whenever people perceive that they are competing for finite resources, with their results being determined by the outcome, the environment may become very competitive with a strong "us versus them" mentality and a lack of consideration for the needs of the whole.

Ultimately, selfishness wrecks teams of all descriptions, and people become selfish when they are fearful. To enable others to reach the cooperative level, all of the factors previously discussed in this chapter need to be in place: no blame, understanding of and tolerance of risk, flexibility, goals orientation, and attention to the individual. In addition, processes must be implemented that will overcome the scarcity mentality and provide rewards based on contribution to results rather than comparison. **As long as feelings of scarcity are allowed to perpetuate, competition will persist, and the achievement of higher levels of performance will remain elusive.** Overcoming this limitation is, I believe, one of the greatest opportunities for growth available to modern-day corporate leaders.

Traits of High-Performing Teams

The traits necessary to maximise the success of a team can only be encouraged and developed in the kind of supportive environment described so far in this chapter, where people feel valued and confident to try new things.

We have already discussed the importance of flexibility, goals, valuing the individual, and collaboration. Other important traits are covered now.

Play to Win

Just like any individual's approach, the team must play to win rather than seek to avoid losing. Many people are able to adopt this approach when things are going well; the challenge is whether they can maintain it when times are tough. Playing to win requires a high level of emotional awareness and self-leadership to be able to respond rather than react. The ability to change is also essential.

Teams will require much practice and encouragement to overcome existing beliefs and paradigms. These habits are not erased by a short seminar that only works at the level of the conscious mind. The culture and norms need to be changed, which will require hands-on, direct attention from the leadership and the acceptance of mistakes, as employees learn to behave in new ways and to move from a competitive to creative mindset.

Never Less Than 100%

It is often said, and it has been covered in this book already, that failure is not the falling down but the failure to get up again. As such, **failure is a decision**. One of the main characteristics of top teams is that they never give up. Neither do they lose their focus or reduce their efforts when things are going well. They simply change their strategy as often as necessary to ensure that they remain on track and avoid getting stuck down blind alleys, recovering rapidly from any bad results.

One team that epitomises these characteristics is Manchester United Football Club. Take, for example, its win against Roma in the Champions League in the 2006-2007 season. With five minutes to go, even though they were 7-1 up, Sir Alex Ferguson, the manager, was still on the touchline shouting instructions. No one was permitted to relax.

Their win in the Champions League in 1999 against Bayern Munich provides an even better example of the never-say-die attitude that is common to most extraordinary achievements. At 1-0 down and with only injury time remaining, having been outplayed for most of the first 90 minutes, the players never allowed themselves to become disheartened. They knew that three minutes of play still remained and that until the whistle blew, one moment of creative genius could change everything. Of course, every team knows this intellectually but it is easy to spot the ones that truly **believe** it from their behaviours in such situations. When Manchester United scored to level the match with two minutes remaining, the Bayern Munich players looked as though they had already lost. Within the next two minutes they did, as United scored again almost immediately. Bayern Munich may have won the first 90 minutes, but United won the last three. No one on that team ever gave up.

Faith in Each Other

Team members must have genuine trust in one another if they are to function effectively as a whole. The spirit that is necessary is one of interdependence. Any member should be able to suggest that another member of the team take on a task because they would be better at it, without feeling that they would be viewed less positively as a result.

The penalty kick in rugby is always given to the person who is likely to do the best job of it based on their strengths and the degree to which they are currently "in form." The leader must make sure that the best person for the job is positioned to it and get egos out of the way. For example, this could mean allowing a member of their team to lead for a particular assignment rather than doing it themselves. This type of "kinetic leadership" allows the different strengths of all of the team members to be fully utilised. Trust, then, creates the interdependence that is a primary feature of a Level 3, cooperative, team.

Teams become trusting most easily when they bond at the personal level. The military provides us with some of the most outstanding examples of this. In situations where people are asked to risk their lives, it is often the commitment to the people in their unit that motivates the greatest sacrifices, not the task or the greater battle. **For teams to be really successful, teammates need to know that they will look out for one another.**

People can be equipped to work effectively together by making sure that there is a high level of mutual understanding. Awareness of self and others is not just for the team leader: everyone needs this so that they can perform well together. They need to understand why people do what they do and have the ability not to judge and criticise others just because they have different methods. Each member of the team needs to be made aware of the

> FOR TEAMS TO BE REALLY SUCCESSFUL, TEAMMATES NEED TO KNOW THAT THEY WILL LOOK OUT FOR ONE ANOTHER.

influences that affect not only their own behaviour but also the behaviour of those around them, so creating the understanding and empathy that is the foundation of trust and openness.

Value Contributions

Possibly the greatest inventor of all time, Thomas Edison, knew the secret of success – you don't do it all by yourself. He relied upon a vast team of people to make things happen for him. Having communicated his vision he then had to trust that others would do their job.

Every person's role contributes to the bigger picture. Captain Charles Plum was a graduate from the U.S. Naval Academy whose plane was shot down after 74 successful combat missions over North Vietnam. He parachuted to safety but was captured, tortured, and spent 2,103 days in a small box-like cell.

After surviving the ordeal, Captain Plumb returned to America and received the Silver Star, Bronze Star, the Legion of Merit, and two Purple Hearts. However, **he never lost his humility or stopped valuing others**.

Shortly after coming home, Charlie and his wife were sitting in a restaurant. A man got up from a nearby table, walked over and said, "You're Plumb! You flew jet fighters in Vietnam from the aircraft carrier *Kitty Hawk*. You were shot down!" Surprised that he was recognised, Charlie responded, "How in the world did you know that?" The man replied, "I packed your parachute." Charlie looked up with surprise. The man pumped his hand, gave a thumbs-up, and said, "I guess it worked!" Charlie stood to shake the man's hand and assured him, "It most certainly did work. If it had not worked, I would not be here today."

> WITHIN A TEAM THERE WILL ALWAYS BE PEOPLE WHO ARE "PACKING THE PARACHUTES."

Charlie could not sleep that night, thinking about the man. He wondered if he might have seen him and not even said, "Good morning, how are you?" He thought of the many hours the sailor had spent bending over a long wooden table in the bottom of the ship, carefully packing parachutes, each time holding in his hand the fate of someone he didn't know.

Within a team there will always be people who are "packing the parachutes." The task may be small but it is still a vital part of the whole. To encourage the personal sacrifice necessary for the team to perform at its best, all contributions must be encouraged and rewarded by the team leader and other members of the team. Over time this increases the level of identification with the team.

Another aspect of recognising contributions is to value diversity. This means respecting others who are different: that is how better ideas will be created. If you look out over a field of grain, it is expansive but can only produce one commodity. If you look at a garden, it will usually contain plants of many different types with different characteristics. They work together in great harmony and produce a much more varied and interesting area than the field with its one plant. Similarly, to sing in harmony does not mean singing in unison, but that the effort of each person complements the efforts of the others rather than conflicting with them.

So it is with diversity in a team. It is very natural that we should find the ideas of people who are similar to ourselves the most acceptable because such ideas will be in harmony with our own paradigms. We see this reflected in the fact that most people recruit and support people like themselves, thus tending to reduce diversity.

Where diversity is not valued, those that do not "fit in" will tend to leave. Most people value esteem from others and don't like going where they are not liked. They also know that if they are marginalised it makes it more difficult for them to deliver what is expected of them. If a company has an environment that doesn't accept and encourage the differences in individuals, it will create a very homogeneous workforce of like-minded individuals. **With this loss of diversity the flow of new ideas, vital to the future development of the company, will also diminish.**

Building the Team Requires Effort

You don't do the right things once in a while; you do the right things all the time. Winning is a habit. So is losing.

~ Vince Lombardi

There is overpowering evidence that, for those prepared to put in the effort to build an effective team environment, "we"-thinking creates the ultimate results. However, as many of those who have tried know, this is easy to understand but may be very hard to do in practice. Few people have been conditioned to operate in this way; therefore, to achieve change does take time and ongoing attention. The collective unconscious of the company, in the form of its culture and norms, needs to be shifted.

THE ONLY WAY TO ACHIEVE CODEPENDENCE AND COOPERATION IN A TEAM IS FOR THE LEADER TO BE FULLY CONGRUENT IN WORDS AND ACTIONS, DEMONSTRATING TEAMWORK FROM THE TOP DOWN.

In the most demanding team challenges, such as the extreme sport of adventure racing, "we"-thinking leads to an attitude of "we all finish together or no one finishes." Internal competition within the team is completely removed and everyone accepts responsibility for success and failure as a team. The motivation to achieve this level is simple: they cannot be successful in any other way.

For many, this is not a realistic expectation in business, probably because they have an intuitive understanding of the difficulty of taming individual egos on the team. Unless cooperation is essential to even remain in the game, it may seem unlikely that competitiveness in the team can be tamed.

Before you decide what you feel to be possible, I recommend that you consider this: whatever goal you choose, you are unlikely to exceed it. Why not aim high and seek the best? If you remember the metaphor that I used earlier in the book, it is only through the contemplation of the laws of flotation that anyone was able to work out how to build ships out of steel. Similarly, it is only by repeatedly asking yourself how your team could reach the highest level that you open up the possibility of finding an answer.

The achievement of codependence and cooperation in a team is an outcome of true leadership. **The only way to make it happen is for the leader to be fully congruent in words and actions, demonstrating teamwork from the top down.** The Level 5 Leaders described by Jim Collins knew this, as evidenced by their humility and unwillingness to take the credit for team successes. The resultant team performance in these circumstances will always be much greater than the sum of what the individual alone could have achieved.

Transformational Technique: Cultural Evolution

No organisation can be successful unless it has developed the ability to learn. This requires cultural issues to be addressed, not simply the development and implementation of training programmes, and is one of the most challenging aspects of leadership. The impact of culture and norms is to maintain the status quo, luring companies into developing overly rigid processes and procedures that limit their ability to respond effectively as their market changes.

To fully mobilise the workforce requires a set of corporate and team goals that are aligned and within which each individual has a clear role. Specific focus is required to ensure that everyone has objectives that align with their personal aspirations and to which they feel committed.

Once everyone knows how they can contribute to maximise performance, teamwork must be addressed. The goal is to reach a level of cooperation and collaboration that avoids the wasted energy of internal competition, and instead creates synergy among the members of the team. This must be led from the top; reward structures must be aligned with the new behaviours that are sought, and a climate must be fostered that simulates creativity, is tolerant of mistakes, and in which everyone feels that they are valued. The overall effectiveness of the team will be limited to the degree that any of these elements is not achieved.

MASTER OF YOUR DESTINY

The future depends on what we do today.

~ Mahatma Gandhi

Unlock Your True Potential

The business environment is changing so quickly that yesterday's methods rapidly lose relevance. As established managerial approaches become less effective we have to respond, but in the effort to stay ahead, it is unlikely that incremental changes will be adequate – a transformational response is required.

My intention in writing this book has been to help you and, if appropriate, your business to make the shift necessary to be successful. I hope that you will be able to make a non-linear leap in performance, not by working harder or making minor adjustments to the way that you have done things before, but by working on transforming yourself so that all of your interactions with the world become more effective and more profound.

I am firmly convinced that every person, at some level, desires success and the feeling of fulfillment that comes from making a positive impact in the world and from growing internally. This is a natural characteristic of the human condition. Furthermore, the evidence is overwhelming that we all have a startling ability to do so, once we allow ourselves to believe in our potential. The foremost brain research in the world today has demonstrated that it is impossible even to identify a definable limit to our potential.

ALMOST EVERY ONE OF US IS BORN WITH GENIUS CAPABILITIES.

For many, perhaps most people, the immediate reaction to this statement is to challenge it, possibly even to dismiss it. I urge you not to do so: as we have seen, your beliefs will determine what you are capable of doing. Before you reject the idea let's look at some of the evidence.

The limiting factor that determines the number of thoughts, memories, behaviour patterns, and habits that you are capable of is thought to be the number of patterns of connections that the brain can create. I referred to the research of Professor Anokhin in Chapter 4. He dedicated much effort to understanding this capacity and, after several years work, concluded that the number of patterns that the brain is capable of, if typed out, would be a one followed by 10½ million *kilometres* of zeros. What this means is that in practical terms, **there is no limit to the number of possible thoughts that we can think**. The capability of the brain is inexhaustible and no one, not even the greatest genius, has come close to fully utilising its potential.

Another way to express this concept is that there is nothing that anyone has ever thought of, or ever will think, that we, too, do not have the capability to think. We have the ability to tap into thoughts, which can then be organised into ideas, formulated into plans, and executed in actions to address any area of our life that we choose to focus on. If we are stuck, in any area, it must point to the fact that we are stuck in our thinking. We must seek new ways of doing things. As Einstein himself said, "It's not that I'm so smart, it's just that I stay with problems longer."

Another study of the brain by Harvard University reached the exciting conclusion that **almost every one of us is born with genius capabilities**. The research evaluated the presence of "the genius mind" in various age groups by assessing the degree to which they used multiple modalities (visual, auditory, kinaesthetic, intuitive, etc.) in their interaction with the world: a measurable characteristic of genius that can be used to evaluate young children. The researchers found that 99.9% of babies operate at genius level. By the time we are five, that figure has dropped to 20% and at age 20, only 2% of us are still able to tap into the innate genius capability that we were born with.

The most fascinating and valuable aspect of this study is the team's conclusion about the cause of this dramatic decline in our ability to access the power of our mind. It concluded that **the cause is "the learned voice of internal judgment."** In other words, although it may have been initiated by the conditioning that we received from others as a child, **the destruction of our ability to access our true potential is ultimately our own doing**. This is probably what Earl Nightingale, one of the pioneers of the

YOU ARE YOUR MOST IMPORTANT CRITIC.

personal development industry, was referring to when he said, "Many people of real ability do small things all of their lives because they are the victims of discouraging self-suggestion."

What this means is that **you are your most important critic.** I believe that this represents a huge opportunity, because **anything that you created, you must also have the ability to undo, which means that the genius that you were born with can be reclaimed.** To do so, you must become aware of the silent conversations that you have with yourself – they are much more important than most people realise and have a huge impact on what you are capable of achieving. We all talk to ourselves in virtually every waking moment of our lives and are seldom aware that we are doing it. The question is, are you nurturing of your dreams and ideas? Do you forgive your failures and disappointments or do you tend to be very critical of yourself? Perhaps it is worth asking yourself, if someone else was to talk to you the way that you talk to yourself, how much time you would want to spend with them? This will give you a clear indication of the degree to which you need to improve the management of your internal dialogue.

Personal Change Is Both Possible and Necessary

One of the characteristics of successful people is their ability to focus on what they want irrespective of what is happening in their external world. We need to be able to interrupt negative patterns of self-talk to create space in the mind to begin to think differently, and recognise that what we have achieved so far in our lives reflects only our thinking to date. It bears no relationship to our potential. We must learn to take advantage of the inexhaustible power of our brains to support creative thought: this is the starting point for all human progress.

Success originates from within, from our conditioning in the form of millions of habits and beliefs in the subconscious mind, and is not dependent upon anything external to ourselves. **This conditioning is at the core of our identity and determines our destiny** because no one can create results that are inconsistent with their identity or self-image. Our starting point in achieving better results, therefore, is to alter the identity that we have created for ourselves, thereby changing our actions. It is not possible to lead others effectively until you have made the decision to take responsibility for your own behaviours.

One aspect of conventional wisdom that I have heard many times states that our basic character, our identity, is formed by the time we are 7 or 8 years old. This is summed up by the old adage, "you can't teach an old dog new tricks," the implication being that, even if there are times when we don't like how we show up, we must learn to live with it. Though ridiculous, this statement will still program the subconscious minds of those who don't know that they have the ability to reject it. Many times people have given me their opinion about what I would be capable of in the future based on their perception of what I did in my past, because they have subconsciously aligned themselves with this belief. However, the evidence is conclusive that this belief is completely fallacious.

If you do not believe in the possibility that you can change then you have, probably without realising it, also accepted the belief that you are already all that you are going to be. I've never spoken to anyone who wants to be stuck where they are, and few will argue for any length of time that they have to accept that they will remain at their current level for the rest of their lives. The question, then, becomes purely one of establishing the means by which change can be realised and how quickly this can be done.

For many, meaningful growth only happens when their environment becomes so uncomfortable that they start to really apply their thinking to how to do things differently – they really change only out of desperation. Most of the time their progress is severely limited because they are seeking security within their comfort zone. They do not readily take on new challenges, but instead run their lives looking for quick and easy fixes to solve the current problems that they are facing. Their fear of failure dominates everything and therefore they only set goals that they are certain they can reach.

TOTAL SECURITY IS, IN FACT, AN IMPOSSIBLE GOAL.

Rarely will anyone with this mindset advance very far because they find it so difficult to change their conditioning. As soon as things get tough, they fall back on their old habits; consequently their results cannot improve and may, if the environment changes further, become even worse. As Vince Lombardi, the enormously successful American football coach, said, "Winning is a habit. Unfortunately, so is losing." Such people have sacrificed the prospect of real advancement in an attempt to hold onto the status quo. They have not realised that security cannot be realised in the comfort zone.

The desire to stay with the familiar is so powerful that many people don't make changes even when they can see that to do so would create a clear opportunity to improve their results. Investigation reveals that the source of this problem is that we hold onto old ideas and old things wherever we lack faith in our ability to obtain new ideas and new things. Therefore, by seeking security and hanging on to what we know, we are really expressing a lack of self-confidence. What we experience through this approach is the opposite of our desired outcome – our feelings of insecurity actually increase. **Total security is, in fact, an impossible goal.**

Sadly, people who live life avoiding change pay the highest price because they can never attain true fulfillment. We must be prepared, when necessary, to do the things that are very difficult for us. Just as fish swim against the current as well as with it – only dead fish go with the flow all the time – so I believe it is for us. **Going with the flow is not a strategy for success in life because a successful life will never be one without problems.** To change ourselves is one of the most difficult things that we can undertake, but those that fail to take on the challenge do not realise that in failing to fully live life, they also unwittingly sacrifice their opportunity for happiness. I really like the *Parable of the Cautious Man* as a summary of this idea:

There was a very cautious man

who never laughed or cried.

He never risked, he never lost,

he never won nor tried.

And when he one day passed away,

his insurance was denied,

For since he never really lived,

they claimed he never died.

The path to greatness is to seek personal advancement, doing so proactively in good as well as difficult times, and to develop a preparedness to constantly step through the Terror Barrier and live outside the comfort zone. That means being prepared to take risks. If you want extraordinary results you have no alternative. Your ability to develop your capacity to lead others effectively is dependent on your willingness to risk making mistakes by trying new things. Ironically, as you do so you will develop the security that so many people fail to achieve through their intuitive but flawed approach of seeking it.

A study by leadership experts Warren Bennis and Burt Nanus, looking at 90 top leaders from a variety of fields, reached the following conclusion on the relationship between personal growth and leadership:

> LEARNING HOW TO GET THE BEST OUT OF OTHER PEOPLE IS THE BEST WAY TO GAIN AN ADVANTAGE BECAUSE NOTHING OF VALUE GETS DONE ALONE.

"It is the capacity to develop and improve their skills that distinguishes leaders from among their followers." As a leader you must continue to invest in your personal development if you are to stay ahead. I've said it several times in this book, but this merits repeating: **growing your leadership capability is a process of sequential growth from the inside out**. This means that you must start with your beliefs, values, and habits, not your externally visible behaviours. Attempting to change results by focusing on behaviours will produce short-lived and superficial results, at best.

You can only reach your potential tomorrow by dedicating yourself to growth today. The more effort you are prepared to put into this area, getting expert help if necessary, the greater your ability to realise your potential will be. Gandhi advised us to "Be the change we wish to see in the world," and Goethe similarly stated, "Before you can do something you first must be something." It is excellent advice to always remember that before you can change the world, you must first change yourself. Once you have changed your path you then have the **choice** to help others. As Stephen Covey says in *The 8th Habit*, "Those who teach what they are learning are, by far, the greatest students."

Leadership Is NOT a Position

When I do good, I feel good; when I do bad, I feel bad, and that is my religion.

~ Abraham Lincoln

The highest performers never wait for their conditions to change before they go to work on themselves. They seek to draw out their own excellence, even when surrounded by mediocre people and in the full knowledge that mediocrity attacks excellence. **Everyone can consciously decide to pursue excellence.** It does not matter what stage of your life you are at or what you have done in the past; you will create new results in the future when you change your thinking. This is **personal leadership**.

As you take responsibility for leading yourself effectively, your ability to influence others will automatically be enhanced – and **learning how to get the best out of other people is the best way to gain an advantage because nothing of value gets done alone.** This is the way of great leaders. They go beyond what is expected, setting the pace and looking for ways to empower not only themselves but also those around them. Irrespective of how great your visionary skills as a leader may be, there is no other source of advantage that has the ability to transform performance to the same degree.

As the knowledge economy gains further strength, the growing importance of trust and influence over power and structure will continue. Consequently, although leadership has never been a function of title or position, those that have relied upon position power to get things done will be increasingly disenfranchised and become even less effective. The style of leadership that will replace this approach requires an entirely different mindset. It will combine the determination to be the best that you can be with an attitude of service. Irrespective of the environment, people can have a huge impact as leaders when they seek to give more then they receive.

Such leadership cannot be awarded or dictated. As noted, Mahatma Gandhi did not have any of the recognised hallmarks of power. Yet he exercised true leadership through his power to influence. He demonstrated that **real power is never about overpowering others but is instead the act of acknowledging and encouraging their power**. He showed that authentic leadership is not about having followers or how many people that served him. Instead, he was a living example of why **a much better measure is the number of people a leader chooses to serve and how many other leaders he creates**. Nothing Gandhi did was about personal gain. He epitomised servant leadership and through this approach achieved freedom for 300 million people.

Servant leaders give willingly, precisely because they have the awareness that they have something to give. Their focus, as described by Jim Collins in *Good to Great*, is on achievement rather than recognition. If you adopt any other approach it will limit your ability to create outstanding results.

Building Your Leadership Skills

The world beyond will not belong to "managers" or
those who can make the numbers dance. The world will
belong to passionate, driven leaders – people who will
not only have enormous amounts of energy but who
can energize those whom they lead.

~ Jack Welch

The kind of service-oriented leadership described above is available to everyone when they choose to serve the greater good. Benjamin Disraeli, the 19th-century British Prime Minister, advised, "The greatest good we can do for others is not to share our riches with them, but to reveal to them their own." The starting point in developing extraordinary leadership is to believe in others and help them to grow.

Whatever we may say about believing in others, our true beliefs will always show up in both subtle and very visible ways. On the subtle side, extensive research with people and animals has shown that our genuine expectations will be communicated in all of our interactions via the Pygmalion effect, or self-fulfilling prophecy, that was described in Chapter 5. More obviously, where managers seek to control others (I can't use the term leader here) by imposing order on the activity in the business through rules, dictates, and policies, they really display a lack of belief in either themselves or others, or most likely both. Such a person must know what everyone is doing and attempt to control results by managing at the conscious, visible level. The outcome of this approach is to destroy the vitality and creativity of the people.

There is no doubt that a critical element of leadership in business is the ability to understand strategic perspectives: to see the big picture then create the vision and direction for the business. Meanwhile, the human element of the job often receives much less attention. However, there is little value to be gained from discovering where you want to go if you don't spend the time developing the skills necessary to influence other people to enable you to get there.

Dale Carnegie, the interpersonal skills expert and author of the best-selling book, *How to Win Friends and Influence People*, put it this way, "When dealing with people, remember you are not dealing with creatures of logic but creatures of emotion." No one was ever inspired by logic – to tap deeply into the motivation required to produce outstanding results it is essential to activate the emotions. For this, influencing skills are essential.

> IF YOU WANT LEARNING TO HAVE AN ONGOING IMPACT, IT MUST BE REGULARLY REINFORCED UNTIL IT HAS HAD TIME TO BECOME EMBEDDED IN THE SUBCONSCIOUS.

This is one reason why it is so important for leaders to develop excellent coaching skills: there is no more effective way to increase influence and assist others in reaching their potential. By helping to create other leaders you extend your influence through them to all of the other people that they touch. Through the process of helping other people to get what they want you will automatically benefit. This is an area where most people can develop very quickly with some additional effort.

Unfortunately, most people treat leadership rather like learning to read. They get to an adequate level, of say 250 words per minute, and then read the same way for the rest of their lives, despite the fact that it is well known that it is possible to read tens, or even hundreds of times faster. When people get their first promotion into a leadership position they may spend quite a bit of effort watching leaders around them and learning from them or attending courses, but then the requirements of their day-to-day tasks take over, and they tend to lose their focus. They are in their comfort zone, and the urgency of current challenges seems more pressing and important than continued growth. Even when they do attend training courses, the lack of spaced repetition over a significant period of time to enable deep learning to take place limits their ability to achieve sustained behavioural change. **If you want learning to have an ongoing impact, it must be regularly reinforced until it has had time to become embedded in the subconscious.**

The exciting evidence of experience is that everyone can go to a new level of performance because **every leadership competency can be learned**. The key question is not whether you can do it but how good you want to be. Because so few people really focus on developing their skills there is an excellent opportunity for those that do. In their book, *The Extraordinary Leader*, Zenger and Folkman describe how elevating yourself into the top 10% may be much easier than you would expect if you focus on what you are already good at and then seek to improve it. It requires above-average strength in only a few attributes to achieve a high probability of being seen as a great leader.

Solomon said, "In all our getting, we should get understanding." Because of the importance of this process, experts in every field have a coach to encourage them to take on new approaches, to help them to raise awareness, and to hold them accountable for their actions. Their influence alone inspires maximum effort. Leadership is no different.

Coaches can massively accelerate learning and provide essential feedback when others are reluctant to comment on their leader's performance. People who excel find ways to make their development an ongoing process, even eliciting the help of others to speed it up.

The next stage is to put learning into practice. As we discussed in detail earlier in this book, everyone already knows how to do a better job than they are currently doing. However, one's level of achievement and rewards will never be determined by what one knows. Sustainable reward is always based upon results, and these will only change when people change the way that they behave. Therefore, a different mechanism for implementing learning in the workplace is required that puts the emphasis onto the **effective application** of skills and knowledge.

Purpose-Led Learning

A feature of greatness is the presence of a clear purpose underlying and motivating all activity. Ghandi's power to influence a nation drew upon a single purpose that inspired people to cooperate to an extraordinary degree. World-class leaders create a purpose-led learning environment for themselves and others, connecting everyone to a mission that goes well beyond the immediate requirements of their job.

Purpose, vision, and goals were described in detail in Chapter 6. Whenever we attempt to do anything, the single factor that will have the greatest impact on how we will respond to the inevitable setbacks that we will face is **why** we are doing it. For example, someone trying to raise a large amount of money quickly would almost certainly have much more determination to be successful if it was to pay for a vital operation for their children than if they just fancied an expensive holiday. **Our purpose provides our "why" in the context of our whole life.**

A clear purpose is vital in removing the confusion that many people experience when faced with tough decisions relating to their life, such as choosing their goals or making career moves. Vision and goals provide the vehicles through which the purpose can be fulfilled. Without purpose you are unlikely to experience the feeling of effortless fulfillment or to enjoy the true zest of life.

The powerful desire to succeed that comes from having a defined purpose ignites the critical element of our character called persistence. Napoleon Hill studied many of the world's most successful people in researching his classic book, *Think and Grow Rich!* He identified persistence as the only quality that was present in these people that he could not find in everyone else; he felt so strongly about the subject that he devoted an entire chapter to it.

Persistence fulfills a vital role in everyone's success and for this reason, must be ignited by the organisations that they work for. To make this a reality, organisations need a clear purpose that will engage their employees at the emotional level – not a mission statement, which is unlikely to impact below the conscious level. The motivation for people to do their very best always comes from inside. This is why the majority of motivational speakers and trainers have such a short-lived impact – they do not create a sustained change to the way that people think.

No one ever became successful in any aspect of their life because of what they knew. **Success is about what you do with what you know.** As Napoleon Hill said, "Knowledge is not power; knowledge is only potential power. It only becomes powerful once it is organised and intelligently directed, through practical plans of action, towards a definite purpose." It is in this way that a speaker who truly inspires people will help them to tap into their own inherent capabilities to be able to use more of what they know.

Tuning into a clear purpose gives people the inner motivation necessary for them to be able to prioritise and give of their best. Stretch goals, within the context of a clear vision, help people and companies to outperform the competition. **Nothing can replace clarity of purpose for giving direction.**

If we consider the most successful businesses, we find that they sustain success by focusing on surpassing themselves, with a clear purpose being at the heart of what they do. Any meaningful purpose will always be altruistic at its core, based on the service that will be delivered rather than what other companies may be doing. As with Tiger Woods, who will rework and improve upon his golf swing even though he is already the best in the world, businesses that focus on surpassing themselves are rewarded with sustained improvement. These companies have moved out of the competitive plane and are focused on moving ahead through creativity.

A company is reliant on its people, and its results are a measure of the sum total of the contribution of its people. Therefore, if a company wants to improve its results, it requires a supportive environment in which individuals can learn to do new things and the synergy of the team can be released.

Synergy refers to the energy created when different elements in a system work together so that their combined performance is greater than the sum of the individual elements. Its benefits are well recognised. Many years ago it was noticed that two horses together can pull far more than two horses working as individuals, and this magnifying effect continues as numbers increase. Whereas two horses can pull 9,000 pounds, four horses can pull 30,000 pounds – far more than the arithmetically-derived expectation of 18,000 pounds. Similarly, geese flying in formation can fly almost twice as far as any bird flying alone.

Synergy can also be generated between people in teams and among business units; one of the most powerful factors in doing so is delivered by the motivation of a shared purpose. Whether at the individual level or the level of the team, a well-defined and communicated purpose is one of the bedrocks of success.

IQ versus I CAN

I mentioned earlier in this chapter the detrimental impact of our critical inner voice that has been found to be responsible for our loss of ability to access our natural genius. Denis Waitley, the high-performance coach and best-selling author, advises, "It is not what you are that holds you back, but what you think you are not." Negative beliefs about ourselves are numerous and varied but they all come down to one problem: **we have been conditioned to believe in personal limitation**. This creates a resistance to taking action and a desire to hang on to the comfort zone.

Compounding this issue is the fact that most people also believe in a limitation of external resources. This is visible in the competitive approach that they have accepted as the most effective strategy in life. Generally, such beliefs were picked up in childhood by watching how others behaved. Competition does create some individual successes, yet it will never bring out the best from, or

> WHEN IT COMES TO ATTAINING SUCCESS, AN ATTITUDE OF "I CAN" WILL OUTWEIGH FACTORS RELATING TO IQ EVERY TIME.

unlock the synergy in, a group. Neither will it maximise the capability of an individual in any environment in which success depends upon the use of the mind. To understand what it takes to achieve the highest levels of success we must study those who have achieved it.

Successful people almost always focus on their personal development by setting demanding personal goals and challenging themselves to grow. The focus of their effort is creative rather than competitive and, as with successful companies, their goal is always to surpass themselves. Such people do not suffer from the belief in limitation because they know that their creativity will deliver everything that they need. Thus they move themselves out of the competitive plane. **At the core of their beliefs is the belief "I can."**

Whether we put it down to internal or external factors, what prevents every one of us from getting the things we most want in life are the reasons that we give ourselves why we cannot have them. We then go on to justify these reasons using the flawed evidence of our perceptions. As was demonstrated in Chapter 4, everything we perceive has already been filtered by our beliefs so this approach will always prove that we are right!

Whenever we believe in internal or external limitations our success will also be limited. To achieve anything of note you first have to believe that you can do it. An attitude of "I can" cuts through the false evidence of our perceptions and opens up huge possibility. Once this has been achieved, modern psychology has shown that the enormous power of your mind will be directed to developing whatever capability you place your focus on. Much as the Pygmalion effect generally leads to your expectations being lived out by other people, so your expectation of yourself is also self-fulfilling.

Many highly intelligent people live mediocre lives because of their failure to understand this dynamic. Conversely, it is possible to find many examples of people with a relatively low IQ who have achieved greatness because they were armed with a positive belief system. **When it comes to attaining success, an attitude of "I can" will outweigh factors relating to IQ every time.** It provides us with persistence, that characteristic so vital to our ability to bounce back from failures, and also allows us to tap into our incredible potential and unlock our innate genius capability.

I believe that one of the most important things that we can do with our lives is to recover the genius that we most likely lost in our childhoods. So many other things then follow automatically. Dr. David Hawkins reminds us that "There are very few at the top; the world of the mediocre, however, is one of intense competition, and the bottom of the pyramid is crowded." The most essential element for rising above the competition and getting to the top is a commitment to rapid and continuous growth. You must find a way to identify elements of your conditioning that do not serve you, that limit your belief in yourself, and make a decision to change them.

There is one more critically important point to recognise here. What we are talking about is your true belief, not what you say you believe. Until you truly believe in your own capability, meaning that this belief is embedded in the subconscious, you will be inhibited. If you feel that you believe in your ability to do something but you are not getting the results that you desire, then you need to take a deeper look. For example, if you ask yourself how crowded and competitive your world is you will get an indication of how near to the top you have climbed. Such questions may require a high degree of honesty but if you are up to it, the rewards will be enormous. You will then be able to unlock your ability to access your true genius potential.

There Is Genius in You

My contention is that there is genius in all of us. We were born with it and it is still available to us by reconnecting to the unimaginable potential of our unlimited minds. You have within you an incredibly powerful capability to be, to do, and to have virtually anything that you desire.

We are moving into The Age of the Mind, and the people that will be the most successful will be those who learn to harness their own power. Published in 1937, *Think and Grow Rich!* by Napoleon Hill must one of the most popular and widely read books on personal excellence that has ever been written. In the October 2002 version of *Business Week* magazine's best-seller list, *Think and Grow Rich!* still held 10th position, 65 years after it was first printed. In it Hill made the following observation about the mind, "You have ABSOLUTE CONTROL over but one thing, and that is your thoughts. This is the most significant and inspiring of all known facts! … if you fail to control your own mind, you may be sure you will control nothing else. If you must be careless with your possessions, let it be in connection with material things. *Your mind is your spiritual estate!*"

> AS YOU CHANGE YOUR PERCEPTION OF THE WORLD, YOUR INTERACTION WITH IT AUTOMATICALLY CHANGES.

Even today, so many years after *Think and Grow Rich!* was published, the quality and insightful nature of Hill's statement is still becoming clearer, as leading edge scientific evidence adds ever more validity to it. We know that it is the mind that gives us the ability to create solutions to problems and to visualise things that are currently nonexistent – a capability that is the starting point of all innovation. We are also now discovering that our minds have the power to interact with and strongly influence the physical world.

In this book I have offered eight techniques for using the mind more effectively and working with people, as well as an understanding of why they are important, that can have a transformative impact on your effectiveness as a leader. Several of them directly address the way that you perceive the world because there is no other approach that even comes close in terms of the speed at which benefits can be achieved. It is demonstrably true that **as you change your perception of the world, your interaction with it automatically changes**. Perception drives everything you do because it determines how you evaluate your environment and thereby whether you will react or respond – and in what way.

The quality of our lives is not dictated by what happens to us but by how we respond to what happens to us. Each time you choose to stop and think, rather than allowing your instant reaction to dominate your activity, you create the opportunity to break through and change another aspect of your conditioning. This is the process of growth. We do not wake up one day and suddenly "get it" – life is a journey, not a destination. It is only by thinking that we can identify new choices of behaviour as events are actually occurring and move to a place of responding rather than reacting.

You can only truly claim to know something once you are doing it, and the most important thing for you to do now is to take action. Having read this book you will have gained some new knowledge but, just as it was applied science that took us to the moon, so you must now apply this knowledge if you are to benefit from it. Please, make the decision to take some new actions as a result of what you have read and focus on them until they become habitual. As Bruce Springsteen said, "A time comes when you need to stop waiting for the man you want to become and **start being the man you want to be**." You will never have all of the tools that you think you need to do the things that you want to do, so at some point you must just start.

To be successful **you must be prepared to sacrifice who you are for who you can become**. Most people don't understand sacrifice, thinking that they will have to suffer in some way. However, here it means giving up something of lesser value to get something greater. This is essential to growth. As you learn to let go of inhibiting beliefs and habits you will unleash your potential, begin to recover your genius, and become a true leader, able to lead yourself and others. It is your responsibility as a leader to do this – to make the most of yourself so that you can unconsciously give others permission to do the same.

I sincerely hope that as a result of reading *Being The Effective Leader*, your belief that "I can" will prevail over your conditioning, enabling you to fundamentally change your thinking and approach to leadership. Also, that by following the techniques outlined you will be able to transform yourself and help those around you do the same, to create greater harmony, effectiveness, and prosperity for all.

HAVE YOU ENJOYED THIS BOOK?

I hope so. If you are interested in exploring more deeply the ideas in *Being The Effective Leader*, please join me online for further exciting growth opportunities.

My web site, **www.beingtheeffectiveleader.com**, offers further resources to support your learning and development. The benefits available include

- A **FREE** 1-hour audio download where I discuss key concepts from the book

- A **FREE** report, "The 7 Big Leadership Mistakes"

- Sign up for my free newsletter

- The audio version of the book for immediate download

- Opportunities to network and grow with like-minded individuals

- Information about opportunities to hear me live

- And more …

I would deeply appreciate your feedback and can be reached directly via the contact page at **www.beingtheeffectiveleader.com**.

I am also available to assist you in achieving personal excellence or developing and empowering your team though keynotes, coaching, seminars, and workshops. To find out more, please go to my business web site, **www.optimaltrack.com**.

Thank you, Michael Nicholas